ALFRED THE GREAT

ALFRED THE GREAT

DAVID STURDY

CONSTABLE · LONDON

First published in Great Britain 1995
by Constable and Company Ltd
3 The Lanchesters, 162 Fulham Palace Road
London W6 9ER
Copyright © 1995 David Sturdy
The right of David Sturdy to be identified
as the author of this work has been asserted by him
in accordance with the Copyright, Designs and Patents Act 1988
Paperback edition 1996
Reprinted 1998
ISBN 0 09 476570 7
Printed in Great Britain by
St Edmundsbury Press Ltd
Bury St Edmunds, Suffolk

A CIP catalogue record for this book
is available from the British Library

THIS BOOK IS DEDICATED TO THE MEMORY OF
WALTER DE GRAY BIRCH
OF THE DEPARTMENT OF MANUSCRIPTS
AT THE BRITISH MUSEUM,
NOW THE BRITISH LIBRARY

AND TO ALL HIS COLLEAGUES
BEFORE AND SINCE,
WHO BUILT UP THE COLLECTIONS
AND MADE THEM FREELY AVAILABLE,

FROM SIR ROBERT COTTON, THE FIRST AND
SECOND EARLS OF OXFORD AND HUMFREY WANLEY
TO THEIR SUCCESSORS TODAY

Contents

Illustrations

Preface

The backbone of this book is a new translation of the *Anglo-Saxon Chronicle*, printed in sections through most of the chapters and filled out with details drawn from many sources, particularly from charters, the property documents or title-deeds of the day. I have included far more information drawn from these than any previous biography of Alfred, having myself handled and studied most of the surviving original documents of the ninth century and also very many of the much larger number that survive only as later copies in great twelfth- and thirteenth-century *cartularies* or property books.

The many short lives of Alfred's leading subjects that are included come partly or entirely from the charters. Future scholars will dismiss some of these documents as outright forgeries or hopelessly muddled copies and some of the individuals whom I have attempted to reconstruct will become two or three different people. On the other hand certain charters still under suspicion as later fabrications will come to be explained as shortened versions or paraphrases of genuine transactions. I have suggested that quite a number of Alfred's supporters were in fact relations and proposed that there were many royal connections linked by intermarriage, giving his kingdom much more the character of a family business.

In places I have proposed that a magnate's standing and sometimes his specific post can be deduced from his position in the list of witnesses attached to a charter and, further, that poorly dated charters can be more precisely dated by a careful study of the names and the order of witnesses; the methodology involves treating the names in just the same way as artefacts from the earliest period of Egyptology, but appears valid.

I have tried to use the evidence that these sources provide to remake a world of brave men and cowards, of desperate weeks of battle, action and sometimes flight, of long months of preparation for fighting invaders, while maintaining standards of learning and the civilised arts.

1

Alfred's Dynasty and its Forebears

ALFRED, BORN IN AD 849, grew up in an unstable and violent
society in a country fragmented into rival kingdoms and threatened
by invaders. Like every other part of Europe, the land was a varied
and changing patchwork of kingdoms, princedoms, provinces and
lordships. England in 849 comprised four small kingdoms. Northumbria, which included all the north of England, had been formed
by an amalgamation of the two older kingdoms of Deira and
Bernicia, each of which had taken over British and Saxon chief-
doms and petty kingdoms. In the east, East Anglia comprised the
two counties of Norfolk and Suffolk, and may never have grown
much. In the Midlands, Mercia had absorbed or conquered the
princedoms of Lindsey in Lincolnshire and the Hwicce of the
Cotswolds and lower Severn valley, as well as several others. Wessex in the south had expanded, if legends hold a grain of truth,
from two early nuclei, one in Hampshire and Wiltshire, and the
other in the upper Thames valley, to include Somerset and Dorset
by the 650s and Devon in c.680–730. In 815 Alfred's grandfather,
King Egbert, had ravaged Cornwall in the far south-west 'from
east to west' and reduced the Cornish to submission. In 825, or
soon after, he conquered the former south-eastern kingdoms of
Kent, Sussex and Essex, reduced to dependencies of Mercia long
before. He had greatly increased the size of the realm in the forty
years before Alfred's birth.

Wales was divided into a number of small princedoms, most of
them under the overlordship of Mercia, Scotland into three or
four small Pictish kingdoms, and Ireland too into several warring

3

Celtic kingdoms. By the time Alfred was born, Norse traders and adventurers had explored and settled Orkney and Shetland, the Hebrides and, more recently, the eastern and southern coasts of Ireland.

We should not imagine, as tidy-minded historians tend to, that any of these kingdoms were cohesive areas with people of a single distinctive racial origin and culture within a trim and obvious boundary. They were casual agglomerations of territories brought together by conquest, inheritance, marriage and purchase. People at the nucleus of a kingdom probably considered most of the outlying provinces as having different customs from their own and being rather alien, as if all those parts of the kingdom were frontier lands, conquered territories, which in most cases they were. A king could spring from or acquire a territory outside the main limits of his kingdom. He or his wife might also be patrons or devotees of a church, and to some extent protector of its lands, beyond his main frontiers. Bishop Asser's statement that Alfred 'was born at the royal estate called Wantage in the district known as Berkshire, so called from Berroc Wood, where box-trees grow very abundantly'[1] shows that Alfred's parents had a residence somewhere in or near the modern town of Wantage or had some other reason to be there. It does not necessarily prove, as the great historian F. M. Stenton thought it did, that the whole of the later county of Berkshire then lay within their kingdom of Wessex.[2] The province of Hampshire, or Hamtunscire as it appears in the *Anglo-Saxon Chronicle*, to which King Sigeberht was confined in 757, when Cynewulf (757–786) seized the throne from him, may well have been only the southern part of the modern county.[3]

While in detail the peoples of each kingdom, their settlements and their fields were mixed and varied, and not at all homogeneous, the social fabric of all the English kingdoms, and indeed all European countries, was very similar, with a tiny ruling class whose close relatives occupied the highest ranks of the Church. There may not have been an aristocracy as we think of it, of noble families distinct from the royal family, but rather all kings, all provincial governors and some lesser officials, all archbishops and most bishops thought themselves to be descended from ruling kings or chiefs. All were more or less closely related to each other by descent or marriage; and no doubt all of them considered themselves fit to rule if the chance came up.

All the surviving records of the period were compiled for the benefit and prestige of these ruling families; many of the surviving documents were written by junior members of the families in secretarial posts. It is thus extraordinarily difficult to reinterpret the very scanty and intensely personal records in broad social or economic terms. The few individuals of whom we know anything at all had such immense social prestige and overwhelming economic power that they defy conversion into graphs and trends. Alfred's personal impact on his age was inconceivably vast, ruling his people as he travelled round holding court, giving judgement as he stood washing his hands, while acting as a final court of appeal,[4] choosing the site of new fortresses and fighting many bloody battles in the centre of the battle-line, sponsoring a cultural revival by translating and adapting the classics himself. His family, his actions, his fame and his personality dominate our thinking.

We think of the great men of the age as 'Anglo-Saxons' of Germanic stock as opposed to 'Viking' kings and jarls of Scandinavian race or 'British' kings and chiefs of Celtic stock or descended from Roman civil administrators and military officers. Even back in the fifth and sixth centuries these distinctions probably meant little or nothing. The Empire had been a vast melting pot of peoples. The Roman army had recruited many Germans, especially in the fourth century, and settled them as frontier troops, so that it may have been virtually impossible to distinguish who were 'Britons' and who 'Saxons', except by the family traditions of the individual kings and chiefs. In early centuries, long before Alfred's time, the rival ruling classes had lived side by side and intermarried, as is clear from 'Saxon' rulers with 'British' names like Cadwalla, king of Wessex in the 680s. This absence of any real difference was, no doubt, also still true of the ninth century, except that both Anglo-Saxons and Britons were Christian and, to some extent, literate, while the Danes were illiterate and pagan, or so we are supposed to believe. All of them equally retained heroic traditions and values.

Kings normally established their eldest sons, and sometimes younger ones too, as rulers of subsidiary kingdoms in some outlying part of the realm. But disputes among the ruling families were common and the junior kings habitually rebelled against their fathers, made war on their brothers and dispossessed their relatives at every possible opportunity. Sometimes several brothers or cousins divided up a kingdom and ruled as equals; sometimes an over-king ruled one or more under-kings, whom he had conquered or appointed from among his relatives. Sons did not usually succeed their fathers; more often a successful cousin killed or drove out other less powerful claimants. Thanks to complex intermarriages in the past, a prince (or *atheling* in Old English) might have a valid claim to more than one kingdom, and different branches of the royal families, or rival groups among the royal clans, competed for any vacant throne.

When one of Alfred's brothers appropriated their father's throne, refusing to hand it back on his return from a visit to Rome, they settled the matter without civil war. This will have surprised Charlemagne's three grandsons, the Emperor Lothar and his brothers, King Louis of Germany and King Charles the Bald of France who had just entertained Ethelwulf at his court, giving him his daughter Judith in marriage. Their record of capturing and imprisoning their father, intriguing against and making war on each other and worse, shows a much more robust view of politics and acceptable behaviour. Their nobles followed their example and the great provincial governors regularly plotted against their monarchs, rose in revolt or sided with an invader; and were often indulged and forgiven. They too will have been amazed when Alfred disgraced a governor of Hampshire for failing to turn up to fight the Vikings, in their eyes more of a casual omission than a very major sin.

Alfred's dynasty was one of the best ordered and of all European kingdoms Wessex the least troubled by family feuds and rivalries. Between 802 and 1016, in an unusual and remarkably amicable record of succession, fifteen kings came to the throne in seven generations, the crown passing from father to son, from brother to brother and from uncle to nephew. No king and only one claimant fell in battle against his close blood relations; there were only a few armed confrontations and just one suspected murder, none admitted openly. The widely accepted European practice of mutilating and blinding actual or potential rivals and disaffected bishops was unknown, or at least never mentioned in any record.

Our main historical record of the time, the *Anglo-Saxon Chronicle*, intended to convey the history of Wessex, notes quite inciden-

6

tally that in the other English kingdoms during the ninth century six kings were slain in battle and another five driven out. In his teens Alfred saw the other three English kingdoms collapse; when he was in his twenties he lost control of his own kingdom for a few winter months and won it back by courage and determination.

Epic poems, now long forgotten, told Alfred and his contemporaries of their forebears, the early kings who, they believed, established the kingdom. Alfred claimed descent from the legendary Cerdic, founder of Wessex, through Ingild, brother of King Ine of Wessex (688–726). We know of Cerdic and his successors only in a rationalised and tidied-up form in the ninth-century *Chronicle*. Bede's *History of the English Church and People*, written in the 720s, tells us a little about the early kings, and a few early charters have scraps of information about some of the later ones.

One version of the poetic legend told of Cerdic and his son Cynric invading Britain in 495 and taking over the kingdom of Wessex in 519. Another version had Cynric as Cerdic's grandson, ruling from 534 to 560, and father of Ceawlin, king from 560 until he died in 591. This legend locates these pagan princelings around the Solent, in Hampshire and Wiltshire. A third strain of the legends, not consistent with these two, glorified a chief called Cuthwulf, victorious in 571, and two others, Ceawlin and Cuthwine, who won a battle against the Britons in 577. These epics located the nucleus of the kingdom on the upper Thames, in modern Oxfordshire.

The long genealogy which the compiler of the *Chronicle* included at the death of King Ethelwulf should not be taken very seriously, but looked on rather like the architectural 'chant' or incantation of the names of great thinkers, scholars and learned men inscribed on the exterior of some great American libraries. It does not indicate for certain that their works are available within, but gives a broad idea of the authors that the founding librarian believed to be good company for his readers. To the Anglo-Saxons, Woden and Methuselah were the right kind of figures to have as ancestors; so too, perhaps, were Cynric and Cerdic, the founding fathers of Wessex.

The *Chronicle*'s ostensibly exact dates in the 400s and 500s were calculated several centuries later by chroniclers who supplemented them with summaries of the poems. Lists of church benefactors, from the time St Birinus began the conversion of Wessex to Christianity in 635, may have included notes of the length of various reigns. In all this guesswork there must be very substantial errors in the 600s and 700s and much worse ones in earlier centuries. We can enjoy Ceawlin and his fellows as legend, but can scarcely hope to find any reliable foothold of historical truth, unless they are confirmed by some other kind of evidence, such as archaeology.

The archaeological record of the fifth, sixth and seventh centuries is abundant, but very unbalanced, with few finds of settlements – now seen as a major priority, noted in the past as rather dull pits and post-holes – but very many discoveries of burial grounds, as skeletons with grave-goods, such as gilt-bronze brooches, have drawn the attention of antiquaries and collectors. Since the early 1800s many large cemeteries and some settlements have been found on the gravel terraces along the upper Thames, indicating quite dense 'Anglo-Saxon' occupation from the early fifth century. The chalklands of Hampshire and Wiltshire have produced scantier evidence for settlement mostly of a rather later date.

Although many scholars have devoted immense effort and ingenuity to reconciling the material evidence for this period with the written, they do not match at all well. Interpretations and expectations of the evidence from the ground change with new discoveries every year. While the documentary evidence has remained unchanged, our opinions of it have altered greatly. Thirty years ago most scholars believed that the 'dates' and 'events' of the *Chronicle*'s early centuries were reasonably close to the truth. We now tend to look on them as legends of a recognisable and widespread type or types casually strung together by arbitrary chronological calculations long after they 'happened'.

The *Anglo-Saxon Chronicle* is a year-by-year account in Old English of the history of the kingdom of Wessex from the 400s, with a brief introductory section of highlights of history from the Roman Empire and the Christian world and fairly summary accounts of the reigns of Alfred's grandfather, father and elder brothers as kings of Wessex. It was compiled in about 890 by an unknown writer, perhaps a priest or monk of princely blood.

The *Chronicle*, as it will be referred to throughout this book, has

8

had an overwhelming effect on historical studies over a very much longer time-span than Alfred's lifetime. All biographies of Alfred, and all accounts of the late Saxon period, are based primarily on it. So many writers have simply paraphrased the text, adding in their own and second-hand speculations without comment, that we will do much better to indicate just what the text says, in indented sections. The *Chronicle* is a composite work, compiled from a range of sources. The early parts of the text read as scrappy notes, as it were the main 'headlines' of each period, jotted down, but never revised or comprehensively rewritten, so that it seems really rather unfinished. The coverage is uneven, as we can see from a glance at the number of entries per century:

First century BC	1
First century AD	27
Second	8
Third	2
Fourth	3
Fifth	18
Sixth	27
Seventh	68
Eighth	94
Ninth (to AD 890)	73

The earliest items, up to the fourth century AD, seem to be extracts from a world history, some lost book of antiquity which has not been identified. The entries for the fifth to the eighth centuries are very mixed, coming from lists of kings of some of the English kingdoms, supplemented by the titles or brief summaries with one or two short snatches, paraphrased into prose, of once-familiar epic poems about kings and great men. The author or compiler was able to assume that his audience had a particular background knowledge, completely different from ours. In those days the mere mention of a hero's or a villain's name instantly recalled a range of dramatic appearances in an oral literature now almost totally lost. As he wrote, the author or compiler included an increasing amount of detail on church history and organisation, which interested him as a priest, from sources which we cannot now identify, surprisingly little of it from *History of the English Church*

9

and People, which the Northumbrian monk Bede had compiled in the 720s.[5]

For forty years from the late 830s the *Chronicle* is largely a first-hand statement of the kingdom's decline into near oblivion, an austere, elegant and dignified piece of writing with no obvious local focus or special emphasis of any kind, but with powerful tension as the writer sets the scene for the spectacular and dramatic events of 878. The notable absence of personal detail about King Alfred's father and elder brothers, and the extreme reticence about Alfred himself, may imply that the compiler had never been part of an intimate circle around any of them, but lived at some remove from court without access to Alfred himself or to intimate gossip and chit-chat about him. But it may be a calculated and very sophisticated literary device that takes for granted a familiarity with many details that are missed out. Also omitted is any mention of 'friendly' Vikings as mercenaries or allies, roles in which they constantly appear in Irish and Frankish annals. This must be deliberate censorship to clarify and enhance the drama.

However, some passages for the late 860s, much of the text for 875–878 and practically all the entries for 879–890 read like the words of a Viking chief whose adventures had ranged across England and much of the Continent. The sudden changes of viewpoint, as the 'enemy' suddenly becomes the main focus, may have been designed for dramatic emphasis. The information is so precise that its source can only be, not a victim or potential victim such as a Frankish monk, but an active participant in the events noted, well accustomed to reciting both a general outline of his misdeeds, as we have it in the *Chronicle*, and also more detailed epic versions of his fighting, rape and pillage. We must assume that a Danish commander, an earl, prince or 'king', had taken service with Alfred, as many did with Charles the Bald of France and his relatives, or had perhaps retired to an English monastery, claiming exemption from war-crimes charges as a godson of the king. The *Chronicle* allows no hint of his identity to emerge and makes sure that he gets no glory as an anti-hero, like General Rommel in World War II.

Once it had been put together in something like its present form, even if we may really consider it a mere sketch or outline in need of editing, correcting and completing with extra data, the

Chronicle was often copied and updated by being extended onwards, but the established wording was only occasionally altered and adapted. Seven versions of the standard text up to 891 survive, one of them (at Corpus Christi College, Cambridge) actually written at that time or very soon after with curious errors in the dates, which show that this text must be a copy of a copy of the original as they are in different places one, two and three years out. The other versions are all later copies, mostly of the eleventh or twelfth centuries. Each of the seven has a complex history of later continuations. Two of them were partly rewritten to include extra items of North Country origin and interest from the 280s to the 690s. An eighth version, put into Latin in Alfred's lifetime, is incorporated in Asser's *Life*. A ninth was produced eighty years afterwards in the 970s, when governor Ethelward, a minor member of the royal family, wrote his *Chronicon*, a strange and almost incomprehensible high-flown Latin translation of a slightly different text, fuller in many details than our standard version, but with the same error in the dates.[6] Translations and paraphrases of the *Chronicle*, or of Asser's adaptation of it, have remained the basis of our knowledge of the period, as these pages show.

Alfred's grandfather Egbert won the throne of Wessex in 802. His father Ealhmund was, the *Chronicle* tells us, king of Kent in 784 and must have been born in the 750s or 760s.[7] He was perhaps a younger brother of King Egbert II of Kent, who ruled in about 765–780, perhaps gaining independence from King Offa of Mercia in a battle at Otford in Kent in 776. Offa and his son-in-law King Brihtric of Wessex had, the *Chronicle* tells us, driven the younger Egbert out of England into exile among the Franks for three years;[8] to be old enough to be a threat worth driving into exile, he must have been born in the 770s or early 780s as Offa died in 796.

By 802 Kent was again under Mercian domination and Egbert did not try to claim that throne, but made a successful bid for Wessex when Brihtric, who had ruled since 786, died in 802. The *Chronicle* does not name any rivals, but a Mercian army crossed the frontier in 802, presumably bringing armed support to some other candidate and against Egbert and his supporters. The *Chronicle* tells us that

Egbert succeeded to the kingdom of Wessex and that same day
governor Ethelmund and a force from the province of the Hwicce in
Mercia invaded by way of Kempsford [in modern Gloucestershire].
Governor Weohstan and the warriors of Wiltshire fought him in a
great battle. Both governors were slain and the men of Wiltshire had
the victory.

This battle was clearly not an incidental sideshow, but was specially
noted because the battle cleared the way for Egbert to take the
throne.

The *Chronicle*'s coverage of the rest of this reign is so sparse
that we must assume that Egbert's life was already familiar to all
potential readers, and well documented in poems, a chronicle or
even a biography. Omitting church appointments and similar matters of special interest to a priest compiling the *Chronicle* in the
890s, but including references to the next-door kingdom of Mercia, there are only twenty-three entries for Egbert's reign. Before
821 there are only two entries, Egbert's accession and one other.
This selection omits church politics and foreign affairs:

815
b. King Egbert devastated Cornwall from east to west.

821
a. King Cenwulf of Mercia [796–821] died and Ceolwulf succeeded
him.
b. Governor Eadberht died.

823
a. Ceolwulf [king of Mercia] was ejected from his kingdom.

824
a. Governors Burghelm and Muca were slain.

825
a. The warriors of Devon fought the Cornish at Galford.
b. There was a battle between King Egbert and King Beornwulf of
Mercia at Ellendun [Wroughton in Wiltshire]. Egbert won with great
slaughter.

d. The East Anglians and their king, fearing the Mercians, sought help from King Egbert and an alliance with him.

e. The East Anglians killed King Beornwulf of Mercia [823–825].

826

a. King Ludeca of Mercia was slain with five of his governors and Wiglaf [827–840] succeeded.

829

b. King Egbert crushed Mercia and the rest of England south of the River Humber.

c. He became the eighth 'High King'.

The first was Ælle of Sussex [about 500]

the second Ceawlin of Wessex [560–591]

the third Ethelbert of Kent [560–616]

the fourth Redwald of East Anglia [about 620]

the fifth Edwin of Northumbria [616–632]

the sixth his successor Oswald [633–641]

followed by his brother Oswiu [654–670]

and Egbert was the eighth.

d. Egbert led his forces to Dore [in modern Derbyshire]. The Northumbrians submitted and made peace, marching away the same day.

830

a. Wiglaf regained the throne of Mercia.

c. King Egbert invaded Wales and subjugated all the people.

835

a. The Vikings pillaged the Isle of Sheppey.

836

a. King Egbert fought the crews of a fleet of thirty-five ships at Carhampton [on the north coast of Somerset, near Dunster], with heavy loss as the Vikings held the killing ground.

b. Bishops Herefrith and Wigthegn [both of Winchester] and governors Duda and Osmod died [perhaps not in the battle].

838

a. A large Viking fleet invaded the land of the Cornish, who joined them to oppose King Egbert of Wessex. He mustered and led his army there and beat their combined force in battle on Hingston Down.

839

a. King Egbert died. Before he became king, he had been an exile for three years among the Franks, driven there by King Offa of Mercia and King Brihtric of Wessex, who had taken Offa's part as his son-in-law.
b. Egbert was king for thirty-seven years and seven months and then . . .

This very basic record of the reign mentions Egbert's major triumphs, especially his defeat of the powerful Midland kingdom of Mercia in battle at Ellendun near Swindon in 825, after which he sent his son Ethelwulf to enforce the submission of Kent, his father's old kingdom, and the other south-eastern provinces of Sussex, Surrey and Essex. These districts had been under Mercian rule since the 760s, apart from a period of independence under Egbert's uncle and father in the late 770s and 780s. Egbert's conquest or rather recovery of Kent is related as a kind of poetic justice.

In 829 Egbert conquered and took over Mercia and marched his army to Dore in Derbyshire, where the king of Northumbria submitted to him and made peace. The following year, in 830, Mercia again became independent under Wiglaf, king since 827. It is not at all clear whether he was installed as Egbert's protégé or whether he had led a successful revolt.

For the last five years of his reign, from 835, Egbert faced increasingly serious raids and invasions by Danish Vikings already attracted or more likely bribed to attack the Dutch and Belgian coast, then known as Frisia, a province of the Frankish Empire.

We can say a modest amount about Egbert's court and his leading noblemen who composed it on their visits for special purposes and tours of duty, and when they all gathered for great assemblies. We will defer a discussion of courts as a whole and their functioning in government until the next chapter, and concentrate first on the men themselves. The *Chronicle*'s coverage is skimpy, mentioning five or six Wessex governors in a reign of thirty-seven years.

Of them Eadberht (821), Burghelm and Muca (both 824) do not appear in any other written source, unless Muca was the Mercian governor documented in 822 and 823;[9] perhaps he and Burghelm of Wessex killed each other in battle. Dudda and Osmod (836) each appear twice in witness-lists of charters. The *Chronicle* gives us not the slightest clue as to why these five men deserved mention nor what they were doing when they died. Only one of Egbert's governors, Wulfhard, figures as commanding a military force. But perhaps everybody knew them as the heroes of a long series of poems in which Egbert was the main star.

This compares with the *Chronicle*'s somewhat more generous record of eight governors mentioned during the nineteen years of the following reign of Egbert's son Ethelwulf, with Wulfhard as the only man common to both. Ethelwulf's governors were mentioned because they fought battles, though two of them were defeated and killed.

We seem to have the names of twenty of Egbert's governors altogether, ten of whom are recorded only once. The complete lack of any royal charters of Wessex, and consequently of witness-lists, for the years 802–823 makes a study based on this material uneven and heavily biased to the second half of the reign. Despite this weakness, we can usefully look at the careers of six men who served Egbert in high office and look for some general conclusions. Two of them, Ethelwulf of Kent and Monneda, who are not mentioned in the *Chronicle*, had careers which we can follow for over a decade. Another, Ethelwulf of Berkshire, a namesake of one of them, governed his province for at least thirty-five years, first as part of Mercia, but for most of his life as part of Wessex. This is just a brief introduction to a man who will reappear often in this book until, not far short of seventy, he died in battle leading his warriors at Alfred's side in 871. After seeing them here first as individuals, we will establish some methods and procedures for using the same chance-saved legal papers about land as a source of information on both government and personal data.

Dudda of Surrey or Sussex, documented 828–836
Born perhaps about 800 Dudda, like Osmod, may have been brought in to govern Surrey or Sussex after Ethelwulf had conquered Kent and the south-east and annexed the whole region. He

appears on only two witness-lists, both for charters about Kentish property,[10] and may have been in his late twenties or thirties when he died, according to the *Chronicle*, in 836.

Ethelwulf of Kent, documented 838–844
Governor Ethelwulf of Kent was born about 800–805, served as a minister after Egbert's conquest of Kent in about 827 and was appointed governor perhaps in his thirties and died in his early forties. He appears as a minister in Kent in 828.[11] In 838 two governors named Ethelwulf witnessed a Kentish charter.[12] The other must be Ethelwulf of Berkshire, who attested a charter of the Mercian King Wiglaf in 836 and then took service with the kings of Wessex, appearing on this occasion in Kent on tour with King Egbert of Wessex. Ethelwulf of Kent then attests exclusively in Kent from 839 to 844. In 841 and 842 he is followed by governor Ealhhere.

Hereberht of Kent, documented 830–841
Alfred cannot have known governor Hereberht. Born about 805, he may have been a kinsman of Bishop Herefrith of Winchester (*c*.825–833). He did not hold office in the Mercian regime in Kent and was no doubt brought from Wessex by King Ethelwulf. He appears in only three witness-lists, first as H . . . rd, in a charter by which King Egbert gave or confirmed land in Kent at Warehorne and Flotham to 'my faithful minister' Ætheric, probably in 830.[13] In 838 he appears, next after Ethelwulf as king of Kent and Archbishop Ceolnoth, as third of fourteen witnesses to a charter by which the king gave the archbishop a small farm called Eastrestadelham and land at Lyminge.[14] In '880', a date which scholars have corrected to 855 and to 844, but must be about 840, he witnessed King Ethelwulf's grant to Malmesbury abbey of Minety in Wiltshire.[15] The *Chronicle* tells us that in 841 'Governor Hereberht, with many of his fighting men, was slain in the Marsh [that is Romney Marsh] by the heathens.' He was then perhaps in his late thirties.

Monneda, documented 825–839
Born in about 780–800, Monneda was a governor for at least fourteen years, on the very incomplete evidence of four witness-lists, and died or dropped from the record at the age of perhaps

forty, after 839. The lack of any royal charters of Wessex in 802–823 means that he might well have been governor for twenty or thirty years and may in fact have been much older when he died.

He appears in two genuine charters and in two which have been denounced as forgeries. The first, of '825', from a twelfth-century volume from Winchester cathedral, now in the British Library, is a grant by King Egbert to Winchester of land at Worthy, which the cathedral long owned, and proclaims that it was 'written with the army at Creodantreoth when King Egbert was on the march against the Britons and signed at Omtune,' intriguing information not available to a later forger from well-known sources like the *Chronicle*. The witness-list of six names must be a shortened copy of an authentic list, perhaps formerly attached to another charter altogether.[16] Monneda seems not to have had any Kentish connections and was presumably escorting King Egbert on tour when he witnessed a charter about a grant to Rochester at a council of 828 which we will soon take as an example of government in action.

Osmod of Sussex or Surrey, documented 828–836
Born perhaps about 800, Osmod is documented as governor in only two charters five years apart, in 828 and 833. He was no doubt brought in with Dudda after Wessex conquered Kent in about 827 to govern Surrey or Sussex. He may have been a kinsman of Oslac, 'King Ethelwulf's famous butler', who seems to have come from the Isle of Wight and whose daughter married King Ethelwulf to become Alfred's mother. He was probably in his thirties or even twenties when he died, as the *Chronicle* tells us, in 836.

Wulfhard of Kent and Hampshire, 824–840
Alfred cannot have known his father's closest supporter and adviser in his early years, governor Wulfhard first perhaps of Hampshire, then of a part of Kent and then of Hampshire. Born in about the 780s, he may have been, to judge from his name, a kinsman of the wealthy and aristocratic Wulfred, archdeacon and later archbishop (805–832) of Canterbury, perhaps even his brother, and of Bishop Wulfhard of Hereford (801–822/4). He was possibly a comrade of King Alfred's grandfather Egbert, in exile with him among the Franks before he came to the throne, perhaps by force, in 802.

He was a governor in Wessex in the mid-820s and possibly in

the poorly documented twenty years before that. King Egbert gave him a Hampshire estate in 824; the assembly at which this gift was made serves as an example of a royal council below.[17] We cannot be certain that Hampshire was then the shire that Wulfhard governed as Saxon kings may have preferred, like William the Conqueror more than two centuries later, to make sure that their great magnates had scattered estates, not large compact blocks of land. He also appears as a witness to two charters of 825 whose main text is interpolated or at least partly spurious.[18]

In about 827 King Egbert sent his son Ethelwulf to conquer his father's old kingdom of Kent, now a Mercian sub-kingdom or province, with Wulfhard as his senior military commander and Bishop Ealhstan of Sherborne in charge of administration, logistics and spiritual affairs. Leaving Archbishop Wulfred who may, if he was a relative, have welcomed the invasion, they made a clean sweep of the Mercian top brass, keeping on just a few juniors, including the ministers Aldred, Ealhhere and Oshere. Wulfhard took charge of Kent, or of part of Kent, under Ethelwulf as king of Kent and the south-east, governing his new province there for at least eleven years. In 828 he was the senior of four governors, with Monneda, Osmod and Dudda.[19] The last two appear in other Kentish charters and may have governed other parts of Kent, Surrey or Sussex. Wulfhard witnessed other Kentish charters in 833 and 838.[20]

When Alfred's father Ethelwulf took over Wessex on his father's death in 838, Wulfhard seems to have gone back with him to become governor of Hampshire for a year or two. As the *Chronicle* notes, he defeated the Vikings at Southampton in 840 and died the same year, probably well into his fifties, having evidently established a prosperous landed family to rival the old princely Os-family. Two later governors of Hampshire, Wulfhere and Wulfred, were presumably grandsons.

Our initial conclusion, from scanning the spare evidence which has allowed us to construct these skeletal biographies, is that many of the leading men came from a fairly close circle of noble and princely families.

2

Alfred's Parents and Family

ALFRED WAS BORN IN 849 at Wantage in Berkshire, youngest son
of the brave and pious King Ethelwulf of Wessex and his wife
Osburh, daughter of the royal cupbearer Oslac, descended from
the old princely line of south Hampshire and the Isle of Wight.
Four of Alfred's elder brothers survived to adulthood and all
became king in turn, but none lived much beyond their mid-
twenties. We know of an elder sister who married King Burgred
of the neighbouring kingdom of Mercia. Her marriage took place
in 853, so she must have been at least ten years older than Alfred.
She died in Italy in 888 at the age of fifty or more. For the time
the family was unusually secure and loving. There is no record or
hint of murder or open brutality to each other. They maintained
some standards of decency despite the inconstancy and violence
of politics and of society generally, and despite the unstable and
fragmented condition of England and threats from abroad.

Alfred's mother Osburh and her family are worth getting to
know as well as we can. King Ethelwulf's elder children may have
been born to an unrecorded earlier wife or companion. If Osburh
was indeed the mother of all five sons, she must have been in her
early forties when Alfred was born. His eldest brother Athelstan
took over the family's junior kingdom of Kent in 839 and was
presumably at least fifteen by then. If Osburh was considered fit
to marry and bear children at about fourteen and was Athelstan's
mother, she must have been born in 809 or a year or two earlier.

The Welsh Bishop Asser, Alfred's close adviser, whose *Life of
Alfred* we will consider and analyse later, describes her as 'a most

religious woman, noble in character and noble by birth, the daughter of Oslac, King Ethelwulf's famous cupbearer'.[1] He goes on to add some rather distant and at least semi-legendary family background:

> Oslac was a Goth by race, for he was descended from the Goths and Jutes, and in particular from the line of Stuf and Wihtgar. Their uncle King Cerdic and his son Cynric, their cousin, put these princely brothers in charge of the Isle of Wight. They killed the few local Britons at 'Wihtgarabyrig'. The rest had all been massacred or fled into exile.

Oslac appears only once more in the historical record. He does not appear as a witness to any of King Ethelwulf's own charters, more than thirty of which survive, many with reasonably full witness-lists, a major source of information for us, among which we could expect to find him named. There may have been a custom that a king's most intimate retainers did not witness his charters. Soon after Ethelwulf's death, he appears as the tenth of twenty-three witnesses to a charter of 858 by which Alfred's third brother Ethelbert, then king of Kent, exchanged land at Wassingwell, Kent with his minister Wullaf for a property at Mersham in Kent. The original charter, or a file-copy of that time, is among the founding collections of the British Library.[2]

Asser's reference to Oslac as a 'Goth by race' may indicate that his contemporaries considered that he came of a princely family reduced, like so many others, in status to become royal servants and governors. Several modern writers have commented that Asser was simply mistaken and should have called him a Jute, following Bede's comment, written in the 720s: 'from the Jutes are descended the people of Kent and the Isle of Wight and the province of Wessex opposite it who are still called Jutes today.'[3] But we should not dismiss Asser's precise contemporary evidence. He must have put down a phrase that he heard at Alfred's court in the 880's, when the word 'Goth' had some special meaning that we cannot appreciate and had perhaps already been forgotten. It might indicate that Oslac had a vague family tradition that they came from Sweden, Yugoslavia, Italy or Spain, all areas held by Goths of one sort or another in previous centuries.

Two other ruling families, in Northumbria and the Severn valley, frequently gave their children names with this particular root in Os–. A link between these has been claimed and denied, but no one has ever suggested a connection between either and the princely Os– clan, from which Alfred's mother came, with property and influence in south Hampshire in the eighth and ninth centuries.

The *Chronicle* tells of two men with Os– names in eighth-century Wessex. An *atheling* or prince Oswald son of Ethelbald son of Cynebald son of Cuthwine son of Ceawlin (the last two being names familiar from the legendary early years of Wessex, fought against King Ethelhard of Wessex in 726 and died in 730. Perhaps his Os– name was a compliment to his mother or grandmother.

When the *atheling* or prince Cynehard assassinated King Cynewulf of Wessex in bed with a girlfriend at Meretun in 786, governor Osric led the main party of the royal bodyguard, with his own guards and minister Wigfrith with his retinue, to take vengeance, killing Cynehard and his eighty-four retainers and leaving only one of them, his own godson, alive but wounded.[4] We can suggest that this Osric was the father of governor Osmod, whose life we have already pieced together, and the father or grandfather of governor Osric, whom we will shortly meet.

Osmod and minister Oshere both witnessed charters of King Egbert in 828 and 833.[5] We may suspect that there were several marriages between the Os–s of Hampshire and Alfred's family at about the time Ethelwulf met and married Osburh and even before. Oshere married Ealawyn, daughter of governor Ealhhere of Kent, while Ealhhere's son, Osberht, a minister in 839–845, may well have been named in compliment to his mother or, perhaps more likely, grandmother.

In the next generation, during King Ethelwulf's reign, various mentions of a governor Osric in Dorset and Hampshire can all be identified as one man, perhaps a brother of Alfred's mother, active through two full decades, first as governor of Dorset, then transferred to Hampshire where his estates and main interests lay. This is a more elegant and economical solution than having to believe that two men of the same name governed adjoining counties a few years apart. We reconstruct and examine his career at the end of this chapter.

Gold ring bearing the name of Ethelwulf, king of Wessex, Alfred's father; a high official's badge of office. Found in a cart-rut in Wiltshire, 1780.

Various ministers and priests with Os– names appear from time to time in Alfred's lifetime in the witness-lists of charters. Quite a number may have been related. Two of them, whom we will meet later, were certainly Alfred's kinsmen with very evident royal connections. Oswald was of royal birth, the son of one of Alfred's elder brothers, and perhaps ten years younger; he died very young. Osferth, born about the same time as Oswald, was a cousin of Alfred on his mother's side; at least he was very close to the royal family but never referred to as if he had royal blood. He became one of Alfred's closest supporters and long outlived him, holding high office into his late sixties or seventies, until the reign of Alfred's grandson Athelstan (924–939).

Alfred's father King Ethelwulf was probably in his late forties when Alfred, his youngest son, was born. He first appears in the historical record as a successful warrior-king aged, we can only presume, at least fifteen but most likely in his twenties. The *Chronicle* relates some of the main events of his reign as part of a long introduction leading up to its main subject, King Alfred himself. Presumably the author quotes from a separate 'Ethelwulf Chronicle' or from epic poems that court bards composed to glorify Ethelwulf's considerable achievements and military prowess.

Before he inherited the throne of Wessex, Ethelwulf had conquered and ruled Kent as a junior kingdom for his father. The *Chronicle* tells us, under the year 825, how King Egbert defeated Beornwulf of Mercia at Ellandun (Wroughton in modern Wiltshire) and then sent from the army his son Ethelwulf and Bishop Ealhstan and governor Wulfhard to Kent with a large force. They drove King Baldred [under-king of Kent, ruling for the Mercians] north across the Thames and the men of Kent and Surrey, and the South and the East Saxons [Sussex and Essex] submitted to him because they had been unjustly forced away from his kinsmen.

While the battle was fought in 825, it has been suggested that this expedition to conquer Kent took place two years later.[6] Mention of the bishop and governor might hint that they were there to help and advise and could imply that Ethelwulf was quite young and inexperienced. To be fifteen by 827, Ethelwulf may have been born as late as 812; but other considerations make about 800 a more satisfactory date for his birth.

In 839, Ethelwulf succeeded his father on the throne of Wessex, leaving his eldest son Athelstan to take over his role as king of Kent and the south-east. As we shall soon see, Wessex suffered repeated Viking raids in nine of the first sixteen years of Ethelwulf's reign. Alfred was born in 849, near the end of the only long break in the raids, a break which lasted from 846 to 850, when the renewed raids escalated with the Vikings taking up winter quarters on offshore islands like Thanet. When Ethelwulf died in 858, he was well past his mid-forties, probably about sixty.

We will follow Ethelwulf's reign in the full text of the *Chronicle*, which we will rely on heavily for the rest of this book. Brief lives of the noblemen and churchmen mentioned, and of members of the royal family, can be found through the index, as can the places and battles.

839
b. Egbert's son Ethelwulf succeeded to the kingdom of Wessex. He entrusted to his son Athelstan the realm of the men of Kent, the kingdom of Essex and the provinces of Surrey and Sussex.

840
a. Governor Wulfhard fought the men of a fleet of thirty-three ships at Southampton and beat them, killing many. He died the same year. Governor Ethelhelm and the warriors of Dorset met the Vikings in combat at Portland, drove them back for quite a time, but lost the battle and his life.

841

a. Governor Hereberht was killed with many of his men on the [Romney] Marsh by the Vikings; later there were killings in Lincolnshire, East Anglia and Kent.

842

a. There were brutal massacres in London, Quentovic and Rochester.

843 [844]

a. King Ethelwulf fought the Vikings from a fleet of thirty-five ships at Carhampton. They held the battleground [for a Frankish record of this serious defeat, see p. 101].

845

a. Governor Eanwulf and the fighting men of Somerset with Bishop Ealhstan and governor Osric and the men of Dorset fought a Danish raiding force at the mouth of the Parrett, beat them and inflicted heavy casualties.

[846–850: No entries]

851

a. Governor Ceorl and a regiment of the men of Devon fought a pagan army at Wicga's Hill. The English won, with much slaughter.
b. The Vikings camped over the winter on Thanet, for the first time.
c. Three hundred and fifty Viking ships came into the mouth of the Thames and the crews devastated Canterbury [Archbishop Ceolnoth survived] and London. They routed King Brihtwulf of Mercia and his troops and crossed the Thames southward into Surrey.
d. King Ethelwulf and his son Ethelbald with the army of Wessex fought them at the 'Oak Glade' and won, with the greatest slaughter ever known.
e. King Athelstan [Ethelwulf's eldest son, junior king in Kent] with governor Ealhhere fought a sea-battle, beat a great Viking armada at Sandwich in Kent and captured nine ships, forcing the rest to flee.

[852. No entry]

24

853

a. King Burgred of Mercia and his councillors invited King Ethelwulf to help subdue the Welsh. He did so, marching his army across Mercia, and they subjugated the Welsh.

b. King Ethelwulf sent his son Alfred to Rome. The noble Leo, then pope in Rome, anointed him royally and sponsored his confirmation.

c. Ealhhere and the men of Kent with Huda and the men of Surrey fought the pagan army on Thanet with initial success. Both governors were killed and many on both sides were slain and drowned.

d. Later, after Easter, King Ethelwulf gave his daughter [Ethelswith] in marriage to King Burgred, sending her from Wessex to Mercia.

855–858

a. The pagans wintered on Sheppey for the first time.

b. King Ethelwulf ordained that one-tenth of all his estates throughout the kingdom should go for God's worship and for his salvation.

c. He went to Rome in great state, stayed there for twelve months and returned. King Charles of France gave him his daughter as queen. After that he came home to his people, who rejoiced.

[860]

d. He died two years after his return from France and was buried at Winchester after a reign of eighteen and a half years.

e. Ethelwulf was the son of Egbert [king of Wessex, 802–839], son of Ealhmund [king of Kent in the 780s], son of Eafe, son of Eoppa, son of Ingild. Ingild was brother of King Ine of Wessex, who ruled for thirty-seven years [688–726] and then went to St Peter's and died there [in Rome]. They were the sons of Cenred, son of Ceolwold, son of Cutha, son of Cuthwine, son of Ceawlin [third king of Wessex, '560–591'], son of Cynric [second king of Wessex, '534–560'], son of Creoda, the son of Cerdic [the legendary first king of Wessex, '519–534']. Cerdic was the son of Elesa, son of Gewis, son of Wig, son of Freawin, son of Freothogar, son of Brand, son of Bældæg, son of [the god] Woden, son of Frealaf, son of Finn, son of Godwulf, son of Geat, son of Taetwa, son of Beaw, son of Sceldwa, son of Heremod, son of Itermon, son of Hathra, son of Hwala, son of Bedwig, son of Sceaf the son of Noah. He was born in Noah's ark. Lamech, Methusaleh, Enoch, Jared, Mahalaleel, Cainan, Enos, Seth, Adam the first man and our father that is Jesus Christ.

BEZEL OF RING.   INSIDE.   SIDE VIEW.

Gold ring with the name of Ethelswith, queen of Mercia, Alfred's sister, on the back. The queen probably wore this herself. Found in Yorkshire, 1870.

This genealogy, which we are not meant to take literally or altogether seriously, is discussed in its place among Alfred's ancestors and supposed ancestors.

The section of the *Chronicle* that we have just read mentions a bishop and eight noblemen, all of them governors of provinces in posts of great responsibility. The author names them for two reasons, neither remotely concerned with disinterested historical information. He was writing for an audience familiar with their deeds and reputations; many of them were the governors' descendants and always enjoyed hearing and reading about them. He also used the names and their battles won or deaths in fierce fighting for dramatic effect, as a means of building up tension.

These noblemen are examples of a type found everywhere in Europe. Over the last century intensive work, largely by German scholars, on Frankish charters and the recipients and witness-lists, has resulted in the reconstruction of their aristocracy as large family groups or 'cousinhoods'. With this very reasonable and likely concept came the claim that these groups of relatives formed rival factions struggling for power and lands. Further scrutiny of the evidence seems to have put the hypothesis out of court, as each 'cousinhood' was itself divided into shifting alliances of mutually distrustful relatives just like the Carolingian dynasty itself. As we shall see, there is fairly good evidence, mainly persistently recurring name roots, like the Os–s, to think that most English governors came from a similar group of cousinly factions, but evidence for rivalries is minimal or has been successfully suppressed.

The court of Wessex, in which Alfred grew up in the 850s, was small and its assemblies rather informal affairs, usually composed of the archbishop and five bishops, never more than eight governors and up to about sixteen ministers, as we can see from more than thirty surviving charters of Ethelwulf's reign. By comparison, before the 840s the neighbouring kings of Mercia had regularly summoned much larger courts of as many as twelve governors and the twelve bishops of the southern province with several abbots and up to sixteen ministers. Neither put on much of a show to compare with the courts of Charlemagne or Louis the Pious with imperial ceremony and bishops and governors by the score, still less of the Byzantine emperors in Constantinople.

All or most of the southern bishops, led by the archbishops of Canterbury, usually attended the Mercian kings' assemblies before the 840s, even after Kent and the south-east had fallen to Wessex in the 820s; we might conclude that Offa's successors clung on to some kind of prestige as patrons of a national Church. From about 840 the Mercian court was rigid and hierarchical, ruled by more ceremony and stiffer etiquette with the governors ranked by strict seniority, to judge from the regularity with which their names are listed in order as they witnessed charters, while only the bishops of Lichfield, who are almost always named first, Hereford, Leicester, Lindsey and Worcester came.

Kings were always attended by an inner circle of their personal staff who, we may suspect, were not normally listed as witnesses to charters, one or more governors and a group of ministers, present perhaps on some informal rota. Forming daily assemblies, these smaller groups can sometimes be recognised in some of the witness-lists. Major decisions were ratified by regular larger assemblies, whose character varied greatly during the ninth century.

By bringing together details from a range of charters, we can draw general conclusions about governments and their running of public affairs, that is the more serious acts of kings and their leading nobles, the governors of provinces and counties, who were regular attenders at the royal councils, assemblies or courts at which public business was finalised. Our raw material is the incidental detail from many of the two hundred charters, such as notes of where the assembly was taking place, comments on the

27

circumstances and the lists of witnesses, often shortened and sometimes omitted. Lists of names, a vital and neglected class of evidence of great importance in many periods, require careful study for us to bring out all the information that they contain. We are concerned in this chapter with these men as groups acting together, in the next with them as individuals. We can extract a good deal more information from this data and incidental references in other sources, such as the *Chronicle*, than seems possible at first glance, even if much of it is a matter of probabilities and possibilities.

At the greater assemblies the leading men of each kingdom, and sometimes a woman of high rank, met with great ceremony in formal royal council and, no doubt among much diplomatic and military business, political intrigue and social chit-chat, transacted the legal business whose record alone survives in any quantity. After war-plans, financial affairs, church doctrine and foreign policy were discussed and decided on, we may assume that the assembly became a court of appeal giving final judgement on, among other things, land ownership and land tenure, before concluding with routine matters such as straightforward sales and leases of property. A few of the surviving charters are evidently court judgements; with most it is impossible to tell whether they were disputed cases or routine transfers.

The sons of kings and no doubt also of governors were present from an early age so that years later, when problems surfaced for any reason, they could recall the details from well-trained memory, as they could also recite many epics of ancient and current heroes. This is why we can identify very young children, such as Alfred at five, among the witnesses and presumably also why the future King Charles the Bald was prominent at the age of three at the ceremonies for baptising the Danish King Harald.

The lists of witnesses to ninth-century charters must, as a general rule, represent the order in which the main participants stood or sat at the assemblies. This allows us to say that the young Alfred and his next brother Ethelred were regularly attended by two abbots, Wullaf and Werferth, and by the minister Esne who was no doubt their guardian or governor while the abbots were their tutors. But sometimes he had a holiday with one of the governors.

The surviving legal papers and property records of the ninth century and of Alfred's lifetime in particular hold precious information about events of the time, about Alfred himself and about many other leading men and women whom he knew. There are about two hundred extant charters, leases, wills, agreements and court settlements from the two kingdoms of Wessex and Mercia for the ninth century, practically none from the kingdoms of East Anglia and Northumbria. These charters contain a great detail of information, about property deals and church endowments; about royal policy towards such matters; about royal and ecclesiastical courts and assemblies and their movements and rotations; and about the topography and agriculture of many of the scattered estates involved. The number is not really adequate for making comparisons and drawing conclusions about local legal customs and a common English legal tradition.

About a tenth of them survive as original documents, all on parchment. The rest are later copies, most of them in great manuscript volumes, the property books or *cartularies* compiled between the eleventh and the fourteenth centuries by priests and monks whose main aim was to be able to produce evidence in court to prove that their abbey or cathedral had owned a particular property for centuries, if their ownership was ever challenged, and to enable their church to lay claim to property that they had once owned and then lost. Hardly any of these monks had the least interest in history for its own sake and none had any compunction about making up and adding in a few extra charters that they could not find, but felt should have existed. Thus some charters were forged for particular motives, but by no means as many as used to be thought.

This change of attitude was due largely to the late Professor H. P. R. Finberg of Leicester University, who took the view that only a few charters are complete forgeries and that most are essentially authentic or, if tampered with or 'improved' in copying, still have a basis of truth. He pointed out that some of the copies are translations or paraphrases from Old English into Latin, or from Latin into Middle English. Careless, lazy or over-confident scribes shortened others, by missing out or abbreviating whole sections such as the lists of witnesses. All these factors caused most scholars, for much of this century, to consider almost all charters suspect for one reason or another. Most scholars now think that most charters are authentic, although they disagree over details.

29

Now and again we find extraordinary errors and misjudgements.

Like all historical and much other data, charters can only be used by systematic listing and reordering of lists; lists and indexes are the lifeblood of history. The charters, our second most important source of evidence after the *Chronicle*, have been systematically listed and published several times over since as long ago as the 1830s. The historian's first action, after scanning through the data for a theme or period, must always be to list the basic sources, his immediate data, and then to rearrange the data in various ways. He will always be on the look-out to supplement his original material with more information sniffed out or found by chance. And he must also search for parallels and comparisons in other regions or countries.

Here, in the particular context of Alfred and ninth-century Wessex, we must extract what information we can from the *Chronicle* and the charters and their attached witness-lists, by listing the charters, the participants and the witnesses. Then we must reorder our lists into names and assess each name to see how many individuals of the same name might be represented. Before we can make any generalisations about career structure, political rivalries, age at appointment and at death and so on from this scanty evidence, we have to attempt to write a 'Life' of each nobleman. We must do the same for Mercia for two main reasons, to gain comparative data and to find background information about the very large portion of Mercia which Alfred added to his kingdom in the early 880s.

We must now glance at some meetings of royal courts from the 770s to the 850s, recorded by chance through property charters, as selections from our lists. These assemblies, which met in many different locations and varied greatly in composition, are best examined with actual examples from Wessex, from the south-east and from Mercia over a fairly long period of time.

Let us begin by assembling and examining nine charters issued between the 770s, seventy years before Alfred's birth, and the 850s, to get an impression of the traditions within which his grandfather and father ruled and in which he grew up; and examining them to gain an overall view of the assemblies at which they were issued, where they were held and who was present; and whether they were flexible and adaptable or followed unchanging traditions.

We can scarcely avoid mentioning the particular transaction which has caused the record to be preserved, but our main objective is the assemblies themselves rather than the business they carried out. We will see Alfred himself as a small boy at one of the last of these assemblies, and later meet him holding his own courts.

We will see how one region, Kent, was run under three different regimes, by an independent king, as a Mercian dependency and as a junior kingdom for the heir to the throne of Wessex. We will see how the government of Mercia was managed as well as how Wessex was ruled. Of course the fact that they were held at all indicates that kings were not autocrats, but ruled by reaching a consensus with their leading men. The lists of names are an essential component of our survey.

1. In 778, at Canterbury, King Egbert II of Kent, namesake and perhaps uncle to Alfred's grandfather Egbert of Wessex, held court with the archbishop of Canterbury, a priest and eight others, no doubt the magnates, petty equivalents of later governors. Egbert, one of several obscure kings or joint kings in Kent at this time, seems to have ruled independent of Mercia. Another minor king, Sigired in the 860s, was perhaps the father of the Sigired named among the witnesses. They were from a princely and wealthy family whose distinctive Sige– names recur, like the Ceol–s in Kent or the Os–s in Hampshire.

Among other business the king gave or confirmed to Bishop Deora of Rochester (*c*.768–783) half a farm at Bromgeheg and a marsh called Scaga. The estate is either Broom Hill in Frindsbury, now a western suburb of Rochester, just across the Medway, or Bromhey Farm in Cooling (7km to the north).

The document used in the ceremony still survives as a single-sheet vellum charter in the British Library of about this date; or if not, it is an early file-copy.[7] In another charter of the next year Egbert confirmed or repeated the transaction, with eight witnesses, none of them churchmen, only two or three of whom were the same.[8]

31

Churchmen	Others	Witnesses in 779
archbishop	UBA	BOBA
IAENBERHT of	BOBA	BALTHARD
Canterbury 765–	UUALHARD	UUEALHARD
792	UBBA	BANTA
priest ESCUUALD	ALDHUN	BILLNOTH
	SIGIRED	OSUULF
	ESNI	BUBBA
	EANIARD	BALTHARD*

2. In 789 King Offa of Mercia, who had regained control of Kent, held an assembly at Chelsea near London, attended by two archbishops, six bishops, two abbots, another king of Mercia (his own son Egfrith), and ten others, clearly his governors. The second archbishop was Offa's own principal bishop at Lichfield, whom he had contrived to have promoted; three of the other four Mercian bishops were present, with the local bishop of London (for Essex) but Hereford was absent; from Wessex, Winchester had come but not Sherborne; from East Anglia, Elmham but not Dunwich, while Selsey was also absent and Rochester, the recipient or plaintiff, is not listed. Church affairs were evidently not very high on the agenda, but every southern kingdom was represented.

Whatever other business was gone through, Offa gave or confirmed to Bishop Wermund of Rochester (*c.*783–804) a farm at

> Broomgeheg with the Uuodafleot on the east, a spring on the south and ditches or hedges on the other sides; and a marsh known as Scaga, round which flowed the Iaegnlaad.

This is evidently the farm which Egbert had granted half of in 778. Perhaps Offa had seized the property as a gift made by a rebel king without his consent and the bishop had to pay dearly to recover it. Offa also took estates that Egbert had given to Canterbury, which were recovered with great trouble.

We recognise Ubba as a survivor from Egbert's regime, but his

---

* All these names appear in the charters spelt in a wide variety of ways. In the witness lists, these appear as in the original documents, but in the text of this book in a unified modern spelling. I have put the names of important individuals in capitals, and of those of lower rank in lower case to distinguish between them.

other magnates have dropped from the record, perhaps into exile with the younger Egbert. A namesake, probably a grandson, of Ceolmund will appear in much later charters; Ceolheard was no doubt a kinsman in the Ceol– family.

This charter[9] is known from a copy in the great twelfth-century Rochester property book, the *Textus Roffensis*, first printed in 1720 by the Oxford antiquary Thomas Hearne, who had already published Spelman's *Life of Alfred* in 1709. It is still at Rochester cathedral.

Churchmen	Others
archbishop IAENBERHT 765–792	BERHTUUALD
archbishop HYGEBERHT 779–803	EADBALD
bishop CEOLUULF of Lindsey 767–796	BRORDA
bishop HEARDRAED of Worcester	ÆTHILHEARD
781–*c.*799	CEOLMUND
bishop UNUUONA of Leicester *c.*783–802	UBBA
bishop CYNEBERHT of Winchester	HEABERHT
*c.*783–802	FORTHRED
bishop EALGHEARHD of Elmham	UUIGCGA
*c.*783–809	CEOLHEARD
bishop EADGAR of London *c.*788–791	
abbot EALGMUND	
abbot BEONNA	

3. In about 797 Offa's son-in-law and dependent king, Beorhtric of Wessex, held a court at an unknown spot in his realm. Both his bishops and seven governors attended. The scribe gives dignity to this small and subservient court by proudly calling the governors prince, prefect, count, patrician and under-king or viceroy. One of them, Wor, died in 802, the same year as King Beorhtric, as we read in the *Chronicle*, which also tells us that governor Weohstan was killed later that year in battle at the head of the men of Wiltshire. He does not figure in this list but appears with Offa's daughter Queen Eadburg (and the bishops of Sherborne and Winchester) in another list of about this date from a charter about land at Crux Easton in Hampshire; this too is printed below.[10]

All we know of their business on this occasion is that the king gave his governor, the 'most faithful prince' Hemele, an estate at

Hurstbourne (36 hides) in exchange for land on the River Meon
which Hemele had bought from King Cynewulf (757–786) 'for the
purest gold'[11]. We will find ourselves on the Meon again shortly.

Both charters survive in the property book of Abingdon abbey,
copied in the late thirteenth century from a confused twelfth-century
compilation which included much legend and the records of some
other ancient monastery. Among the founding collections of the
British Library, this was published, rather to the bafflement of
scholars, among the very first volumes of the 'Rolls Series' in 1858
by Joseph Stevenson; only now is some sense being made of it.

Churchmen	Governors	Governors in B282
bishop ÆTHELMOD	patrician HEMELE	WOR
of Sherborne *c.*770–	prince WOR	WIOHSTAN
791	prefect BEORNFRID	WIGFRETH
bishop KINEBERT of	prefect WIIGFRID	WIOHTBRORD
Winchester *c.*783–	under-king	ÆSE
802	LUNLING	EALHMUND
	prefect WIIGFRID	LULLA
	count WINGBALD	

4. In 824 Alfred's grandfather, King Egbert of Wessex, describing
himself as 'by the generous and bountiful hand of God king of the
West Saxons', assembled a council 'in the celebrated place "in the
Oak Glade", *in loco celebri ubi dicitur Ac Leah*,' which has never
been identified, but was probably Oakleigh in Higham, a short way
(6km) north-west of Rochester. We can infer from the *Chronicle*
that Egbert was at war this year, since his governors Burghelm
and Muca were slain; Kent, his father's old kingdom, was a likely
objective. Between 787 and 810 many assemblies were held 'at the
Oak Glade' and Alfred's father Ethelwulf beat the Vikings in battle
there in 851.

We may note that neither of the bishops and none of the five
governors remained from King Beorhtric's time in the 790s. Alfred
knew and must have respected Bishop Ealhstan, here named Alf-
stan, one of his father's closest associates and a valiant warrior,
and almost certainly a close relative.

Among other dealings the king gave his governor Wulfhard a

large estate on both banks of the River Meon, 'of twenty-two hides as the locals reckon, *xxiiorum manentium juxta estimationem incolarum,*' a transaction which continues the story begun in 797. The scribe explains the reason for the king's action. He did it 'for the good of my soul and to expiate my former misdeeds'.

The text survives in a twelfth-century Winchester volume in the British Library.[12]

Churchmen	*Governors*
bishop WIGTHEGN of Winchester *c.*810–833	BYRHTELM BURHHEARD
bishop ALFSTAN of Sherborne 824–867	WLFHARD HUN (of Somerset, killed in battle in 825) HIOTOMANN

5. In 828, probably somewhere in Kent, Surrey, Sussex or nearby, Alfred's grandfather and father, King Egbert of Wessex and his son, the new king Ethelwulf of Kent, held a council for the south-eastern provinces, composed of the archbishop and three bishops, four governors and eight ministers. Egbert was presumably inspecting his new provinces in the south-east of England which his son had just conquered for him with governor Wulfheard and Bishop Ealhstan as his main helpers.

Egbert brought his other principal bishop, Wigthegn of Winchester, and some governors and ministers; the others, not on tour with Egbert, were evidently the newly appointed local officials. One of the ministers, Ealhhere, had served under Mercia before the conquest and was later promoted to governor in Kent. Like Ealhstan he was probably a close relative of the two kings.

The transaction recorded on the surviving copy of the charter was to free the estates of the church of Rochester from many obligations. This may have been attached later to our list of witnesses, or the list attached to a bogus transaction. The wording of the charter has been suspected, because Egbert's regnal title 'by the grace of God king of the English' was not used until a century or more later, and also because of the general nature of the grant, which may have been concocted by a monk in about 1100.

35

The date given in the manuscript, the twelfth-century Rochester property book, the *Textus Roffensis*, of 823 is also wrong, as Kent did not become a province, or rather several provinces of Wessex until several years after that. Perhaps a copyist accidentally missed the 'v' from 'dcccxxviii', for 828. Despite this problem, the witness-list is unique, shows no sign of having been concocted later and has an authority of its own.[13]

Churchmen	Governors	Ministers
archbishop UULFRÆD of	WULFHARD	Aldred
Canterbury 805–832	MONNÆDÆ	Oshere
bishop WIGTHEGN of	OSMOD	Æthelwulf
Winchester c.810–833	DUDDA	Duduc
Bishop EALHSTAN of		Boba
Sherborne 824–867		Ealhere
Bishop BEORNMOD of		Sigesteb
Rochester c.804–843		Æthelhard

6. In 836 at 'Craeft', or Croft in Leicestershire, King Wiglaf of Mercia summoned a council composed of his queen, Cynethryth, the archbishop and eleven bishops, ten governors and twelve ministers. Wiglaf had ruled Mercia from 827, when King Ludeca had been killed in battle with five of his governors, to 829, lost it to Egbert of Wessex in 829–30 and 'again obtained his kingdom', as the *Chronicle* tells us, in 830.

At this combined royal council and church synod, a kind of assembly regularly held by the Mercian kings of this time, he freed Hanbury minster in Worcestershire, an ancient church set in a prehistoric hill-fort, from entertaining kings, governors and other magnates in return for a life interest in Idsall in Shifnall parish, Shropshire (20 hides) and other estates for himself and in Crowle, Worcestershire (10 hides) for governor Mucel, son of Esne. In this period the bishops acquired as many old endowed churches as they could, perhaps 'on trust' in an attempt to re-establish them securely or simply to increase their personal income.

One of the junior governors, Humberht, soon obtained a special status in Mercia as the senior governor, which may indicate that he was considered deputy head of state or even a kind of prime minister. For more than a quarter of a century, from 840 to 866, he appears first among the governors in practically all Mercian witness-lists. The bishops of Lichfield appear first of the churchmen so commonly that they must have had a similar special status, perhaps as head of the government secretariat.

Thirty-five years later one of the witnesses, the young Mercian governor Ethelwulf, was killed in battle at Alfred's side as a veteran warrior leading his men of Berkshire. The dates between which a man can be safely identified are given in brackets after the governors' names. We can see, with some surprise, that half of them held their posts for more than thirty years, one for over forty years, giving them a formidable wealth of administrative, financial, legal and military experience.

The original charter is in the British Library's founding collections and we can see how the vellum sheet was folded up and labelled, or *endorsed*, for filing in pigeon-holes in the bishop's office.[14] The words of the text are also preserved in the great eleventh-century Worcester property book in the same library.[15]

Churchmen	Governors	Ministers
archbishop	SIGRED (814–845)	Wicga
CEOLNOTH	MUCOEL Esne's son	Aldred
833–870	(814–855)	Aldberht
bishop CYNEFERTH	TIDUULF (831–836	Aelfred
of Lichfield c.832–	only)	Hwithyse
843	ÆTHELHARD	Werenberht
bishop RAETHHUN	(831–840)	Wulfred
of Leicester c.815–	CYNEBERHT (811–	Wiglaf
840	845)	Eanuulf
bishop EADUULF of	ÆTHELWULF	Alhmund
Lindsey 796–836/8	(836 in Mercia,	Berhtuulf
bishop HEABERHT	838–67 in	Ecghard
of Worcester 822–	Wessex; killed in	
845/8	871)	
bishop EADUULF of	ALHHELM (836)	
Hereford c.828–	HUMBERHT (836–	
837	866)	
bishop ALHSTAN of	ÆLFSTAN (831–	
Sherborne 824–867	848)	

bishop BEORMOD of   MUCOEL ii (855–
   Rochester *c.*804–   868)
   843
bishop HUSA of
   Dunwich *c.*836
bishop CUNDA of
   Elmham *c.*836
bishop
   CEOLBERHT of
   London *c.*820–853
bishop CYNRED of
   Selsey *c.*820–842
abbot EANMUND
abbot UUEOHTRED
abbot BEORNHELM

7. At Wilton in 839 Alfred's father, King Ethelwulf of Wessex, summoned a council, perhaps the first after he succeeded his father Egbert and moved from his junior kingdom of Kent to take over the throne of Wessex. It was composed of two bishops, five governors, a deacon (perhaps the council clerk) and eight ministers. They confirmed the decision of a church synod at Kingston in 838 that Malling, Kent should be returned to the church of Canterbury.

Two of the governors, Wulfhard and Monneda, had been with Ethelwulf and his father Egbert in Kent eleven years before, in 828. Another, Eanwulf, will appear in later lists and in the *Chronicle*. We cannot be sure which of the two Ethelwulfs serving as governors at this time was present, while Ethelhelm of Dorset went down to defeat and death at Portland two years later, still probably very young. The dates between which they can be identified as governors are given in brackets; the letter 'd' marks the known year of death.

The original charter survives in the British Library with two others in the series. Together they allow us to follow the legal processes by which Canterbury regained the estate.[16]

Churchmen	Governors	Deacon	Ministers
bishop	WULFHARD	Eadberht	Æthelheard
ALHSTAN of	(824–840d)		Ecgberht
Sherborne	ÆTHELWULF		Alhstan
824–867	i (838–844)		Osmund
bishop	or ii (836–		Huda
EADHUN of	871d)		Osric
Winchester	EANWULF		Ceolræd
c.835–838	(833–867d)		Uulflaf
	MONNEDA		
	(825–839)		
	ÆTHELHELM		
	(839–840d)		

8. At Ethandun or Edington in Wiltshire in 854 King Ethelwulf called together the royal council of Wessex, composed of his two Wessex bishops, seven governors, two abbots, his two younger sons, Ethelred and Alfred, then five, fourteen ministers and a priest, some time before setting off for his visit to Rome.

He repeated a grant, made thirteen years before at Æscantun in 841 to the deacon Eadberht, freeing from taxes and duties the modest (15 hide) estate of the church at Halstock in Dorset 'for his faithful service as well as for the honour of almighty God and for the love of St Michael whose church lies in the said little minster'. Eadberht was the 'council clerk' in 839 (Council 7).

The charter was preserved in the twelfth-century Sherborne abbey property book now in the British Library.[17] This volume or a copy was in Oxford in 1712, when the industrious antiquary Thomas Hearne copied eleven Anglo-Saxon charters from it into his notebook-diary; he took down the full lists of the witnesses of the first two charters, but with this, the third, he gave up this detail and simply copied the first name. He printed some of the charters in various of his many books; this charter remained unpublished until 1889 when Charles Doble, in the third of the eleven-volume series that took from 1884 to 1918 to publish much of the gist of Hearne's research notes, reached Notebook xxxix for 1712 and published the text. The property book itself was by then in the vast Phillipps collection and Birch, unusually for him, had missed this particular charter in 1887 when his Volume ii came out with practically every other ninth-century charter. It was only in 1964 that Finberg published the complete charter and list.

Churchmen	Governors	Princes' household	Ministers	Priest
bishop ÆLFSTAN of	ÆTHELBALD	abbot	Cynewulf	Eahmund
Sherborne 824–67	EANWULF i	WULFLAF	Cyneheah	
bishop SWITHUN of	OSRIC	abbot	Cuthulf	
Winchester 852–62	WULFHERE	WÆFERTH	Nithmund	
	ÆTHELBREHT	ÆTHELRED,	Ecgheard	
	EANUULF ii	later king	Osmund	
	LULLEDE	ÆLFRED, later	Milred	
		king	Ecgulf	
		minister Esne	Lullric	
			Ulfred	
			Alfstan	
			Kyma	
			Aldred	

9. At Oswaldesdun in 855 the new King Burgred of Mercia, in crisis with Viking raids, held a council with his queen, Alfred's sister Ethelswith whom he had married earlier in the year, four of his five bishops, ten governors and ten ministers. They witnessed Burgred free four of the bishop of Worcester's estates from most taxes in return for two heavy gold armlets, 'when the heathen [Vikings] were in the province of the Wrekin-people'.

Governor Humberht appears, as so often, as senior governor or perhaps deputy head of state. Mucel's granddaughter married Alfred in 868. Beornnoth was to survive all the troubles of the 870s, when Mercia was overrun by the Vikings and Burgred fled into exile abroad, to bring his province over to Wessex and give his loyalty to Alfred.

The charter survives as copies in both the early eleventh-century and the late eleventh-century part of the great Worcester property book in the British Library.[18] The list gives the names in two columns alternating.

Churchmen	Governors	Ministers
bishop CIORED of	HUNBERHT	Baldred
Leicester c.839–878	MUCEL	Eadgar

bishop ALHUN of	ÆTHELHEARD	Mucel iii
Worcester c.846–	ÆTHELWULF	Eadwulf
872	BEORNNOTH	Æthelwulf iv
bishop BERHTRED	O[S]MUND	Werberht
of Lindsey c.837–	BEORNNOTH ii	Baldred ii
872+	BERNHARD	Aldberht
bishop CUTHWULF	ALDBERHT	Æthelheard
of Hereford c.837–	CEOLMUND	
861	WERBERHT	

Of the eight governors named during Ethelwulf's reign by the *Chronicle*, we have already discussed Hereberht and Wulfhard, who were active in the previous reign. The remaining six all appear in other sources, and most of them are not well documented, although at least we know their shires. We examine the lives of Ealhhere, who was probably a kinsman of Ethelwulf and is well documented, and of Eanwulf later, and glance at the other four now.

Ceorl of Devon, documented 841–851

Born perhaps in the 810s, Ceorl is very poorly documented, appearing as a witness in only two charters, of 841 and 844. The *Chronicle* tells of his victory at Wicganbeorg over Viking raiders in 851. He may have been one of a leading West Country family and died young, perhaps in his twenties. The first grant of the Halstock charter noted at 8 above in 841 lists him first and hints that he had some seniority; but in 844 he is listed last of five governors.[19] We cannot say whether or not he was the father of governor Odda of Devon, who also defeated the Vikings in 878.

Ethelhelm of Dorset, documented 839–840

One of the worst documented of this group of governors, Ethelhelm appears in the witness-list of a single charter of 838, one of the group by which Canterbury recovered Malling in Kent (7 above), and once, when he was killed in battle, in the *Chronicle*. Ethelhelm's name suggests that he was of royal or princely blood; he was perhaps a kinsman of King Ethelwulf, appointed governor very young and killed in his early twenties.

41

Huda of Surrey, documented 842–853

Born perhaps about 820, Huda appears twice as a minister in Kentish charters, in 842 as the sixth of nine ministers listed in a royal grant of land at Rochester to governor Ceolmund which survives as a copy in the Rochester property book,[20] and in 843 as fifth of seven in a royal grant of land at Chart to governor Ealhhere's brother, minister Ethelmod, later himself a governor.[21] This survives as a particularly interesting original charter in the British Library; attached to the bottom corner by the witness-list is a rough copy of the list taken down during the ceremony at Mereworth in Kent, where the court was meeting. One scribe wrote the king and royal staff in a fine hand in the left-hand column; another jotted down the archbishop and his eight priests and deacons on the right in a crude scrawl. The fifteenth-century scribe who abbreviated a Malmesbury charter of 850, missing out at least half of the text and more than half the witnesses, may have disguised Huda as 'Tudda', who is otherwise unknown.[22] The *Chronicle* kills off this rather short-lived governor in perhaps his early thirties in battle on Thanet in 853, together with his much better substantiated colleague Ealhhere.

Osric of Dorset and Hampshire, documented 844–860

Born perhaps in about 820, Osric may have been Alfred's uncle, his mother's brother. He was often at court and witnessed as many as fourteen charters between 844 and 860. Perhaps he was appointed emergency governor of Dorset when Ethelhelm was killed in 840. In 845, as the *Chronicle* tells us, as governor of Dorset he joined Bishop Ealhstan and governor Eanwulf of Somerset to defeat a Viking force at the mouth of the River Parret. We learn from the same source that in 860 governor Osric of Hampshire and governor Ethelwulf of Berkshire defeated a sea-borne Viking army which had stormed Winchester.

3

Alfred's Visits to Rome
in 853 and 855, and
his Boyhood to 866

KING ETHELWULF OF WESSEX had begun to plan a journey to Rome in 839, ten years before Alfred's birth, when he sent an embassy to obtain King Charles the Bald's permission to travel through France.[1] He had to wait sixteen years before he was able to fulfil this intention, which two of his forebears had carried out, King Cadwalla in 688 and King Ine – who founded a church, which still exists in a rebuilt form, close to the great early Christian basilica of St Peter – in 726; both of them died in Rome.

In 853 Ethelwulf sent his youngest son Alfred to play his first major role in public affairs and diplomacy, not in England, but in central Italy. The four-year-old prince rode a thousand miles to Rome to represent Ethelwulf at the papal court. We have already glanced at the *Chronicle*'s brief note of this epic journey:

> King Ethelwulf sent his son Alfred to Rome. The noble Leo [IV], then pope in Rome, anointed him royally and sponsored his confirmation.

The particular occasion may have been the first anniversary of the inauguration of the 'Leonine City', the new fort constructed around St Peter's church by Pope Leo IV, an energetic restorer of churches and builder of fortresses, and a skilled fund-raiser and publicist of both his projects and himself. He may have sent

43

Ethelwulf an invitation without really expecting anyone to show up.

For a prince to be initiated into public duties at such an early age was not at all unusual at this time. Charles the Bald himself had been three when he and the palace doorkeeper Gerung led his father, the Emperor Louis the Pious, and the Danish King Harald for the latter's solemn baptism in formal procession into the church at Mainz ahead of the leading counts of the empire, the arch-chancellor, who was English, and the arch-priest, who came from Ireland. Charles must often have wished in later life that Harald had stayed at home and not been given such a glimpse of imperial splendour; he and his sons were to prove themselves fearful thorns in his side as they played their parts, now bandit, now imperial governor, in the Low Countries.

Thirty years later Alfred told the Welsh Bishop Asser, one of his religious advisers who was regularly at court, about the ceremony in which Pope Leo had anointed him solemnly, perhaps as an honorary consul of Rome. Historians debate this occasion fiercely, some claiming that a letter from Pope Leo to King Ethelwulf, informing him that 'we have decorated him, as a spiritual son, with the dignity of the [sword-]belt and the vestments of the consulate,' was concocted three centuries later by priestly forgers desperate to create evidence in a tremendous row about the standing of the German emperors in the eleventh century.[2] So many historians have nervously denounced so many documents of this time as forgeries that we are tempted just to sigh deeply and agree. But a wiser solution is to present the evidence and outline the problem, without taking sides.

Some time perhaps in 853, when he was four and in England, Alfred was recorded as taking a formal part in legal ceremony at his father's court. King Ethelwulf's grant to minister Ealdhere of an estate of one ploughland at Ulaham in Kent lists 'Elfred the king's son' after three governors and before a fourth.[3] The original charter survives in the British Library; but we must add that the date is far from certain and the list of witnesses also includes Ethelwulf's third son as 'Ethelbearht king'; all other evidence implies that he cannot have become junior king in Kent before 855, when the royal party left for Rome and the second son Ethelbald left Kent and took over Wessex. Perhaps therefore the

charter really dates from 856–858, when Ethelbert had to share
Kent with his father Ethelwulf and Alfred was, aged about seven
to nine, more likely to be with his father than in Wessex with the
disloyal Ethelbald.

Alfred was consistently listed in 854, at the age of five, among
the witnesses of a series of charters by which his father gave a
generalised group of privileges to churches and bestowed a strict
legal title, clear of most dues and duties, on particular estates which
he and his ministers could then use for endowing churches in
perpetuity.[4] These survive in a number of rather scrambled copies,
most of them in property books of the twelfth to fifteenth centuries.
The earliest version is a loose vellum charter, usually thought to
be an eleventh-century file-copy, in the British Library which
relates to minister Wiferth and a property at Hardenhuish in Wiltshire (1 hide), listing as witnesses the king and his two Wessex
bishops, grand old Ealhstan of Sherborne and Swithin, the future
weather-saint, of Winchester, six governors, two abbots 'Hunlaf'
and 'Hunerferth' (for Wullaf and Werferth), minister Esne, the
two king's sons 'Æthred' (for Ethelred) and 'Ælfred', minister
Cynewulf and thirteen other ministers.[5]

The two princes, the two abbots and minister Esne appear
together during these years so regularly that they must have formed
an inner group within the royal household. Two other ministers,
Cynewulf and Cyneheah, also appear quite often with them and
may have accompanied the young princes as specialists in hunting,
riding, sword- and axe-fighting and other princely skills.

In 1964 Finberg made sense of this group of charters and stated
some of the uncertainties very clearly;[6] he eliminated four[7] as concocted by Winchester monks of the Norman period on the basis
of authentic charters and, in one case, other forgeries. He recognised one as a memorandum written at Winchester in Old English
some fifty years later to convey the gist of an authentic charter
without all the details;[8] and accepted six as copies of genuine
documents of 854, the charter-copy and texts from property books
and registers from Abingdon, Glastonbury, Malmesbury and Winchester.[9]

Finberg added to the series of charters of 854 as clearly related,
one from the Rochester property book, a charter recording King
Ethelwulf's grant to his minister Dunn of

45

a close south of HROBI's fort [Rochester] with ten yokes of land next to the hamlet and two yokes of meadow and ten honest waggonloads [of firewood] from the king's wood on the hill and grazing-rights on the saltmarsh, as belonged to the township by right from ancient times.

The grant, dated DCCCLV for 855, was made 'when I went overseas to Rome'; perhaps this implies that the transaction was arranged before he left and validated on his return. The actual 'paperwork' was presumably carried out after Ethelwulf's return to England some time in October 855.[10] He is listed first of the witnesses, then the archbishop, King Ethelbert (the middle son), governors Lullede and Ethelmod, Alfred the king's son, governors Eadred and Ethelric and eleven ministers. Many of these had perhaps accompanied the royal party to Rome; they may also have constituted a 'loyal' group opposed to King Ethelbald (the second and eldest surviving son) usurping the senior kingdom of Wessex.

Before he left for Rome in 855 or while he was abroad, Alfred lost his mother Osburh who slipped quietly from the record as she had lived. Her death cannot have been long before he left, as he was old enough both to crave ownership of a book of English poems and also to learn the contents off by heart before all his older brothers could, to win the book itself as his reward. Asser tells us how Osburh had shown them the book, pointing out its finely decorated capital letter (or letters) and offering to give it to the first of them able to understand it, as an incentive for them to learn to read. Alfred took it off to his tutor, presumably one of the abbots, Wullaf or Werferth, to recite to him until he had it word perfect, came back to Osburh, declaimed the poems and scooped the prize.[11]

By the time he was seven Alfred had crossed the full width of Europe four times, twice with his father. When he revisited Rome he could show Ethelwulf how the generous donations he had made had been spent on defence works essential to the preservation of Christianity. We can only judge the donations he made in his lifetime by his bequest, which Asser records, of three hundred mancuses a year to Rome, that is nine thousand silver pennies a year, one-third to St Peter's for oil for the lamps on Easter eve, one-third to St Paul's (another great church at Rome) also for Easter oil and one-third for the pope.[12]

Asser wrote briefly, during Alfred's lifetime and after prolonged periods spent at court with Alfred, about this second visit:

> King Ethelwulf . . . journeyed to Rome with great ceremony, bringing his son Alfred for his second trip, loving him more than his older sons. They stayed a whole year and then returned home accompanied by Judith the daughter of King Charles.[13]

It has been claimed that, despite their close daily personal contact for some years, Alfred deliberately muddled the good bishop and, for public relations and to give himself a better reputation, managed to convert a single visit to Rome into two trips; but this claim is not proper use of documentary sources. Clear contemporary evidence tells us that Alfred went twice to Rome as a child and it is not really up to us to deny it.[14]

Asser was a Welsh priest and later bishop who knew Alfred well and had been summoned to his court in 885 to advise and help him. He commemorated Alfred in a biography or *encomium* based on the *Life of Charlemagne* which Einhard, a monk who had known Charlemagne well and was private secretary to his son, the Emperor Louis the Pious, compiled in the 820s.[15] Asser was writing for a Celtic-speaking audience, perhaps the Welsh princes who paid tribute to Wessex, their priests and their more educated subjects.

The biography begins with a long chapter on Alfred's birth and ancestry and a shorter one on his mother and her background. Most of the book (paragraphs 3–86) is Asser's own expanded Latin translation of the *Chronicle* from 851 to 887, amended to include extra details that he had been told about or thought his particular audience needed, such as explanations of the meaning of English names. He was using a text that differed in various details from the established main text that has come down to us. Asser then recalls helping King Alfred make a sudden breakthrough to be able to read and understand Latin (paragraphs 87–9). The final part of the book is Asser's assessment of Alfred's religious, legal and technological innovations and achievements (paragraphs 90–106). To judge from a mention of Alfred as being in his forty-fifth year, he wrote it in 893. The book ends abruptly at a chapter describing Alfred's vigorous attempts to improve standards of

Monograms of Pope Leo IV (left) on a papal bull; on a stone from the entrance-gate of his fortress at 'Leopolis' (centre); for comparison (right) a monogram of London on a silver penny struck for Alfred.

learning and thus of justice among his great lords. As with the *Chronicle* we seem to be left with a draft rather than a fully finished work.

In 1964 the most eminent living English medievalist, the retired historian V. H. Galbraith, made the ridiculous claim that Bishop Leofric of Exeter had faked the whole of Asser's *Life* two centuries after the event, arguing the case over forty pages of print. After a reasonable pause for thought, a scholarly specialist in Anglo-Saxon literature, Miss D. Whitelock, comprehensively demolished the learned but over-conceited professor and re-established Asser's credit, a task that may need repeating every few decades.[16]

WESSEX AND ROME

Rome, once the greatest city of the West and capital of the Empire, now leader and spiritual focus of the Western Church, was in many ways a second home to the royal family of Wessex. A century and a half earlier King Ine, Alfred's grandfather's grandfather's great-uncle (there may be an ancestor or so too many in the *Chronicle*'s family tree), had founded the church that is now San Spirito in Sassia, the church of the Holy Spirit 'in the Saxon quarter', and had retired there after his abdication in 726. He was following the example of his kinsman and immediate predecessor on the throne of Wessex, the pagan Cadwalla, who had abdicated and gone to Rome for baptism in 688. Other English monarchs, nobles and churchmen visited or retired to Rome.

The kings of Wessex may have sent offerings to Rome almost every year; the *Chronicle* records a series of missions between 883 and 890. The envoy was usually a nobleman, often a governor. The great man and his gifts must have been led by an experienced guide with up-to-date knowledge of safe routes, guarded by an escort of at least thirty to eighty warriors, perhaps many more, well-mounted enough to outride and well-armed enough to out-fight any opposition. We can only imagine that, for Alfred's visits to Rome, accommodation along the route varied from welcoming courts where the hundred or so fighting men of his escort could feast and drink while their young prince slept, to bleak wayside shelters without food or fire. No doubt English innkeepers, priests and mercenaries had settled here and there along the way. When a king such as Ethelwulf rode to Rome, there must have been a great bustle of couriers making arrangements, while detachments of the royal guards reconnoitred the route, with exchanges of gifts and much ceremony at the courts of kings and counts as he travelled.

By the 850s Rome had long ceased to be the capital of a world-wide empire and the greatest city in the West, as it had been in the first and second centuries. But it was still the great religious centre of the West. The settled areas comprised a few scattered villages, almost hidden among the gigantic ruins of antiquity. Each village lay around one of the great early Christian basilicas, some inside and some outside the vast city walls, which had far too long a perimeter for the few Romans of the ninth century to defend. The most closely settled part of Rome, where the English had their local base, lay outside the ancient walls near St Peter's.

In 846, three years before Alfred was born, a sea-borne Arab raiding army had attacked and sacked what remained of the city, looted St Peter's and despoiled the apostle's shrine. The local people had made no attempt to shelter behind the vast circuit of city walls, but had simply abandoned their homes and churches and fled. The 'schools' of the Franks, Frisians and English, which presumably means the residents and pilgrims with any envoys and their guards who happened to be present, had stayed to form a battle-line, to defend the city and fight to the last. The Emperor

Lothar's commanders caught up with the raiders a long way off and attacked them, inflicting some casualties, while local forces dealt mercilessly with a second smaller Arab force and wiped it out.

In 848–852 as a direct result of the sack of Rome in 846, Pope Leo IV (847–855) built a sizeable walled fort covering an area 1700m by 320–370m, from the great mausoleum of Hadrian towering over its ancient Roman bridge to the crest of the Vatican hill. Much of the circuit of the walls, well over 3km long, has disappeared under vast Renaissance gun-defences, but sections survive in the Vatican Gardens and a continuous length of more than 600m remains, widened and partly refaced, with the Renaissance popes' fifteenth-century funk-passage running along the top, to link the papal palace to the Castel Sant' Angelo, as the mausoleum became. Hastily built of recycled Roman brick and tile laid in 'undulating, even drunken' courses with many large blocks of tufa and marble dragged from the ancient ruins stuck in here and there, the wall was 6–8m high and probably no more than 1.3m thick. Some original battlements and five square towers survive.[17]

The labour squads of 'militias' from the rural estates, the 'Domuscultae', around Rome set up inscriptions, composed in the worst Latin imaginable, to mark the towers and lengths of walls that they had built, however unwillingly, under Leo's firm authority.[18] We can suggest that each estate was also obliged to keep its stretch of wall in good repair and provide warriors to man it in time of war, possibly even to keep a watch in peace. Local cities and monasteries were also ordered to contribute and a lost inscription tells of a stretch built by Arab prisoners.

After five years' work, Leo IV inaugurated the new fortress on 27 June 852 with a solemn processional service, leading his clergy, barefoot and with ashes in their hair, as for a Good Friday service, around the new defences. They halted to bless each of the three new gates with a specially composed prayer. These, which were recorded, are more practical and modest than the high-flown and would-be poetical sentiments put up over the gates.[19]

With an eye to morale-building and good publicity, Leo named the new fortress after himself, calling it the Civitas Leoniana, or Leonine City. He set up grandiloquent inscriptions, written in deplorably bad Latin, over each of the three gates, extolling himself and his distant overlord, the Emperor Lothar, Charlemagne's grandson, who was usually based in the north of Italy. The one at the south gate, the Posterula Saxonum or Saxons' Gate adjoining the Schola Saxonum or Saxons' Hostel, read:

> You who come and go, Traveller, note this glory
> Which the fourth LEO the pope, has gladly built.
> The beauteous summits shine with exact* marble
> Which fitting deeds please by the hands of man.
> This work of the invincible emperor Holothair
> Which you espy. the rejoicing bishop carried out.
> I trust that the wars of evildoers will no more harm you
> Nor will there be a victory beyond your enemies.†
> Rome the head of the world,
> Rome the splendour and golden hope
> Bountiful, behold, as the labour of your bishop shows.
> THIS CITY IS CALLED LEONINE, ITS FOUNDER'S NAME[20]

After Charlemagne conquered the Lombard kingdom in northern Italy in 773–774, the popes acted effectively as superior counts of the Frankish Empire on its furthest southern borders. Other dangerous frontier zones were entrusted to *markgrafs* with authority over a group of counts, or in the Byzantine Empire *doukoi* set over groups of *strategoi*.

The energetic Pope Leo III (795–816), who crowned Charlemagne emperor in 800, invaded and conquered the lands south of Rome as far as the mouth of the Garigliano, where in about 810 he founded a fort or *civitas*, and named it, after himself, Leopolis, Leo's Town in Latinised Greek, to be the seat of a local governor, his rector or consul.[21] He also started to build a wall around St Peter's. This was unique for the time, as Charlemagne had deprived his other bishops of secular authority and taken over their strongholds.

In 842 Gregory IV (827–844) built some kind of defence work at Ostia, perhaps only mud-brick walls filling gaps and doors in a group of ruined Roman apartment blocks, if remains found in excavations long ago have been correctly recognised.[22]

---

* This seems to be a mistake for 'precious'.
† This is probably a mistake for 'in front of our gates'.

In addition to establishing his central fortress around St Peter's, Leo IV settled a group of Corsican refugees on the site of the long-abandoned harbour-town of Portus, putting his own nephew Bishop Radoald as governor over them. As an important part of this second defence project, Leo made them self-sufficient by granting them farmland and promising them livestock.[23]

Leo's third defensive project was to relocate the displaced citizens of the old coastal town of Centumcellae in a hill-fortress well inland, naming it Leopolis, again claiming credit by name. Inscribed marble blocks have been found at the gate here, with monograms of 'PAPAE', Pope, and 'LEONIS Q[*uarti*]', Leo the Fourth, with fragments of a long inscription, surrounded by debased interlace and reading in the same exceptionally bad Latin as on the Leonine City:

> This City no work of man can damage . . .
> May the warrior turn away from here . . .
> May the enemy turn away [from] wrongdoing . . .
> . . . not this . . .
> . . . to violate the city . . .[24]

Leo IV's fortifications in and around Rome in the 850s may have inspired other chains or systems of defence elsewhere in Europe. His relocation of several groups, the Corsicans and the displaced citizens of Centumcellae, if not improvised on the spot, must have been carried out with some knowledge of the usual Byzantine frontier practice of rural resettlement and perhaps of their frontier works in this area and elsewhere. Leo's assignment of lengths of the Leonine wall to separate monasteries and estates to construct was no doubt the normal way all rulers carried out major projects at the time and had since the days of the Roman Empire; King Godfrid of Denmark had split up his frontier barrier, the Danewerke, into lengths for his nobles to construct.

ALFRED IN 856–866

While Alfred appeared in the *Chronicle* in his father's reign as a child of four, he did not appear again until he was nineteen, after the end of this group of entries. We do not lose touch with him, however, as the evidence of charters shows him taking a busy part in court life throughout his boyhood and as a teenager.

In the *Chronicle*'s account of the years 858–866 we can follow the deteriorating state of the English kingdoms (and continue to assess the character of this crucial source) in the reigns of his second and third brothers, Ethelbald and Ethelbert (855–866), until he was seventeen.

858

f. Two of Ethelwulf's sons succeeded to his realm, Ethelbald as king of Wessex and Ethelbert to the kingdom of the people of Kent, the kingdom of Essex, the people of Surrey and the kingdom of Sussex.

860

a. After ruling for five years, Ethelbald died and was buried at Sherborne. [He had married Judith, his father's young widow.] His brother Ethelbert succeeded to the whole kingdom and ruled in peace and harmony.

b. In his time a great sea-borne Viking army went overland and sacked Winchester. Governor Osric with his Hampshire troops and governor Ethelwulf and his Berkshire forces engaged the army. They drove it in flight and held the killing ground.

c. Ethelbert ruled for five years and was buried [in 866] at Sherborne.

d. The saintly Bishop Swithin [of Winchester 852–862] died.

865

a. A Viking army camped on Thanet and agreed a cease-fire with the men of Kent, who promised payment to get peace.

b. With the armistice in force while the cash was collected, the army went inland and pillaged all east Kent.

866

a. Ethelbert's brother Ethelred succeeded as king of Wessex.

b. A great pagan army invaded England and spent the winter in East Anglia, where they got horses. The East Anglians paid tribute.

These nine entries cram a vast amount of information into a few words. Before they set off for Rome in 855 Alfred's father King Ethelwulf had made the division referred to in 858, entrusting Wessex to the second, but eldest surviving son Ethelbald and his former junior kingdom of Kent to the third son Ethelbert. When he returned, in October or November 856, Ethelbald refused to hand back power in Wessex. Not wanting civil war, Ethelwulf agreed to leave him in control and ruled Kent and the south-east jointly with Ethelbert until he died a little over a year later, in January 858.

We can identify several men in the court circles of his brothers who must have had an influence on Alfred as he grew in these years from the age of nine to seventeen.

Eanwulf of Somerset, active 833–867

Governor Eanwulf of Somerset witnessed fourteen charters between 833 and 860 and died, aged about sixty, in 867. He must have been a familiar figure throughout Alfred's boyhood and no doubt showed him the site of his own victory over the Vikings in 845 at the Parrett mouth, discussing his tactics with the boy on the spot. The battle site, whatever its precise location, cannot be more than 13km from the 'isle of the princes' or Athelney.

Born in about 800–810, Eanwulf does not appear as a minister in any surviving charter of Egbert's reign of the 820s or 830s, but as he presumably came from the west and all charters listing ministers in this period are Kentish, we cannot be at all certain about his early public career. In 842 King Ethelwulf gave him Dicheat (25 hides), on the Fosse Way near Castle Carey and Lottisham (5 hides).[25]

When the court met at Cheddar or Somerton we may imagine Eanwulf, as governor of the shire, taking the young princes hunting in the marshes there and in particular giving Alfred the knowledge of the area where he later took refuge in the blackest days of 878, while governor Ethelnoth, Eanwulf's successor and perhaps his son, stood guard nearby. His death in 867, presumably in his fifties or sixties, is recorded in Ethelward's *Chronicon*, but not in the main text of the *Chronicle*.

Bishop *Ealhstan* of Sherborne

When King Egbert appointed him to Sherborne, the second bishopric in Wessex, in 824 Ealhstan must have been young or very
young, most likely in his early twenties. His name in Ealh– hints
at a very close kinship with Alfred's family and he can almost
certainly be looked on as a Kentish princeling, a brother or cousin
of Ealhhere and Ethelmod noted below, and a great-uncle or some
close older cousin of Alfred. He may well have been an influence
of great significance in Alfred's later boyhood, certainly for bold
courage and perhaps also for saintliness.

During his forty-three years as bishop he marched into Kent
with the young Ethelwulf, as adviser on logistics and perhaps
morals, in about 827. He led his retainers victoriously into battle
at the mouth of the Parrett in 845; we should think of him pointing
out details of the battle and, also with Eanwulf, hunting across the
Athelney marshes with the young princes including Alfred. He
must have been close on seventy if not older when he died in 867,
the same year as Eanwulf.

Ealhhere of Kent, documented 825–853

Alfred will have met, and will have been able to remember, a
governor who was killed in battle in 853, the year of his first visit
to Rome when he was four years old, Ealhhere of Kent. Born in
about 800, he was a local man; his predecessors as governor,
Wulfhard and Hereberht, came from Wessex to govern Kent after
the conquest by Wessex. The name in Ealh– suggests that he was
a younger son, nephew or grandson of Alfred's great-grandfather
King Ealhmund who ruled Kent in the 780s, and thus one of
Alfred's own family. A reliable bulwark of Alfred's father's regime
for twenty-eight years, this Kentish governor was probably his
uncle or close cousin.

He first appears as a junior minister in 825, when Mercia still
held Kent, fifty-ninth of sixty-five witnesses to some of the legal
proceedings at a church synod at Clovesho.[26] In the late 820s and
830s he was a minister in witness-lists to Kentish charters of King
Egbert of Wessex and his son King Ethelwulf of Kent: in 828 sixth
of eight ministers and sixteenth of all witnesses; in 833 fourth of
five ministers and sixteenth of all witnesses; in 839 second of
twenty-three unspecified men, perhaps all ministers, and seventh

of all witnesses.[27] We can see a regular progression upward in seniority as Ealhhere remained a minister in Kent for sixteen years or so from 825.

Ethelwulf, king of Wessex from 839, no doubt promoted Ealhhere governor after Hereberht's defeat and slaughter in 840; at least we meet him as a governor in Kent in 841. That year, as the second of two governors listed, he witnessed a charter by which King Ethelwulf of Wessex gave Hoborough in Kent, nominally a 240-acre farm, to Bishop Beornmod of Rochester.[28] He appears in several other charters of the time.[29] In 851 he and Alfred's eldest brother, King Athelstan of Kent, defeated the Vikings in a sea-fight at Sandwich, as we read in the *Chronicle*. We learn from the same source that after twelve years as governor he, like governor Hereberht before him, was killed by the Vikings, with governor Huda of Surrey, in a battle on the Isle of Thanet in 853, aged probably about fifty.

He may possibly have been the 'Alchere' whose brother, the reeve Abba, gave a food-rent to Folkestone church; he had a son Osberht, who was a minister in 839 and 845, and two daughters, Ealawyn who had property at Finglesham which paid one hundred pence a year to Canterbury and another, who married Oshere and had a son Eadwald, who eventually inherited family estates at Brabourne and Chart. His sister Ealburg held land at Bourne and Brabourne with her husband Ealdred.[30]

This rich detail is unusual for great English families of the ninth century; the conjunction of names in Os– and Ealh– strongly hints that the marriage of Alfred's father Ethelwulf to Osburh was one of a number between two closely linked dynasties in Kent and south Hampshire.

Ethelmod of Kent, active 841–859

A most familiar figure throughout Alfred's boyhood and perhaps his great-uncle, Ethelmod was Ealhhere's younger brother, born in about 815 or earlier. He appears as a minister in 841, and was a senior minister throughout the 840s. In 842, 843 and 845 we find him listed first of all ministers.

A scrap of vellum attached to an original charter of 843 in the British Library names the king's staff in the left-hand column in a fine clear hand, while the archbishop's priests are scrawled crudely on the right. This charter is of special interest in our immediate context, as Ethelmod himself was the recipient or purchaser of an estate at Chart in Kent (10 hides) which he later left to his wife. The vellum scrap is evidently the original witness-list written during the actual legal ceremony of giving, before the charter was completed. Ethelmod, named first of the ministers on the charter itself, comes next after the governors on the vellum scrap, but is called *'cel'*, as is the next-named man, Diora (Dera on the scrap). They were no doubt King Ethelwulf's two *cellarii*, or royal stewards. Such particular officials can only very rarely be recognised.[31]

Soon after his brother Ealhhere fell in battle on Thanet in 853 we find Ethelmod as governor. No doubt King Ethelwulf, who clearly knew him intimately, appointed him to succeed his brother to govern, most likely, west Kent. He appears on charters in 853, 855, 858 and perhaps 859 and then drops from the record, aged perhaps almost fifty. He left his widow Cynethryth his estate at Chart, to pass after her to his great-nephew Eadwald Oshering.[32]

We will continue Alfred's personal story after surveying the state of Europe at this time through a close examination of some of the chief places of some countries with close (and occasionally rather distant) English connections. We must inquire into the origin and nature of the Scandinavian raiders whom we have already encountered in the *Chronicle* in 860, 865 and 866 and see how they very gradually came to be a devastating threat.

4

The Chief Places of Christian and Pagan Europe: trade, forts and the origins of towns before the 860s

━━━━━━◆◆◆━━━━━━

A FULL UNDERSTANDING OF THE PLACES named in records of the time is the central historical problem of Alfred's kingdom of Wessex, as it is of every other European kingdom. This requires a whole battery of different skills, rules and methods. The chronicles and other sources name many places, some very familiar to us in their present form as great cities, such as London, Paris and Rome, or well-known towns like Oxford, Beauvais or Orleans. We must however set aside all our present-day images of them.

Raids, attacks, burning and plundering endlessly recur in all the chronicles and other records. A need for defence is the ninth century's most constant theme. From the 850s we encounter it in an increasingly and recognisably bureaucratic context and often wonder what these places were really like.

Many of the most important settlements of the ninth and tenth centuries have the element –burh, –burg or –borg in their name, from Burgos in Spain to Merseburg in eastern Germany and from Aggersborg in Denmark to the Borgo at Rome, as the Leonine City is called today; we have already visited it and other fortifications around Rome. As the word means 'protection' or 'fort', we will refer to the central focus of every chief place in Europe at this time as a fort.

We will review a selection of forts and their surrounding settlements before the 870s, beginning in Wessex with the one most familiar to Alfred's father and grandfather at Southampton, and continuing with London, which Alfred lost and recovered. We will include Oxford, a place long linked with Alfred, as a cautionary tale about the dangers of jumping to conclusions. Before reaching any further conclusions we will glance at a chain of forts built or improvised across northern Spain in the 850s, Bulgar stone forts and a Byzantine brick fort in the Ukraine.

In the next two chapters we will examine the Viking impact on the West, particularly on France up to the 860s, first from a Danish, then from a French viewpoint. Later we will follow King Alfred building forts in the 880s, and then be able to put his achievements into a broader European context.

The evidence of archaeology, our main tactical source of data, must be deployed on the topography, the surface of our subject, with a strategy based on the records. Topography, architectural and structural analysis and below-ground archaeology each have their own principles and procedures, which most historians and many archaeologists themselves fail to grasp. None of the three approaches is complete without the other two and, in this period, the use of all three depends largely on documents, a fourth approach to our subject. All these approaches depend on developing and checking hypotheses but they differ greatly in many ways. In archaeology a level, such as a floor or yard-surface, found above another level, such as a deposit of topsoil, must be of a later date, an absolute rule which does not apply to standing buildings, where earlier stonework can often be found surviving above a row of arches inserted through a wall.

At Southampton the principal place of trade and manufacture, and by far the largest settlement known in Wessex during the reigns of Alfred's father, grandfather and earlier forebears, lay north-east of the medieval walled town, which faces the broad tidal River Test. Different elements of this settlement lay on either side of the lesser River Itchen, the fort on the east and a trading settlement on the west. As we have seen, governor Wulfhard slaughtered most of a Viking force of 'thirty-three' ships here in 840.

The initial nucleus was a Roman fort (called Clausentum), containing in Anglo-Saxon times, we have to surmise, a royal hall and

59

housing for the king's officials, 3km from the mouth of the Itchen on its east bank. This was the Ham-Tun or 'town on the river bend' from which both the county of Hampshire and the modern city of Southampton take their names. It was the centre of a great royal estate with many hamlets and villages engaged in farming and other activities. In a passage written well over a century after the event, the *Chronicle* refers to Hamtunscire, Hampshire, as a district under the year 757, and also mentions the shire in a military context in 860 and 878.

The largest of the subsidiary settlements, the Ham-Wic or Hamwih, the 'trading mart on the river bend', which has been extensively excavated, lay on the eastern slope of an irregular brick-earth peninsula between the Itchen and the Test, a ferry-crossing and fifteen minutes' walk south of the Roman fort. Early boat-builders' yards and other such activities may one day be discovered in silted creeks on either shore of the Itchen above and below the Roman fort.

As the eastern suburbs of the later town were developed, pits dug for brick-earth revealed the rubbish-pits of the trading settlement. As early as the 1770s finds, including a surprising number of coins, had begun to attract antiquarians from the nearby town and drew the regular attention of professional men, a pleasant stroll from their homes and offices between the 1820s and the 1870s. The collectors included a banker, a surgeon and an Anglican priest in this time when Southampton was a fashionable resort. Post-war development of the suburban streets has given many opportunities for rescue excavations which have continued since 1946.

From a river frontage of less than 300m with marshes on either side, the trading settlement sloped gently up for as much as 1000m from the shoreline. With a width of up to 600m, the settlement covered over 40ha. Judging from documents, coins, pottery and radio-carbon samples, none absolutely precise for this period, the settlement began about 700, perhaps at the end away from the river, where the densest evidence for occupation has been found.

The road network can already be discussed in general terms, which will no doubt need refining with further discoveries. The modern topography has preserved only a partial skeleton of the old town plan. So far nine streets have been excavated or can be inferred on the line of medieval and later field-lanes which have survived as streets today. Three streets ran roughly north–south, and, as yet, we know of five running roughly east–west. While the plan has a semblance of regularity, it was not laid out at one time on a grid-plan, but evidently grew by stages in a reasonably regular way. One area around the old church of St Mary, quite near the river, has produced very few finds and structures and may have been a large open market-place.

The existing church of St Mary has a very large churchyard and, claiming to be the town's 'mother church', monopolised all burials in Southampton throughout the Middle Ages. This was not the case in Saxon times, from which nine burials or groups of burials have been found, four of sufficient size to be called burial grounds; one had a recognisable timber church.

The Anglo-Saxon residents dug through the ground surface to get clay for house walls and to make wells, storage-pits, rubbish-pits and cess-pits for themselves. Much of this surface was destroyed by foundations, drains, pipelines and brick-pits in the nineteenth century and later. In the limited areas left undisturbed ancient post-holes and stake-holes, investigated and recorded in the excavations, represent parts of many houses, but can seldom be interpreted as reasonably complete structures. One house seems to have been 10m or perhaps even 15m long and several were 5.5m long by 4.5m wide. There were a few shallow sunken huts, but no large cellar-pits so characteristic of tenth- and eleventh-century towns. Evidence of industry and manufacture is widespread and quite abundant. The inhabitants, who may have numbered as many as two or three thousand, included blacksmiths, coppersmiths, bone- and antler-workers and weavers, and no doubt other craftsmen whose debris is harder to identify or more liable to decay. Foreign-made pottery, markedly more abundant near the river, the presumed market-place and St Mary's church, may indicate the area where traders and merchants lived. Merchants and shipmasters had a long Channel crossing to the Normandy ports, the mouth of the Seine and the great mart of Quentovic south of Boulogne.

The extent to which the settlement was developed by successive kings of Wessex, or local magnates of Alfred's mother's family, the Os–s, drafting in artisans and consciously attracting merchants, is uncertain and our views will change with fashions of interpretation and as more evidence comes to light. The author of the latest major survey of the excavated sites and finds, A. D. Morton, suggests that Hamwic was 'in many ways an artificial creation' which was 'expanded in a number of controlled stages'. He draws attention to King Cadwalla's action when he captured the Isle of Wight, just across the Solent from Southampton, and tried 'to destroy all the people and bring in colonists from his own territory'.[1] Such forced movements of people were a normal procedure in the Byzantine Empire and are well documented also in Italy and Spain.

About a century and a half after the settlement came into existence, the 'archaeological evidence indicates that Hamwic had largely disappeared in the middle of the 9th century'. Neither coins nor pottery help us to be more precise about the date when the settlement was largely abandoned. Hamtun thus lost this large manufacturing and trading element at about the time Alfred was born. Its decline roughly coincides with the battle of 840, with the sporadic Viking attacks of 851–860 on Wessex and with the invasion of England that began in 866.

The excavations of the last fifty years have all been urgent rescue operations undertaken by successive improvised committees, societies and the local museum, far better than nothing, but often hurried. As a general rule the excavators decided to bulldoze off the shallow, but potentially very informative, upper layers before digging by hand. This has entailed the loss of such features as slightly raised floors and house walls built of turf or clay that survived only above the old ground surface. All this intensive archaeological work, made necessary by modern development, has led to sensible, scholarly and well-presented conclusions about the settlement up to 850. The city's Cultural Services Department has produced a clear statement of all the old findings and is well placed and organised for continuing work on this most important site.[2] Alfred used the old Roman fort as one of his chain of forts.

In Winchester (the Roman town of Venta Belgarum) extensive excavations by M. Biddle have revealed the plan of the church founded by the recently converted king in '648' (a very dubious date calculated in about 1100 in a Canterbury monk's adapted copy of the *Chronicle*, the F-text), which became a cathedral in about the 660s. The whole site of the Roman city, which had been largely deserted in the fifth and sixth centuries, seems to have been the bishops' property from the seventh to the late ninth century, together with a large area around.[3] There is no documentary or archaeological evidence for a royal palace in the sixth–ninth centuries, although Biddle has often claimed there was one. In the 880s Alfred took Winchester over as one of his forts.

The small Roman walled town of Dorchester-on-Thames, whose Roman name is unknown, manifestly succeeded the late prehistoric river-fort close by, now called 'Dyke Hills', which in turn must have succeeded the prominent hill-fort just across the Thames on 'Wittenham Clumps'. That the place remained of local importance well into the Saxon period is attested by many finds of early Saxon burials and huts.[4] The imposing abbey church, whose visible fabric is largely of the thirteenth and fourteenth centuries, can claim to be the mother church of both the Midlands and of southern England. At a date supposed to be about '635', Cynegils, the semi-legendary fifth king of Wessex (or perhaps rather of one of the petty kingdoms that became, or was absorbed by, or perhaps was later simply claimed by, Wessex), gave Dorchester to the missionary (later saint) Birinus as the first seat of his bishopric. Despite many small-scale excavations there are many unknown or obscure points about the place. The bishopric was soon moved to Winchester, but Dorchester became a Mercian bishopric for a time in the late seventh century and then again from the 880s to 1072. All this time the main royal centre in the area seems to have been at Benson, 4.5km to the south-east.

London, the seat of a bishop from 601 or soon after, fell into the power of the Mercian kings in the mid-eighth century, when they annexed the western part of the kingdom of Essex and may have usurped some of the bishop's authority. In the 820s Alfred's grandfather, Egbert of Wessex, seized London from Mercia in turn and also seems to have eliminated or downgraded the old ruling dynasty of what remained of Essex. The *Chronicle* tells us of a massacre at London in 842, of its capture in 851 by a large Viking force which was then defeated with heavy loss and of its seizure by a Viking army as a winter base for 871/2. But a charter of 867 shows that it was part of the realm of Alfred's next brother Ethelred.[5]

The whole settlement, it has recently been realised, sprawled along the north bank of the Thames for almost 4km. The extensive walls of Roman Londinium enclosed the eastern half of this large area, which contained very few buildings of any kind in the Saxon period. Even the great forum, one of the largest Roman public buildings north of the Alps, was totally demolished before the end of the Roman period.[6] Presumably there was a church at St Paul's cathedral, but deep layers of dark topsoil between Roman and late Saxon levels, found in many recent excavations, indicate that most of the area of the walled Roman city was under cultivation between the fourth and the ninth centuries.

From the seventh to the mid-ninth centuries the western half of the area, outside the walls from the Fleet river and the Strand to Westminster, contained a large straggling settlement. Called Lundenwic, it is the best-documented English trading mart of Saxon times, and may have been much like Hamwic at Southampton.

Treasure discovered in the 1200s at the church of St Martin-in-the-Fields, at the corner of present-day Trafalgar Square, may have been an Anglo-Saxon coin-hoard or burial deposit. In the 1720s, when this church was rebuilt in its present form, two glass bowls, now in the British Museum, were found in an antique stone coffin. Other scattered finds of the sixth to eighth centuries AD, from a wide area between Westminster and the City, included a Saxon building found in 1961 on the corner of Downing Street and Whitehall, interpreted then as one of a number of farmsteads scattered about to the west of Roman London.

No one realised the full significance of these finds from the West End until site-watching and excavation in advance of massive redevelopment in the boom years of the 1980s, particularly in Covent Garden, revealed pits and artefacts in many places and led to the sudden realisation by A. Vince that the merchants and artisans of Saxon London lived outside the Roman walled city to the west. This rich, important and well-documented settlement, whose actual location is a notable and unexpected discovery of the last ten years, is a striking reminder of how much remains to be discovered, or just to be recognised.[7]

Elsewhere in England there seems to have been a major trading centre, perhaps established by the kings of Kent, at Fordwich, which may have had outports or satellites at Sturry, Sarre and

Sandwich to suit the gradual silting up of the Wensum Channel between the mainland and Thanet. This may have been another trading settlement, close to the protection of the walls of Canterbury (the Roman Durovernum), its wares picked to satisfy the tastes of the wealthy priests of the churches there. The merchants faced the shortest crossing to the famed trading mart at Quentovic near Boulogne. Another trading settlement of the sixth to ninth centuries at Ipswich, well attested by many finds and excavations since the 1940s, faced a longer sea-crossing to the Rhine mouth, and the prosperous trading settlements of Walacria and Dorestad. No Roman fort or town has been identified here, as there has in all cases mentioned so far, to serve as a defended nucleus, although there are many Roman finds; the site itself was surrounded by an extensive rampart.[8]

In south-west England there is good evidence for British reuse of hill-forts in the fourth and fifth centuries, but Anglo-Saxon forts of the seventh and eighth centuries have not been made much of. One example in Wessex is Malmesbury in Wiltshire, where the Irish missionary Maildubh founded a church in the 660s.[9] This hill-fort, which may be prehistoric, was later used by Alfred as a fort.

Another early church of much the same date is Abingdon in modern Oxfordshire (formerly Berkshire). A very large late-prehistoric river-fort has recently been discovered surrounding the site of the late Saxon abbey. But the actual location of the seventh-century church is far from certain and may have been on a hill nearby.

Alfred's own kingdom of Wessex has particularly few records or hints of forts before the 860s. Alfred's grandfather Egbert (802–839) and father Ethelwulf (839–860) must have had a good many defended residences with walls, ramparts and stockades of some military value. The shortage of evidence can only mean that the documents have never been adequately assessed and the places properly investigated. Field-workers and archaeologists still have a good deal of work to do here.

In the adjacent kingdom of Mercia a number of forts are implied by place-names, as at the three adjacent townships of Charlbury, Spelsbury and Cornbury in the Oxfordshire Cotswolds, where nothing has yet been noted on the ground to be confirmed by excavation. A fort at Hereford has been identified by rather optimistic interpretation of small excavations; it is probably the work of Alfred or his family in the late ninth century.

Oxford lies at the south end of a long peninsula or tongue of well-drained gravel with, to west and south, the 1600m-wide flood-plain of the River Thames and the narrower flood-plain of the Cherwell to the east. The question of the town's original focus has been debated since the twelfth century and all sorts of claims have been made, strange ideas put forward and evidence concocted, misunderstood and misrepresented. Two authentic pre-urban nuclei have been identified on the gravel tongue and two others which have no substance have been claimed in recent years. The first two are a settlement and a Roman crossing, the second pair, the bogus nuclei, are a more recent crossing and a church with strange ancient legends.

Early Oxford, of the fifth to eighth centuries AD, lay around St Giles's church nearly a kilometre north of the central crossroads of the medieval town and modern city, which developed out of Alfred's fort of the 890s. A gold pendant or 'bracteate' of fifth-century date was found near the church in the 1640s and a bone 'weaving tool' nearby in 1938; both are in the Ashmolean Museum. An adjacent field was called the 'croft de tribus burhhes', 'Three Barrows Close', in the 1150s, showing that three burial mounds survived here until the twelfth century. Iron spearheads and shield-bosses, found in foundation-digging for an infirmary in this field in 1770, confirm the date as Saxon.

The other authentic Saxon location, recorded in medieval times as the Oxenford, is 1600m west of the city centre, near the village of North Hinksey where a Roman road crosses the Thames, pointing straight towards the St Giles' site just noted. A number of middle and late Saxon spearheads and other artefacts have been dredged up from the river nearby.[10] A large meadow beside the crossing has always been called Bulstake Mead, implying that a bull's head was carved, or a bull's skull displayed, on a post there. The conjunction of oxen and bulls is curious and may be more than a coincidence, as may the name Bullingdon, the 'Hill of the People of the Bull', for the area directly east of Oxford, a name used for the medieval hundred and its successor until the 1970s, Bullingdon Rural District.

In 1973 an eminent history professor, R. H. C. Davis, frivolously dismissed the medieval documents referring to the Oxenford as fraudulent and claimed that they resulted from an attempt by the town councillors of the 1380s to extend their jurisdiction.[11] He ignored a lease from a local monastery which gives the name before the council's claim that the town boundaries reached so far. In fact there is no reason to doubt that the name Oxford was first applied to the crossing at North Hinksey.

The two bogus locations must now be dismissed. The first, a modern myth, promoted by some archaeologists in the last twenty years, concerns the main road running south from the city centre, now called St Aldate's (as far as the Thames) and the Abingdon Road (beyond the river). Its old name is Grandpont, the 'Great Bridge', well documented as having been built about 1080. A narrow stone-arched causeway of this date lies under the middle of the widened modern road. Three of the arches built by its early Norman engineers have always been visible by boat. The road runs ruler-straight for 750m south from St Aldate's church, the straightness indicating that it was planned and constructed in a single operation with no existing encumbrances.

Excavations beside the road in 1961 revealed, 12m west of the eleventh-century stone causeway, part of a pit or gully cut into river-silts and lined with wattling. B. K. Durham, the excavator, chose to interpret the silts, found extensively across the flood-plain of the river, as a 'clay bank'. In 1979 it was naively hailed as a 'late-8th-century causeway'. The date came from samples of wattles lying in the gully or pit, beside but not forming any part of the supposed causeway. They gave radio-carbon 'dates' of between AD800 and 830.[12] As scientific determinations such results should be presented as a broad range of possibilities and should not be, and should never have been, equated with precise calendar dates. In common-sense terms the wattling is quite likely to be of some date between the seventh and the twelfth century.

Of course a bank of mud will quickly be washed away by floods and storms and cannot ever make an adequate or even a possible causeway. The excavations, and subsequent ones in the area, have not revealed a causeway earlier than the eleventh century. The date, coming as it did from deposits against but not in the 'clay bank', was never valid even if the 'bank' had been a man-made feature.

Stimulated by this interpretation and dating, R. H. C. Davis compounded the issue with a third violation of method. Not content with denouncing the authentic medieval documentation of the Oxenford, he brazenly ignored the well-documented medieval name of Grandpont and claimed the mud 'bank' as the 'true' Ox-ford. This is an example of the well-developed human ability to hold three contradictory opinions at once.

The consequences of this archaeological mishap are considerable, as all the conclusions piled, like Pelion on Ossa, on the date that is no date and the causeway that was never a causeway must tumble and slide into the mud. Pottery fragments from deposits around the 'clay bank' are far more likely to date from the eleventh and not from the eighth century. As they form the basis for a whole dating system, all sites whose dates depend on these 'findings' must be critically re-examined. Indeed similar pottery has already caused problems when found in London and Northampton, where it has to be given later dates. And notions of an ancient long-distance route on this line must be abandoned.

The other doubtful site, advanced by ancient legend and a modern historian, is Oxford cathedral, the twelfth-century priory at St Frideswide, at the southern tip of the gravel tongue. No objects, carving or foundations earlier than the twelfth century have yet been found here. Some burials excavated south of the church in 1985 have produced radio-carbon 'dates' between 886 from an early grave and 772 from a later one dug through it.[13] The discrepancy of a full century in the wrong direction should warn us not to accept such data uncritically. Properly assessed in calendar years, the burials are probably of some date between the seventh and the twelfth century. These results do not prove that there was a church here in the 700s. The site seems to lie outside the fort that King Alfred laid out in the 890s and the burials might well be a good deal later than that.

The twelfth-century monks noisily asserted that their church was the town's oldest, senior to the larger and wealthier abbey of Oseney in the western suburbs, which was of the same Augustinian order. They claimed that the obscure saint, Frideswide or 'Bond of Peace', whose relics they had, was a local princess who founded a nunnery on their site in 727, concocting lively legends about her to attract pilgrims and donations for their building fund. This publicity drive attracted a rather down-market clientele with skin diseases and other unpleasant complaints. W. J. Blair has claimed, with all the zeal of an ayatollah, that the legends have a basis of historical fact.[14] But as no confirmation has yet come to light, neither the legends nor the radio-carbon 'dates' can be accepted as adequate evidence.

Scanning Europe from west to east, we come first to Spain, then largely Moslem, apart from the Basque country in the western Pyrenees – which was normally in revolt against either the Frankish emperor or the Emir of Cordoba, modern Catalonia, which was a more regular Frankish province – and the small Asturian kingdom in north-west Spain. This provides vital parallels to England, in charters and chronicles, in art and architecture, in social structure, and in fortification and resettlement policy.[15]

King Alfonso II (792–842) of the small Christian kingdom of the Asturias, a contemporary of Alfred's grandfather, fortified a new capital in about 800 at Oviedo, where he built a palace with baths and an aqueduct. At the same time his bishop, Odoario, occupied Lugo (Roman Lucus Augusti) 140km to the west, with its sulphur baths and great Roman defensive walls with eighty-five towers until the nineteenth century. At Naranco near Oviedo a stone palace of this time, later converted into a church, stands to its full height, and several other churches of this date also survive intact or partly complete. In 834, as we know from a building inscription, the Arabs built a citadel at Merida (Roman Augusta Emerita) in central Spain to the south.

During the next two generations the Asturian kings systematically conquered lands lost to the Arabs in the seventh century and consolidated their gains by building forts and settling colonists around them until they had seven strongholds in the 860s, about twenty by 910 and perhaps thirty by 915. King Ordoño I (850–866), a younger contemporary of Alfred's father, established a line of five forts in land that had long been abandoned as no man's land at Tuy (Roman Tudae) on the River Miño near the west coast, in 854; Orense (Roman warm springs of Aquae Originis)

65km up the Miño, also in 854; Astorga (Roman Asturica Augusta) 140km further east, astride the main route to the north-west, in 854; Leon (base of the Legio Septima Gemina) 50km further east; and Amaya.

A charter of 916 informs us that Count Gaton refounded Astorga with men from his province of Bierzo, 60–70km back up the road to the coast. He planted vineyards and built houses for them, shared out farmland, ploughed the fields, sowed the crops and settled their flocks. This example of large-scale transfers of population seems to have been widespread general practice.[16]

As we shall see later, Alfonso III (866–884) extended his kingdom southward in the late 870s and early '80s, defending his conquests with another chain of forts, while Alfred was fighting desperately to survive, triumphing and then extending and protecting his own kingdom.

The nearest partner in Frankish territory across the Channel to the English trading settlements was Quentovic, south of Calais. Of very many Roman towns that became later royal or episcopal centres, it is difficult to pick out a few as well-documented examples that have been thoroughly analysed on and above ground and explored below, so that we can understand them reasonably well.

Walacria, near Domburg on the island of Walcheren in Frisia (covered by sand-dunes in the eleventh century; many artefacts were salvaged when it was lost to coastal erosion in the last century), and Dorestad, near the lost Roman fort of Lefevanum on the Rhine, abandoned in the late eighth century, were both large manufacturing and trading settlements like Hamwic. Vast excavations at Dorestad have revealed sixty houses, three cemeteries and an almost endless series of piers or wharves built out into the former river bed. Many other forts and marts are known, with so much research in progress that it seems too early to take any distinctive and representative example.

Modern Germany spans the frontier of the Roman Empire and can give us examples of Roman cities which became royal or episcopal centres, the frontier itself with lines of forts, and the lands beyond with examples of the pagan tribes of northern, central and eastern Europe who generally occupied territories centred on hill-forts. These are so common that throughout central and eastern Europe the whole period from the sixth to the eleventh century is called the 'the hill-fort time', in German Burgwallperiode.

In 741 the English missionary, and later saint, Boniface established a bishopric in the Marienberg, a prehistoric hill-fort which towers above Würzburg and is named in documents from 686. He set up another in 742 in a hill-fort of late seventh-century date, the Büraburg above Fritzlar, as a base for the conversion of Thuringia and, less successfully, Saxony. This has been quite extensively excavated.[17]

In the west there were many lesser river-marts along the Rhine, as at Mainz, Worms and Cologne. Near the coast of Saxony there was a mart at Hamburg beside Charlemagne's small roughly circular fort, about 100m across inside, built in 810 and sacked by Vikings in 845. Civic pride allowed excavations before the bomb-devastated city centre was rebuilt.[18]

In Scandinavia the Danish King Godfrid established Hedeby in 808 on an inlet at the south-easternmost tip of the Baltic below a small hill-fort. The *Annals of the kingdom of the Franks* record his invasion of a Slavonic tribe, the Obodrites, in alliance with the Wilzi, whose lands were on the far side of them. Charlemagne had lately deported a Saxon tribe and let the Obodrites take over their lands. Rounding up the merchants from a trading mart in this area, Godfrid took them home with him to gain the benefit of their dues and taxes, landing them in Schleswig bay on a new site, which he protected with a long strategic earthwork right across the Jutland peninsula. In about 825 an enterprising financier here began to mint copies of the standard small silver coins of Dorestad. A large rampart was built round the settlement at some date.

Hedeby, a green-field site now generally known as Haithabu in Schleswig, Germany, has been dug on a large scale since the 1930s as an academic project with convict labour. Extensive excavations have produced evidence of close-packed houses, ranging in size from 7m long by 3.5m wide to 15.5m long by 7m wide. They lay in small plots on fairly regular streets which, rather as at Southampton, did not form a rigid geometrical grid.[19] In the eleventh century the merchants and artisans deserted the site and moved to the present town of Schleswig across the bay.

Other trading marts have been discovered in Scandinavia, at Ribe in Denmark, where there is still a medieval town, Kaupang in Norway, Helgö and Birka in Sweden and Paviken on the island of Gotland. Most lay near fortified enclosures or had ramparts. Much work is in progress and still awaiting publication.

Rich and sometimes exotic finds have turned up: the Swedish island site of Birka has produced an Egyptian bronze ladle of about AD 500, a north Indian Buddha-figure of the seventh century and an Irish crozier of the eighth century. This wealth of striking material for study has ensured that archaeologists have devoted much attention to these marts and its spectacular nature has helped publicity for winning sponsorship and research funds.

The Slavs, a tribal society, had numerous forts on hilltops, in marshes or beside rivers. Polish, Czech and East German archaeologists have carried out intensive and systematic studies of their remains, making important discoveries and taking great steps in interpreting the social development from tribe to kingdom with formative ideas on the early development of towns. This work has been stimulated by the very scanty documented history, largely from Frankish and other external sources, and by national pride very properly demanding that they should discover their own origins from their soil; this has led to much excellent archaeology. Place-names suggest that some Czech hill-forts had artisan villages clustered around them, an element which should be expected and looked for in other countries.

As a sample, we may briefly note several sites, all virtually undocumented, in the Czech Republic: a western group in the valley of the Vltava, which flows north to the Elbe and the North Sea, and an eastern group in the valley of the Morava which flows south to the Danube and the Black Sea. Several churches seem to date from before the documented Byzantine mission of 863; Czech archaeologists have long suspected that unrecorded Irish missionaries were active in the early and mid-ninth century; an English one is equally likely.

Reputedly the original centre of the small Czech tribe, Levý Hradec lies on two adjacent rock spurs, each very roughly 200m square, high above the Vltava 20km north of Prague. The timber-laced ramparts, 9m thick and originally 4–5m high, run around both spurs and are 1.5km long. The slightly higher spur contained log-built houses with plank floors, interpreted as housing for the early princes and their companions; the lower spur contained huts of wattle and daub, presumed to be for lesser retainers and servants. This site is associated with the legendary chief Neklan and the documented Prince Borivoj, who built a church here. At Budeč, a hill-fort traditionally associated with Prince Waclav (whom we know as 'Good King Wenceslas'), a round church still crowns the hill.

Around Prague a dense farming population with many hamlets and villages is so well attested in the middle Vltava valley, by numerous finds of the sixth and seventh centuries AD made in brick-earth digging in the nineteenth century, that the earliest phase of hard dark 'Slavonic' pottery is widely known as 'Prague-type'. Legends recorded later imply that this was the heartland of the Czech tribe, which in time absorbed or conquered all the other local Slavonic groups. As well as pottery, silver ear-rings and many other grave-goods from pre-Christian and Christian burial grounds attracted collectors, who preserved them and left notes on the find-spots. Six or more hill-forts occupied in this period lie within the modern city limits, including Vyšehrad, which survived as a strongpoint or citadel at the south end of the very extensive late medieval and Renaissance defences, but not the Hrad itself. The great castle hill, the Hrad, was fortified later, in the ninth century, to become the princes' main stronghold.

In about 825–850 at Stará Kouřim a chief of the Zličane tribe constructed a small fort of 4.8ha as his tribal centre on a prominent spur between two rivers dominating the surrounding country, just above a spring long reputed sacred. Over the next generation it was enlarged to 44ha with three successive ramparted annexes on the side away from the rivers, the first enclosing the spring and a small area to one of the rivers. Across the other, larger, river a low hillock was also occupied at this time. The place was severely damaged by fire at the end of the ninth century and destroyed about 950, approximately the time when the Czech tribe absorbed this tribe. The site, excavated by M. Šolle of the Czech Academy of Sciences in 1948–52, has been fully published.[20]

The powerful Presmyslid princes of Bohemia governed the area from St George's, a small new promontory fort close by, from the eleventh to the thirteenth century, when the existing market town was laid out on lower ground nearby on a rigid grid-plan with a large central market-place.

An earlier, lesser, hill-fort on the edge of this tribe's territory was excavated at Klučov; an original small fortified nucleus of 1.5ha with a village or suburb beyond was extended after the village was burnt in about 850 to include much of its area, which was then occupied with sunken huts and storage-pits of a farming community. The site was abandoned after 900, perhaps having been seized by the Czech tribe.

A major centre of the Great Moravian Empire, Stará Město sprawled across 250ha of low hills on either side of a broad marshy side-stream on the north bank of the Morava. The original defended nucleus, a 40ha fort of about 800 on the tip of one of the ranges of hills, was quite densely occupied and contained a small apsed church, which seems to date from before 863, with a churchyard whose fifteen hundred graves produced rich grave-goods.

In about 850 an outer rampart was put up to enclose the tip of the hill and another very long rampart was constructed for 3km from the Morava across both ranges of hills to a second side-stream, enclosing the fort and six or seven satellite settlements which had grown up by then. Those on the other low spur had three burial grounds, one with a small stone church, metal-working sites and evident farms. Several of these areas remained in occupation after the Moravian Empire was destroyed in 905.[21] A number of dug-out canoes, found in draining the Morava flood-plain, date from this period. As at Kourim there is a small planned town of the thirteenth century close by.

Other notable sites in the area include Mikulčice, where a fort of the seventh and eighth centuries, at first 3ha in extent, later doubled in size, attracted a cluster of lesser settlements around it during the ninth century. The fort contained a stone palace and five churches; five more churches were scattered among the lesser settlements. The whole complex of sites, like Stara Mesto, covered a very large area, some 200ha of the broad flood-plain of the Morava, well protected by water-channels.[22]

At Pohansko a sixth-century fort was eventually surrounded by 100ha of lesser settlements, among which a church of about 850 with over four hundred graves has been excavated. A 2km-long rampart surrounded the whole complex.

The Bulgars had settled and begun to absorb the mixed

Romanised native and Slavonic peoples on the Danube before the end of the seventh century. After Charlemagne's troops subdued the Avars in 796, the Bulgar Khans built up a great empire across modern Bulgaria, Romania, Hungary and Serbia. In 811 the Emperor Nicephoros invaded their land at the head of a Byzantine army and burnt their chief centre at Preslav, which consisted of a rectangular 20ha earthwork within which was a stone palace-citadel 110m by 93m; Khan Krum (802–814) annihilated the invaders and converted the emperor's skull into a drinking cup.[23]

His successor Omortag (814–831) founded a new capital at Pliska, which had buildings of fine cut stone, a large nearly square central fort 740m by 612/788m with high stone walls, square gate-towers, round corner towers and half-hexagonal intermediate towers.[24]

An outer rampart no less than 20km long surrounded this huge site. Russian archaeologists began large-scale excavations in 1889 and made spectacular discoveries, several stone palaces and large churches, from the start. Earlier this century Serbian archaeologists persistently claimed that the early Bulgars could not possibly have built such sophisticated structures and the forts must be Roman. Modern Bulgarian archaeologists, working on these sites from the 1920s, took this claim as a national and professional insult and have amply confirmed that some of the stone palaces and the large rectangular forts date from the ninth century.

The Franks were in touch with the Bulgars throughout the ninth century, particularly closely in 864 when Louis the German met Khan Boris to discuss his proposed conversion to Christianity. He received baptism in 865; a year later he suppressed the subsequent violent revolt and sent his son to Rome with gifts, theological queries and a request for priests and bishops. This was only eleven years after Alfred's second visit. Although Boris decided in 870 to link up with the Eastern Church instead, this episode provides plenty of chances for the Franks and ultimately the English to hear of Bulgar fortifications and building practices.

The Byzantine Empire, reduced to much the same low economic state as the rest of Europe, remained the wealthiest, most civilised and most technically skilled of nations. The court and military staff at Constantinople had kept a knowledge of the Roman Empire's traditions of defence and had developed special skills in fortress building and also in the resettlement of warlike peoples in defensive frontier zones, roles for which the Anglo-Saxons, the Franks and many other tribes had been recruited in the fourth and fifth centuries AD, centuries earlier.

The Byzantine military lost the old Mesopotamian *limes*, or defended frontier, to the Persians in 607–615, regained it in 628–629 and lost it for good to the Arabs in 639–646. From then until the eleventh century they successfully maintained a frontier zone across eastern Turkey, stretching from the north-easternmost corner of the Mediterranean to the east end of the Black Sea. They could also mobilise a central striking force of four regiments of Imperial Bodyguards, the *palatini* (Greek, *tagmata*), with a cavalry force or *comitatenses* of light horse (Greek, *trapezetai*) and heavy cavalry (Greek, *kaballaria themata*) living on military tenancies. As their first line of defence they regularly recruited and settled new Armenian regiments, the *limitanei* (Greek, *kleisourai*), as local defence forces in the frontier zone, which fluctuated a fair amount in the five centuries for which it was held.

In 835 the Byzantine Emperor Theophilus (829–842) sent a military mission led by the high-ranking officer, *spatharocandidate* Petronios Kamatiros, to answer an appeal for help by his allies, the largely nomadic Khazars, against attack by the even more nomadic Pechenegs. The Khazars were also great allies against the Bulgars who had settled between the two. The mission travelled deep into Khazar territory, sixty days' journey from the coast, and planned a compact and powerful fortress on the River Don for a permanent garrison of three hundred Byzantine troops, intended to be changed annually. Finding no building stone in the vicinity, the mission organised a local labour force to build brick-kilns and fire the ten million bricks required for the fort, which was an exact rectangle measuring 186m by 126m, with walls 3.75m thick and probably 10m high. A dependent settlement grew up outside and was enclosed within a curved outer rampart.[25]

Eventually, in 965, the Russian Prince Sviatoslav captured the fortress from the Khazars; it was then known as Sarkel or the 'White Town', perhaps because the bricks had been limewashed to look like stone. The most distinctive archaeological features of the later Russian occupation were a number of cellar-pits, so common in western European towns in the tenth and eleventh centuries. Abandoned in 1117, the site was identified by the Russian archaeologist M. I. Artomonov in 1934–36 and extensively excavated in 1949–51 in advance of a hydro-electric scheme. It provides a classic example of a Byzantine fort far outside the Eastern Empire.

The Byzantine foothold in Italy, with the dependent duchy of Naples and three regular 'themes' or counties in the far south, probably meant that high-ranking *strategoi* and other officials were regularly in Rome, where visiting English governors and their staffs could gain a fair knowledge of military procedures and principles in the Eastern Empire.

We can draw a number of conclusions from all this evidence. The places that our sources name were all or almost all government or church centres, defended by walls, ramparts or stockades, new, improvised, adapted or reused; the defences took one of these forms:

1. Long walls or banks, such as Offa's Dyke or the Danewirke.
2. Rectangular stone forts, as in Bulgaria and on the Byzantine frontiers.
3. Fairly rectangular forts, such as Cricklade, Oxford, Wallingford.
4. Circular forts, on the north coast of France, Belgium and Holland, in east Germany, and in Denmark, all echoing Baghdad, a circular city of 763.
5. Fairly circular forts, common in east Germany and Baltic lands.
6. Irregular new hill-forts or river-forts.
7. Reoccupied prehistoric hill-forts.
8. Roman towns or forts, such as Bath, London, Paris, Mainz.
9. Very high hill-top forts, only used as refuges.

We should add that there are many examples of composite forts made up of several elements and many places too that are named but whose defences are not properly understood or have not been identified or investigated. We must presume, regardless of the

77

absence of documentary evidence or identified sites, that every part of Europe had a long tradition of fort-building.

Many of these places contained a cluster of royal officials' houses grouped around a royal hall, used as a courtroom and occasionally to house the king himself as he circulated around the kingdom, and often a chapel. Great royal officials, the governors, *duces* or *comites*, tended to think of themselves as hereditary and constantly tried to take over part or all of a fort or put up new ones for themselves or their families; such tensions are not always apparent on excavated sites.

The rest were cult-centres with a church or 'family' of churches and housing for priests and their dependants, servants and animals. Archbishops, bishops and abbots were often princes or nobles, so powerful that they required their own fortified centres. Another source of tension affecting these two assumptions is that kings and nobles often enlarged their chapels to become separate well-funded churches for their chaplains, who kept their records. The Italian, Irish, English and Greek missionaries who converted the Anglo-Saxons and all the other pagan tribes to Christianity in the seventh, eighth and ninth centuries often located their new churches in Roman towns and forts or hill-forts. These cult-centres regularly attracted kings and nobles to move in and put up halls for themselves, for pleasure or military need, so that they became administrative and military centres as well.

None of these administrative or ecclesiastical centres had at first or necessarily a large population of merchants and craftsmen or very many inhabitants at all. But artisans, dealers and markets, now characteristically located in towns and considered distinctively urban, were regularly attracted to the forts and settled close by. 'Traders at the gate' were a normal and nearly inevitable adjunct of any fort.

While none of these places can be considered quite urban, on any view of the documentary, numismatic, topographical and archaeological evidence, they were the seed from which the medieval town and our modern urban civilisation grew. To understand ourselves better is the best justification for studying them.

5

Pagan Europe: Denmark and the
Franks before the 860s

For the whole of Alfred's lifetime the Danes dominated England. They had long held much of the north German, Dutch and Belgian coastline and had, for a time, taken Dublin from their Norwegian cousins. During the early years of his reign they destroyed the other three English kingdoms, divided them up and settled them. The three great military crises that he faced and survived were Danish invasions of Wessex, the first in 870–871, the second and most dangerous in 876–879 and the third in 892–896. We must discover more about them.

How did they become the great unrelenting enemy, intent on destroying Christian civilisation, as they are portrayed in all surviving records of the time? The scribes who wrote all these records were, of course, priests whose well-endowed churches and rich offerings were singularly attractive and vulnerable to passing gangs of bandits and robbers on the look-out for something to loot, burn and take. We may presume that the accounts, which have conditioned and affected our judgements, were somewhat exaggerated when churches were prime targets. To modern writers too, blindly following false tradition and the sources without close and critical examination, the Vikings are fierce adventurers lusting for plunder and battle. These traders, raiders, conquerors and settlers from Denmark, Norway and Sweden hold a star role on the historical stage from about the 780s, when the Norse began to settle in Shetland, Orkney and the Hebrides, until the battle of Stamford

Bridge in 1066, as the greatest terrorists and robbers in Europe. In fact they were opportunists always ready to make a deal, thankful to find somewhere to settle for a time.

In this chapter, therefore, we will visit Denmark to meet two kings, first Godfrid and then his son, Horic, last survivor and perhaps youngest of five or more brothers who grew to adulthood and became kings. Between them, father and sons ruled in Denmark for half a century, from before 804 to 854. As we read in an account set down by a far from friendly clerical pen of their constant search for peace by diplomacy and negotiation, we get a very different impression of Danish aspirations and forget the Vikings' reputation. The Franks, bloodthirsty looters and conquerors on a heroic scale long before the Vikings, had invaded and ravaged Danish lands before they suffered in turn. At home in Scandinavia the Vikings were just like everybody else.

In this and the next chapter we will encounter Horic's cousin Harald as an occasional king of Denmark, and a rather more frequent exile, and his sons, Roric and a younger Godfrid, as claimants to the throne. All three appear far more often in Frankish lands than in Denmark. As we shall see, they played a variety of roles: as freebooting warriors, as hired mercenaries and as Frankish governors, or at least officially in charge of Frankish counties.

The Danes were a self-reliant people, anxious to maintain their independence, but drawn inexorably into the fabric of many developing European societies, including that of England. The Emperors Charlemagne and his son Louis the Pious constantly interfered in their internal affairs and evidently believed, or liked to think, that they were a subject or tributary kingdom. The main causes of Viking involvement in western Europe in the 830s and 840s were hostile political pressure from the Franks and the chance of serving as mercenaries with warring factions of the Frankish royal family. Scholars have suggested all sorts of reasons, simple and complex, for the Vikings' sudden and violent expansion in the ninth century: overpopulation, economic and social pressures, a desire for trade, or just for adventure, and so on. The blame for letting them loose and training them to become a devastating military and political threat to kings, to their courtiers and warriors and, most of all, to their priests lies with the Emperor Lothar and his brother King Louis of Germany, and, to a lesser extent, their younger brother King Charles the Bald of France, who will be the main character of our next chapter.

There is no reason to suppose that the societies from which the Vikings came were significantly different from the rest of Europe. As elsewhere, downtrodden tenants, serfs and slaves farmed the land, while kings and nobles with war bands ruled them. Scandinavian scholars have claimed too exclusively that their forebears stayed at home in the fourth to sixth centuries and did not take part in the westward emigration of Germanic tribes such as the Goths, Vandals, Franks and Angles. This movement, essentially of chiefs and warriors, has been exaggerated elsewhere and played down in Scandinavia. Notable exceptions have long been recognised, such as the Jutes, who settled in Kent and the Isle of Wight, and the Swedish chiefs who founded the dynasty of East Anglia. No doubt there were always adventurous spirits who left home and sought their fortunes abroad. The compiler of the *Chronicle* may not have been right when he asserted, a century later, that Norse seamen raided England for the first time in the 780s. We can suspect that there had always been raiders in a small way since the fourth century, but that life in eighth-century Northumbria and the other Saxon kingdoms was so chaotic and brutal that nobody troubled to record the incidents as anything special. The Anglian nobility and warrior class here came, as they were well aware, from Angeln at the southern end of the Jutland peninsula. In his *History of the English Church and People* Bede portrays the 730s as a time of peace and prosperity in the north; but this may be true only of a short interlude.

The Vikings who left home to form or join gangs of bandits roaming across Europe and ravaging other kingdoms for decades were not 'free peasants', but members of a warrior caste which had always been prepared to travel for pay and adventure. Their kings, like Godfrid, tried to keep out of trouble abroad, but were frustrated by restless and unsatisfied younger members of the royal family, who led war bands abroad to serve in foreign wars and then to join in on their own account. The Angles and the Saxons, the Jutes, the Franks and the Goths had done precisely this in the fourth, fifth and sixth centuries.

The Danes, pagan and illiterate, were outside the scope of written records, except when they came in contact with more developed kingdoms. They first appear in the 780s in both the Frankish *Annals* and the English *Chronicle*:

782
King Charles began his campaign by crossing the Rhine at Cologne and summoning an assembly to meet at the springs of the River Lippe. All the Saxon chiefs came, except for Widukind who was in revolt. Halptani and other Norse envoys came from King Sigfrid, as did ambassadors from the Avars.[1]

786–802
In that reign [of Brihtric of Wessex] three Norse ships [from Hörthaland, Norway] arrived for the first time in Portland and a reeve [Beaduheard of Dorchester] rode to take them to the king's hall to identify themselves, but they killed him. These were the first Danish ships to sail to England.[2]

793
On June 8 the church at Lindisfarne was plundered and destroyed with much slaughter by pagan raiders.[3]

794
The pagans pillaged Northumbria and looted [King] Ecgfrith's monastery [Jarrow] at the Don mouth. One of their chiefs was killed and some ships wrecked by storms with many of the crew drowned. Survivors who got to shore at the river mouth were at once massacred.[4]

798
At Easter the Nordliudli [a Saxon tribe] across the Elbe rebelled and imprisoned the king's delegates who had gone to decide reparations. They executed some and held the others to ransom. Among the dead was the envoy Godescal whom the king had lately sent to King Sigfrid of Denmark. The rebels captured and killed him on his return journey. The news enraged King Charles . . .[5]

Chronicles of this kind were a standard class of record in many kingdoms, as we have already seen for Wessex. The entries just quoted are of two kinds. The Frankish *Annals* were written at the time or very soon after by men involved in the events noted and

are thus of prime significance. But the English *Chronicle* was compiled a century after the events noted; the killing of the reeve in
what may be '789' is a second-hand quotation from some other
source, while the plundering of the Northumbrian monasteries was
added to the main text from another chronicle put together in
York in the tenth century, and is quoted third-hand. These three
references are all later additions 'stitched in' retrospectively on
different occasions to enhance the interest of these parts of the
Chronicle, whose major theme is the Viking raids on England from
the 830s to the 870s.

The chronicle known as the *Annales regni Francorum*, 'Annals of
the kingdom of the Franks', covers the years 741–829 and gives
a very exact account in Latin of the diplomatic and military achievements of the usurper King Pepin, his son King Charles, who
became the Emperor Charlemagne, and grandson the Emperor
Louis. Composed in the late 780s, it gives fairly brief accounts of
events to the late 760s, presumably taken from some earlier set of
annals. From about 787–788 to 794 it relates public affairs seen
through the eyes of a high court official who preferred to gloss
over conspiracies and U-turns. A second author described the
events up to 807 in simple elegant language; a third with a sophisticated command of Latin brought the story up to 829, telling of
Charlemagne's death in 814 and the succession and early reign of
his son Louis the Pious. Except in the earliest years, it is full and
detailed. The *Chronicle* follows its general lines but in a simpler
and more basic form.

The principal account of the years 830–882, the major source
for Viking history and for events all over Europe, the *Annals of
St Bertin*, is a continuation of the *Annals of the Franks*, kept at first
in a rather routine way by the court chaplains as an official 'diary'
and from the early 830s, largely by Prudentius, a Spanish-born
chaplain at the Frankish court. When the Emperor Louis the
Pious's household broke up on his death in 840, Prudentius joined
the youngest son, Charles the Bald, in his new western kingdom,
where he was made bishop of Troyes in 843. He took his *Annals*
with him and kept them up to date, his viewpoint and concerns
getting ever further from court interests until he died in 861.
Then Archbishop Hincmar of Rheims, by birth a great Frankish
nobleman, obtained the *Annals* from Prudentius's heirs and

continued them from his own personal and rather different stand-point. The manuscript survived at the abbey of St Bertin at St Omer in Flanders. A number of other chronicles, kept at abbeys and cathedrals, also survive. We can judge the character of the main annals from their account of Charlemagne's actions during the first six months of 800:

> The king sent the monk from Jerusalem home with Zacharias, one of his court chaplains, to convey his gifts to the Holy Places. In the middle of March he left the palace at Aachen to inspect the Channel and North Sea coasts, which were suffering from raiders. He ordered a fleet to be built and set up guard-posts in various places and cele-brated Easter at Centula [St Riquier near the Somme mouth]. From here he progressed along the coast [and up the Seine] until he got to Rouen, where he crossed the River Seine and went on to Tours [on the Loire] to venerate St Martin. His wife the lady Liutgarda's illness kept him here for some days until her death on 4 June. After her funeral he returned through Orleans and Paris to Aachen. Severe frosts on 6 and 9 June did not damage the harvest.[6]

Later in the year he summoned his army to Mainz and set off across the Alps to Rome, sending a division off to devastate the area around Benevento. On 24 November he entered Rome with great ceremony and, on Christmas Day, had himself crowned emperor.

The Danish King Godfrid, who was perhaps King Sigfrid's son and who died in 810, had loosely united much of Denmark by the start of the ninth century and ruled capably over the tribes of the Jutland peninsula, and perhaps the islands and the southern tip of Sweden together. The main cause of his success was external pressure from Charlemagne's relentless campaigns against the tribes of Saxony to the south and south-west in 772–804.

Godfrid and his sons could mobilise and lead their chiefs and fighting men on campaign, and keep them in hand during armed confrontations without actual fighting. But they could not keep them all quietly at home and, as we shall see, Danish nobles and warriors got increasingly out of hand during the 840s and were so unmanageable in the 850s that they wiped out their king, Godfrid's son Horic, and almost all the high aristocracy.

We first encounter Godfrid in the spring or early summer of 804, when Charlemagne was carrying out a massive 'ethnic cleansing' operation to the south of Denmark. One element of this was the deportation of all Saxons from east of the River Elbe to areas under Frankish control to the west of the river. He then let the Obodrites, a 'trusty' Slav tribe, take over the area cleared of Saxons. The operation was delayed retribution for the murder of the envoys in 798. With his forces at full strength Godfrid, concerned but not directly involved, faced Charlemagne as an equal, steadfastly refusing to be overawed or bullied:

> At this time King Godfrid brought his ships and horsemen to Schleswig on his frontier with Saxon lands. Although he agreed to meet the emperor for discussions, his advisers warned him to take care. He remained at a distance and conferred through representatives. The emperor at Hollenstedt sent envoys to negotiate the return of Saxon refugees from Denmark.[7]

In 808 Godfrid, who clearly had a keen eye for business, established a new trade mart and constructed the Danewerke, a long rampart to define his frontier and provide some measure of military strength, just as King Offa of Mercia marked his frontier with the Welsh in the 780s by Offa's Dyke; and the Bulgar Khan Omortag defined his southern border with the Byzantine Empire in 815–816, when he made the Ertesiya, an earthwork over 160km long. The official Frankish chronicler gives us some details of Godfrid's year. He had allied himself to the Slavonic tribe of the Wilzi and invaded the lands of the Obodrites, his immediate Slav neighbours, in a profitable summer campaign:

> Before he withdrew his forces, Godfrid destroyed a trading place on the coast, which the Danes called Reric, a great commercial asset to his kingdom because of the dues collected there. Taking the merchants from Reric on board, he sailed with his whole force into the mouth of the Schlei. He stayed there for a few days and decided to protect his borders with a defensive rampart running from the Baltic on the east by the north bank of the Eider to the western ocean, with a single gate for horsemen and carts to come and go. He divided the work up among his commanders and set off home.[8]

85

This casual rounding-up and transfer of a trading community to a new site which was then protected by a strategic defence-line has always been taken to record the foundation of Hedeby (in Danish) or Haithabu (in German) in Schleswig. Reric, their former site, may be the earthwork known as Alt Lübeck on the Trave; it lay in the territory from which Charlemagne had deported the Saxons in 804. Recent excavations have shown from tree-ring dates that the first phase of the Danewirke incorporates logs felled late in 737 or just after. Unless Godfrid used well-preserved timbers from an old structure, he was refurbishing an earlier barrier.

In 809 Count Egbert, Charlemagne's local commander, built a new fort near the frontier as a countermove and to give him a base from which to maintain surveillance on Danes and Slavs, following elaborate three-way peace talks, in the course of which fierce fighting broke out among the Slav tribes. Godfrid, who had sensibly secured the son of the nearest Slav chief as a hostage, kept out of trouble. Later, the *Annals* tell us, he assassinated this chief at Reric, when he was perhaps trying to restart trade there.

In 810 Godfrid sailed west with a large fleet to invade and ravage the Frisian coast, Frankish territory, as a pre-emptive strike. He defeated the Frisians in three battles and forced them to pay tribute, but was murdered on his return.

> While the emperor was at Aachen planning a campaign against King Godfrid he got news that two hundred Danish ships had invaded Frisia, that all the Frisian islands had been pillaged and that the Danes had landed and battled three times with the Frisians. The Frisians had given the conquering Danes tribute of a hundred pounds of silver and Godfrid had returned home. The report proved to be true. In fury, the emperor sent out couriers to mobilise his forces . . .[9]

Godfrid's first successor was a nephew, Hemming, who made peace with Charlemagne in a formal ceremony of oaths on the River Eider and died within a year. A refitted Frankish fleet was mobilised for Charlemagne to inspect at Boulogne. Then two of King Godfrid's nephews claimed the Danish throne and killed each other in battle. Next, two more nephews, Reginfrid and Harald who were brothers of one of the dead claimants, secured the crown. Reginfrid was to die in a civil war in 814, Harald to have

86

a long and adventurous life. Their joint reign did not last much more than a year, before Godfrid's sons surfaced with a strong claim:

> A delegation of Frankish and Saxon noblemen travelled across the Elbe to the Danish frontier on a peace mission asked for by the kings of Denmark and also to return their brother [no doubt he had been held as a hostage]. The same number, sixteen Danish jarls met them at the agreed spot, swore an alliance with them and collected the brother. The kings [Harald and Regenfrid] were away on campaign in the far north-west of their kingdom in the Westfold [southern Norway] beyond the north extremity of Britain, where the princes and tribes would not submit to them. When they had subdued the Britons, returned home and picked up the brother sent by the emperor, King Godfrid's sons, mustering warriors from everywhere, attacked them. Many Danish nobles joined them from exile in Sweden. With these large reinforcements Godfrid's sons defeated the kings with ease and drove them from the kingdom.[10]

This record is a fascinating muddle that shows a touching ignorance of northern geography; the annalist must have scrambled second-hand accounts of two separate expeditions, a short one to Norway and another, long-range one, to Britain.

After Godfrid's five sons seized power by force in 813, one or more of them continued to hold it for the next forty-one years. At first all the brothers were joint kings; from time to time Frankish pressure forced them to accept as a partner Harald, whom they threw out three times and reinstated twice between 817 and 827. The eldest of Godfrid's sons was slain in a short civil war in 814; two more were evicted on Harald's restoration in 819. As late as 828 we read of the sons of Godfrid in the Frankish *Annals*, but from 836 only of the last of them, Horic. He remained king in increasingly difficult circumstances for another eighteen years.

Like their father, the sons of Godfrid were ready to fight to defend their land and equally ready to strike hard when threatened and take reprisals when attacked, but they evidently preferred to keep the Franks at arms' length by negotiation.

In 815 the Frankish commander Count Baldric, sent by the Emperor Louis the Pious to restore Harald, breached the

Danewirke and invaded Jutland in 815 at the head of a heavily armed mission with Saxon and Slav contingents. The brothers and their army gave ground steadily until they could confront the Franks from an island, behind the protection of an arm of the sea and their fleet. As they withdrew the Franks, as always, took hostages and devastated the Danish countryside, setting an example that the Danes were enthusiastically to copy.

From 815 to 834 regular peace talks were enough to avoid military action, with few small-scale disturbances. There was some trouble in 820:

In the Mediterranean Arab pirates captured and sank eight merchantmen sailing home from Sardinia to Italy. Thirteen ships which came from Norse lands to plunder the Flemish coast were driven off by the watch-guards; through momentary carelessness they managed to burn some hovels and take some cattle. In the Seine estuary the watch-guards repelled similar landings and inflicted five casualties. But eventually the raiders scored a success on the Aquitaine coast and devastated the town of Bouin, sailing home with much loot.[11]

In 826 King Harald travelled to the emperor's court at Mainz with his wife and retinue and received the sacrament of baptism in a spectacular and long-famed ceremony in which the future King Charles the Bald played a notable part as a three-year-old. His father, the Emperor Louis the Pious, gave Harald rich gifts and the governorship of the province of Rüstringen, the coastal region of Saxony, as a refuge for the next time his cousins decided to throw him out.

In 827 the sons of Godfrid ejected Harald from Denmark for what turned out to be the last time. No longer a client king, he began a new life as a Frankish official governing his new province, as countless Germanic mercenary chiefs had done on the fringes of the late Roman Empire in the fourth to sixth centuries. When the emperor called on them to explain their action the Danish kings promised that Horic, who was then perhaps the youngest and most expendable brother, would attend an imperial council at Nijmegen, the old legionary fortress of Noviomagus, once the nerve centre of the Roman frontier on the lower Rhine. But, just as his father King Godfrid had failed to present himself before

Charlemagne twenty-three years before, Horic hesitated and, perhaps wisely, did not turn up. At least, this version of events was recorded by the Frankish chronicler:

> The emperor summoned an assembly to meet at Nijmegen as Godfrid's son Horic the Danish king had undertaken, falsely, to appear before the emperor . . .
> Meanwhile the kings of Denmark, Godfrid's sons, robbed Harald of his share of the throne and drove him out of the kingdom.[12]

Near the Danish frontier the planned discussions to confirm the settlement between the Danes and the Franks and agree the matter of King Harald attracted counts and marquises from all over Saxony. When an armistice had been agreed and guaranteed with hostages, Harald precipitately broke it, burning and sacking several small Danish villages. At the news, Godfrid's sons instantly mobilised and advanced on our forces, billeted peacefully along the River Eider. The Danes swept over the border, crossed the river, routed our troops and captured their base. They withdrew with supplies and plunder and then worked out the best way of avoiding retaliations. Their envoy told the emperor that they had been unwillingly forced to take countermeasures and were prepared to give compensation, leaving it to him to fix reparations in order to maintain the cease-fire.[13]

Even after fierce family squabbles had begun to tear the Frankish Empire apart by 833, drawing the Danes inexorably into the fight, Horic remained a dignified and courteous negotiator. The next two episodes, recorded as before by the other side, took place after freelance raiding had begun:

> Horic sent a mission to the emperor complaining that his previous envoys had been killed near Cologne, offering peace and loyalty and disclaiming liability for the attacks on Dorestad that had just taken place. [Later] he sent other envoys to Aachen reporting that he had arrested and executed the raiders and asking for head-money for them.[14]

He sent an embassy led by his most trusted adviser and including his nephew. They presented and received rich gifts to cement the peaceful alliance and complained about inroads by the Frisians [whom Horic's subjects were raiding]. The Emperor Louis sent two senior counts to mediate. In Denmark they concluded a solemn sworn alliance.[15]

Later references to Horic in the Frankish annals show how the whirlpool of destruction that had drawn the Danes into Europe was not only wrecking the Frankish economy but starting to threaten his kingdom:

The Emperor Lothar and his brothers King Louis and King Charles sent an embassy to the Danish King Horic to command him to stop his people making war on the Christians. If he did not, they would invade his kingdom.[16]

In 850 he resolved a civil war that had broken out against him by dividing the kingdom with two of his nephews, preferring this to power-sharing:

Two of King Horic's nephews attacked him in a war that went on until he bought them off by granting them part of his kingdom. Horic's nephew Roric, who had left the Emperor Lothar's service, recruited a great Viking army with ships and plundered Frisia. Unable to defeat Roric, Lothar took him into his service again and granted him Dorestad and other counties.[17]

Another nephew, Guthrum, was kept out, but later found a kingdom in East Anglia.

In the end Horic was killed in battle, with most of his family, in a murderous civil war in 854:

The Danes fought among themselves, battling frenziedly with grim persistence for three days in internecine struggle. Their king Horic was killed, along with other kings and almost all their nobles.[18]

Other claimants, who had just lost their positions in Frankish lands, promptly turned up and chanced their arms in claiming the crown:

The Emperor Lothar granted the whole of Frisia to his son Lothar, and the Danes Roric and Godfrid [Harald's sons] sailed for home to make a bid for the throne.[19]

The relatively peaceful activity that we have read about in the last few pages was curiously out of key with what was happening on the Channel coast and in the Low Countries between 834 and 841. Was it simply a diplomatic charade, intended to cover up military preparations? Let us turn to see how the trading marts there, familiar to Scandinavian merchants and seamen and tempting to raiders, were faring.

In 834, as a direct response to the events of 833, a Viking force attacked Quentovic and Dorestad where 'they destroyed everything, killing some of the residents and enslaving others and burning the whole area around'.[20] This was the first of a series of attacks on Dorestad, which do not seem to have inflicted fatal damage, as large numbers of coins were minted there in the late 830s.

They returned to Dorestad in 835, 'laid it waste and looted it savagely. The Emperor Louis, greatly enraged, travelled to Aachen and made plans to strengthen the coast defences.'[21] A series of large round forts along the north French, Belgian and Dutch coast has been attributed to this initiative, but is probably later. In England too, Kent suffered from raids and the Isle of Sheppey was pillaged.

In 836 the Vikings sacked Antwerp and Dorestad yet again and ravaged Frisia. As we have seen, the Danish King Horic sent an embassy to the emperor complaining that his previous envoys had been mugged and killed on their way through Cologne. He claimed that he had arrested and executed the coastal raiders and asked to be paid head-money. The same year a Viking band sacked the island monastery of Noirmoutier at the mouth of the Loire and caused the monks to abandon it. This or another force landed in the Bristol Channel and defeated Egbert of Wessex at Carhampton.

The Vikings returned in 837 to ravage the island of Walcheren off the Frisian coast, where the trading settlement near Domburg was a tempting target, and pillaged Dorestad yet again, sailing off in a hurry when the Emperor Louis gave up a proposed trip to Rome and marched to Nijmegen. In an imperial assembly at

Aachen soon after, he assigned to his fourteen-year-old son Charles a kingdom comprising the entire Low Countries, north-east France and Burgundy. This put the vulnerable Frisian coast, already suffering from raids, in the hands of the youngest and least experienced member of the royal family.

A Viking fleet set off in 838 for what was becoming a normal season's raiding, but was struck by a storm and went down with few survivors. A 'great force' landed in Cornwall and fought King Egbert as allies of the local Britons, but they were beaten at Hingston Down. An Arab pirate fleet captured Marseilles and carried off all the men and the many nuns into slavery. Another Danish embassy arrived, claiming, as before, that all the coastal raiders had been duly put to death and suggesting that the emperor should invite Horic to govern the Frisians and the Obodrites, the Slav tribes nearest his borders, just as Harald governed the coast of Saxony.

In 839 Frisia suffered from serious floods and Viking ravaging. The regular Danish embassy arrived with rich gifts seeking an alliance and, as we have read, laid complaints against the Frisians. The emperor sent two senior counts to investigate and also sent gifts in return. This mission to Denmark concluded a permanent peace. This did not succeed in stopping the raids which, as we have suspected, may have been sponsored by one of the emperor's older sons. At this time the Emperor Louis' main concern was to broker a succession deal between the sons, one or other of whom was openly in arms against him from 838 until his death in 840. He had just concluded a successful campaign to chase his son Louis the German 'in flight to seek the help of the heathen and tribes beyond our borders, to whom he gave lavish subsidies'.[22]

Who, we must ask, could have persuaded or bribed the raiders to attack the Rhine mouth and Channel marts in 833 and later years? There are two obvious suspects, Charlemagne's two elder grandchildren, disgruntled, unprincipled and actually at war with their father, the Emperor Louis the Pious. Their usual everyday behaviour allows us to accuse the junior emperor Lothar and his brother Louis the German of hiring mercenaries to commit the atrocities as part of their war. Their most likely agent is ex-King Harald helped, if they were old enough, by his sons Roric and Godfrid at the head of a mixed force of *émigré* Danes, Frisians and Saxons under Danish colours. This seems far more likely than supposing this round of Viking raids to be a strictly Danish enterprise, embarked on through an initiative of Horic or any of his home-based nobles.

In 840, while hostilities between Lothar and Louis the German simmered, a Danish force, reported to be of thirty-three ships and thus possibly of over a thousand men, attacked Southampton and was driven off with heavy loss by the veteran governor Wulfhard. They or another band invaded Dorset, killing and defeating governor Ethelhelm at Portland. From this time we will follow the constant Viking presence first in France and then in England.

From a vantage point of the mid-century we can survey and assess the Vikings' reputation and achievement, and also ask what a Viking camp was like and what went on there all day. What kind of military activities and what sort of commerce did they engage in? How did the leaders maintain discipline? We can hardly suppose that they bothered much with the parades and spit-and-polish that obsessed generals in more recent times. No doubt it was rather like any king's or governor's hall. There may have been a good deal of arms practice, some of it in the form of drunken fights. Local farmers brought their produce to sell, so that a market developed at which the Vikings could also sell off unwanted loot. A note in the *Codex Aureus* or 'Golden Gospels' at Stockholm, originally made for a Kentish monastery, records that governor Alfred of Surrey bought it back from the Vikings to give to Canterbury. And no doubt slave-dealers kept their ears out for news of likely new consignments from any raid planned. But slavery by capture was an everyday risk, as it was also for debt.

As well as foraging parties, the Viking leaders no doubt also sent out 'tax' collecting patrols around their hinterland, just as the rival sides in the English Civil War of the 1640s took what contributions they could from their own area and twice over in any areas of 'no man's land'. They must have run 'protection rackets' of all kinds and offered local monasteries armed help and military 'advisers' who could help the bodyguards of the abbots when they travelled.

In none of these activities and presumed enterprises did the Viking leaders behave much worse than any king or governor of the time. In ninth-century England, Alfred's grandfather ravaged Cornwall in 815, no doubt repeating the exercise when he thrashed a coalition of Vikings and Cornish in 838. In 830 he subjugated the Welsh and his son Ethelwulf and grandson-in-law Burgred of Mercia repeated the process in 853, as did his great-granddaughter Ethelfleda in 916, when she took a queen and thirty-three others hostage in reprisal for an abbot's death. Egbert's wars with Mercia, scantily reported in the *Chronicle*, must have been accompanied by plundering and burning royal halls and churches, if wars were still being carried on as Bede reports of the seventh and early eighth centuries. Alfred's own capture of London in 886 was accompanied, Asser tells us, 'with so many towns burnt and so many men slaughtered'.[23] The Frankish kings habitually ravaged their own and neighbouring kingdoms on any excuse.

Society and the economy could absorb ravaging and looting and in many ways depended on it. Kings needed plunder to redistribute among their nobles to hold their loyalty; carpenters could be sure of work, if there were always burnt church roofs and royal halls needing to be replaced. The damage was focused on the chief places, with few permanent residents.

When the Vikings captured and took over an area, killing or driving out the kings, governors, their warriors and the priests and chaplains who were their scribes, they simply replaced these upper ranks of society themselves and imposed their will on the humble farmers not trained to fight, but conditioned not to put up any opposition, lying low when there was trouble. Their duty was to produce food and raw materials. New Scandinavian rulers bought the merchants' imports and farm produce and employed the artisans, bringing in specialist craftsmen to make some artefacts to their own taste. But in many ways there was little change.

6

Christian Europe: France and the
Vikings before the 860s

THE FRANKISH LANDS ARE A CLASSIC EXAMPLE of a fluid and loosely organised kingdom that became a great empire and then broke up again, within two generations, into rather more stable successor kingdoms. These rapid fluctuations of political structures are characteristic of proto-historic societies. How far, we might wonder in passing, can we use them as analogies for the study of prehistory? The dynasty that ruled the Franks from 752 to 887, the Carolingians, can be regarded as an unsurpassed example of perfidious and bloodstained royalty who bullied and robbed all neighbouring countries, whose mutinous children squabbled on every possible opportunity, fought each other for power, seized their relations' estates, captured and imprisoned their parents and regularly used assassination as a political weapon. In this chapter we will examine the career of one of them, Charles the Bald, first king of France, the western part of their territories. We suggested in the last chapter that the Vikings owe their bloodstained reputation to the leadership and example of Charles's brothers Lothar and Louis.

The heartlands of the early kingdom comprised much of northern France, the Rhineland and southern Germany and already by 752 stretched beyond the old Roman frontier, and thus included four different kinds of places where the chiefs and petty kings who had come to power in sub-Roman territories had found refuges and maintained centres for their rule, for keeping what law there

95

was, for collecting ordinary taxes and for profiting from markets held there. In the old civilian areas they huddled within the extensive walls of the derelict Roman cities and towns. In the frontier zones they could find safety within the many Roman forts that stood deserted and ruined. Beyond the frontier they refortified much older prehistoric hill-forts or made new ones. At key locations along the coast and on major rivers there were trading marts, all of them close by a former Roman fort that had been reused or a new fortress.

We have already seen that authors and compilers of lives and chronicles had no concern for a balanced record of events. They wrote to glorify their kings and great lords, to boost their reputation and diminish the fame of their rivals and enemies, and thus win for themselves promotion in the Church or rewards in cash and lands. This gives us confidence in the texts: however heavily edited, biased and muddled they are overall, the compilers had no reason to change the regular month-by-month record of their own king or emperor and his assemblies, hunts and campaigns. We must not think of them as modern heads of state in modern cities, or even as medieval kings in medieval towns. The doleful list, year by year, of places sacked or burnt by Viking forces must give us the main outline of the damage inflicted, but we must not interpret what we read as comparable to the devastation of a modern city by missiles with a TV reporter dodging the fire. There was not much to burn and there were very few people to suffer from the raids, apart from the royal bailiffs in charge, who could ride off in flight and to muster aid, and the priests of the churches, who were the main victims and the keepers of the records.

In this chapter we will follow events in France in a selective summary of the *Annals of St Bertin* through most of the reign of Alfred's older contemporary, Charles the Bald, first king of France (840–877), closest of his European neighbours in time and space.[1] Alfred met him a number of times, first probably as a small child in 853, and stayed at his court for some months in 855, when Charles gave his young daughter Judith in marriage to Alfred's widowed father. He may well have taken Alfred, then six, out hunting or campaigning against Vikings during the five months he and his father were there. Although our evidence is scanty, there must have been constant friendly relations between the two courts.

Forty years later Alfred in turn gave a daughter in marriage to Count Baldwin of Flanders, Judith's son by her third, runaway, marriage.

In 752 Pepin, son of Charles, 'Mayor of the Palace' of the Frankish kingdom, deposed his lawful but essentially ceremonial head of state, Childeric, last king of the Merovingian dynasty, and seized the throne. He enlarged his kingdom by conquering south-west France and attacked Saxony, Lombardy and Bavaria. The usurper's son Charles, later Charlemagne or 'Charles the Great', succeeded in 768. Between the 780s and the 810s, in a long series of annual campaigns which brought him vast quantities of booty, Charlemagne built up a great empire covering most of western Europe and stretching from the Channel, the North Sea and the Danish border in the north to 80km south of Rome and from the Elbe in the east to beyond the Pyrenees. To control these conquests he set up some of his sons, like Pippin in Aquitaine, as kings in outlying regions.

Charlemagne based the security of his newly conquered frontier provinces on forts, establishing a local governor or 'count' in the main ones to control the territory or 'county' around it. This was nothing new; the kings and chiefs he conquered had taken over and ruled their lands through kinsmen, chiefs and nobles, based in hill-forts or within old town walls, in very much the same way. Charlemagne simply organised it all on a grander scale and the chroniclers, taking them for granted, mention them casually and unevenly. Some of the forts were new, others improvised from Roman cities with existing walls.

On the north-eastern frontiers of his realm Charlemagne built Paderborn, first documented in 777, Herstelle near Minden in the centre of conquered Saxony in 797, and Hamburg, a fort for coastal defence, in about 810. In Catalonia to the south-west he founded strongholds at Gerona in 785, Urgel in 789, Barcelona before 797 and Pallas and Ribogorza in about 808. He also had fleets constructed, one in 800 to guard the Channel coasts from its base at Boulogne against minor raids that Norse and Danish seamen, and no doubt others, had begun in the late 780s, the other in 810 in the Mediterranean against the Arabs.

97

National pride, both French and German, has prevented Charlemagne from being presented as one of the greatest gangsters of all time, ruling a clique of amoral warlords by bullying and bribery while terrorising all neighbouring countries, but this judgement is not so far from reality.

Charlemagne's surviving son, Louis the Pious (814–840), succeeded him as emperor with at least nominal control of the whole group of family kingdoms. We have related many events of Louis' reign from a Danish standpoint. Up to 834 the Danes were less trouble to the Franks than the Saxons and Slavs close to them, the rebellious Bretons on their north-west frontier, the Basques and Arabs across the Pyrenees to the south-west and the Carinthians and Pannonians to the south-east, all of whom figure large in the *Annals of the Franks* as worthy opponents.

The Emperor Louis had lost full control long before his death in 840. A widespread conspiracy that began in 830 led to his capture and imprisonment by his three elder sons in 833–834. Louis had made Lothar, his eldest son, king of Bavaria at ten years old in 817 and then, in 829, sent him off to rule Italy. The revolt of 833 was caused largely by Louis' desire to find a kingdom for his favourite youngest son Charles, then just ten. He had earmarked first south-west Germany and then south-west France for Charles, but whatever he chose was instantly objected to by one of his other sons as already promised to him, until finally in 837 they agreed on north-east France with the Low Countries; as we have just seen, the rows led to the first serious Viking attacks there.

We have followed the attacks of 834 on Quentovic and Dorestad where 'they destroyed everything, killing some of the residents and enslaving others and burning the whole area around'[2] and the raids that followed, suspecting that ex-King Harald carried them out with renegade Frisians, Saxons and Danes in the pay of Lothar or his brother Louis the German as part of their war on their father the emperor.

A few months after Lothar became the new emperor in 840, his brothers Louis the German, king of the east Franks, and Charles the Bald, king of the west Franks, combined to defeat him in a hard fight at Fontenoy. Lothar gained the armed support of the Danish ex-King Harald, who with other Danish marauders had inflicted endless damage on the Frisians and other Christians along the coast, damaging the emperor's resources while increasing Lothar's, by granting him the island of Walcheren with the neighbouring counties to govern.[3]

This gift of Frisia shocked the chroniclers, or rather Charles's personal chronicler Prudentius, who expressed his horror that 'the destroyers of Christianity should be set to rule over Christians and Christian people should have to obey a devil-worshipper', conveniently forgetting that Harald and his wife had been baptised at Mainz fourteen years earlier in 826, when the Emperor Louis had given him coastal Saxony to govern. It is not clear if Lothar was adding Frisia to Harald's province, or compensating him for losing it, as he had so often lost his share of the throne of Denmark. Lothar must have been fully aware that Frisia was part of the kingdom that his father had assigned, with his agreement, to his brother Charles. It was just this area too that King Horic of Denmark had offered to take over through his envoys in 838, as his preferred long-term solution. From this time there was a destabilising presence in the west.

At about this time the Channel fleet that Charlemagne had built to prevent raids disappears from the record. We might suspect that Lothar gave or sold the ships to Harald rather than pay them off and scrap them. Also in 841 a Viking force, perhaps led by Harald acting for Lothar, invaded the Seine valley in Charles's territory and captured Rouen (the Roman Rotomagus). Showing good business acumen, they

plundered the town with pillage, fire and sword, killed or enslaved both monks and residents and ravaged the monasteries and settlements along the river, or terrorised them and extracted massive ransom payments.

This force or another band invaded Kent, killed governor Hereberht and many of his warriors on Romney Marsh, and committed atrocities along the east coast of England to Lindsey, the north-easternmost province of Mercia (now Lincolnshire).

In 842 a Viking force took advantage of the political turmoil and captured Quentovic, a famous trading mart on Charles's lands south of Boulogne, in a dawn raid. They 'plundered and sacked it, and captured or slaughtered the residents, leaving nothing except the buildings they were paid to spare',[4] again showing a thoroughly commercial approach and making us realise that protection rackets are nothing new. Perhaps this same band carried out the massacres in London and Rochester this year; the less sophisticated English *Chronicle* makes no mention of cash changing hands. In the same year an Arab raiding party pillaged the Rhone valley and sailed out unhindered with all their loot.

In 843 the three royal Frankish brothers made a final settlement at Verdun by which Louis and Charles left Lothar with northern Italy and a broad dividing strip of territory from the Alps to the Channel between them. After breaking up his empire, Charlemagne's grandsons abandoned two of his policies. He had built and maintained a fleet in the Channel and, except for Rome, had firmly kept bishops out of politics and restricted their territorial power. As we have just seen, the fleet was given up. And as the counts, appointed to serve as provincial governors by royal favour, strove ceaselessly to establish themselves as hereditary magnates, with authority and estates handed down from father to son, so Charlemagne's successors encouraged their bishops to become active counterweights, just as French colonies in the eighteenth century had the authority of a military *gouverneurs* balanced by the civil *intendants*.

The west Frankish territories which Charles the Bald won as his realm were forged into the kingdom of France, after events which we read of in the chronicles as prolonged fighting, constant revolts and decades of Viking ravaging and burning. But, as we have seen, places recorded as looted and burnt were not cities and towns with wealthy merchants, tradesmen and hard-working craftsmen, but very basic government centres or churches, so the damage had relatively little long-term economic effect. As the chronicles make it quite clear that burning cities and ravaging the countryside were a normal and long-established response to any kind of political discord or change, it becomes ever clearer how unfair it is to blame the Vikings for violence in a violent age. The Franks had invaded and ravaged their homeland, threatened them at home with their domineering diplomacy and hired them to serve as hit-men and mercenary seamen.

In 843 a Viking squadron invaded the mouth of the Loire, sacked Nantes, killing the bishop, and went on to ravage the west coast of Aquitaine, then a kingdom ruled by Pippin II, a nephew of Charles the Bald. This was good news for Charles who was trying to drive Pippin out and we can wonder whether he hired them. Another group of Vikings established a base on Noirmoutier, no doubt in the abandoned monastery buildings, which were to remain a raiding base for many years. Other warbands were to follow this example in England, on the offshore islands, as they then were, of Thanet in 850–851 and Sheppey in 854–855.

In 844 Charles besieged Toulouse and forced King Pippin to submit. As he withdrew, the Vikings sailed up the Garonne and attacked Toulouse themselves. Some went much further and raided the Spanish coast as far south as Andalusia, where they suffered a sharp defeat. The major Frankish chronicler was sufficiently interested at that time in English news to note that a Viking force, perhaps of Danes who held Dublin briefly, invaded Wessex by the north Somerset coast; they 'attacked Britain in great force, defeating the English in a fight that lasted three days. Without further resistance they ravaged, pillaged and murdered freely.'[5] As we have already seen, a 'great force' of thirty-five ships, whose crews may have numbered over a thousand men, beat King Ethelwulf at Carhampton, where an earlier force had beaten his father seven years earlier. The major defeat was tersely played down in Wessex: 'King Ethelwulf fought the crews of thirty-five ships at Carhampton and the Danes held the killing-ground.'[6]

The Viking fleet that had attacked Toulouse pillaged Saintes in 845 and spent the winter in the area. Also in 845 a Danish leader called Ragnar, previously a mercenary in the pay of Charles the Bald, led another raiding party up the Seine and sacked Paris, but not so gravely as to stop church councils being held there in 846, 847 and 849. While boasting, home in Denmark, about the great ransom of seven thousand pounds of silver that Charles had paid him to spare the monastery of St Germain, he was struck by a fatal sickness, much to the satisfaction of the monks when they heard the news. The Danes made a strong attack on Germany; King Horic sent a large fleet, reported as six hundred ships, up the River Elbe, where it was defeated, but burnt the fort of Hamburg to the ground, leaving, so the archaeological findings indicate, the trading mart beside it quite intact. Presumably Hamburg lay within Harald's province, or perhaps the attack was provoked by some hostile plan of Louis the German's. The same year a Viking attempt to build on the previous year's victory in Wessex met with a sharp rebuff, when valiant old Bishop Ealhstan and the governors of Dorset and Somerset thrashed the Danes at the Parrett mouth, where the river flows into the Bristol Channel, so effectively that all England was free from raids for the next six years.

In 846 the Vikings, presumably Harald's men from Walcheren, invaded and overran most of the rest of Frisia, keeping control of it for many years, perhaps continuously until the 870s. The status of the great mart of Dorestad is obscure; it may have continued under Viking management, until put out of action by Rhine floods in the 860s. Charles made peace with the Bretons, who had long been in almost permanent revolt against the Franks. The threatening situation forced Charles to make some attempts to improve his defensive security and reform provincial government. The scanty historical records other than the *Annals*, whose compilers show little interest in forts at this time, refer to new fortifications at St Omer in 846 and Angers in 851. The capture and sack of Rome on 27 August by the Arabs resulted in a defence programme there.

In 847, as we have noted, the Emperor Lothar and his royal brothers, Louis of Germany and Charles the Bald, threatened Denmark with full-scale war if King Horic did not hold his warriors back; but everything went on much as before. Some Vikings pillaged Brittany and moved on to aid a revolt in Aquitaine and blockade Bordeaux in 847–848. Charles the Bald defeated a Viking army but failed to save Bordeaux from capture and sack.

In 848 most of the Aquitainian counts abandoned Pippin and accepted Charles as their king. An Irish embassy, boasting a series of Viking defeats, concluded an alliance with Charles, who gave their king permission to travel through his lands to Rome.

In 849, a notably quiet and peaceful year, Vikings burnt Périgueux, intentionally or accidentally helping Charles the Bald who marched into Aquitaine and captured a nephew who was trying to seize power. The Bretons attacked Anjou and the area round and the Arabs pillaged the Provencal coast. After this moment of calm, attacks and raids increased and became more serious.

In 850 a fierce civil war in Denmark, presumably fomented by the Franks, forced King Horic to give two nephews part of his kingdom. The renegade Prince Roric, son of Harald, sacked by the Emperor Lothar from his province of Frisia, got his own back by recruiting a large Viking force and devastating Frisia, Batavia and the lower Rhine area so effectively that Lothar had to hire him again to protect the area from people like him.

In 851 a formidable Viking force, perhaps including men paid off by Roric, ravaged Frisia and burnt the monastery of St Bavo at Ghent, before going on past Rouen to burn Beauvais. A Frankish force attacked their rearguard and inflicted some casualties. The records of this year are difficult to follow and it is impossible to tell how many bands were active along which rivers. A strong force invaded England; after spending the winter, for the first time in England, on the Isle of Thanet they captured Canterbury and London and defeated the Mercians. King Ethelwulf of Wessex crushed them with heavy casualties at the 'Oak Glade'; the victory got a brief mention in the Frankish *Annals*. Two other Viking attacks on Wessex were also beaten off, by governor Ceorl in Devon and by Alfred's brother Athelstan and Ealhhere in a sea battle in Kent.

In October 852 Roric's brother Godfrid, who had been baptised long before and who had served the Emperor Lothar as a mercenary, and a new leader, Sidroc, led a Viking fleet into the Seine valley to raid and pillage. The emperor promptly marched to bring help to his brother Charles, perhaps feeling some remorse for his part in bringing this Danish dynasty to the west. If so, the feeling did not last. After a short winter campaign they made peace with Godfrid. They made friends with each other too, for once, and spent Twelfth Night feasting together.

In 853 the Vikings from the Seine valley invaded the Loire, sacking Nantes and burning Tours. Another force, invading Kent, defeated and killed the governors of Kent and Surrey on Thanet while King Ethelwulf was off with his new son-in-law Burgred of Mercia raiding the Welsh. A four-year-old English prince, Alfred, rode to Rome and back with his bodyguards.

The next year the Loire Vikings captured and burnt Blois and planned to attack Orleans. Hearing that the bishops of Orleans and Chartres had joined forces and raised ships and men to oppose them, they sailed away downstream, but returned to burn Angers at the end of the year. Perhaps the younger Godfrid was still leading them.

After a violent civil war in Denmark late in 854, in which King Horic and most of the leading nobles were annihilated, Viking attacks on France intensified still more. But our knowledge of what was happening in Denmark soon drops away to nothing.

In 855 the Emperor Lothar, who was seriously ill and died soon after, dismissed both Roric and Godfrid from governing Frisia, entrusting the region to his son King Lothar junior. They went home to Denmark to put in a bid for the throne which their father Harald had held with his brother Regenfrid in 812–813 and shared with his cousins intermittently through the 820s. Meeting with no success they returned to their base at Dorestad and continued to govern or dominate Frisia. The Loire Vikings sailed to attack Bordeaux and ravaged the neighbourhood; returning to the Loire, they moored their ships and marched overland to Poitiers. An army from Aquitaine defeated them and inflicted very heavy casualties. King Ethelwulf of Wessex and his youngest son Alfred enjoyed King Charles's hospitality as they rode across Europe to Rome, where they spent the year.

In 856 the Loire Vikings sacked Orleans quite unopposed. The younger Godfrid reappeared on the Seine and entrenched himself on the island of Oissel on the Seine above Rouen. This remained a Viking base for five years. Charles the Bald entertained King Ethelwulf of Wessex on his way home from Rome with his son Alfred, now seven, at his court from July to October, if Bishop Prudentius got the dates right in his *Annals*. Ethelwulf married Charles's young daughter Judith. We can be sure that Ethelwulf told Charles of the newly completed Leonine City and of arrangements for manning and maintaining it. We might perhaps imagine the young Alfred listening to grizzled Frankish counts tell of their campaigns against Viking bands up and down the Somme, the Seine and the Loire and of long marches against King Charles's hostile brothers and nephews and disloyal counts and other enemies in Aquitaine, Brittany, Lorraine and Spain. In December 856, after Ethelwulf had left for home (to find his second son Ethelbald refusing to hand back the throne of Wessex), the Vikings raided and burnt Paris.

They repeated the raid during the following summer and at the end of 857, when they burnt one church and extracted a huge payment to leave three others. In 857 too, a Viking band on the Loire sacked Tours and ravaged the valley as far as Blois. Then, allied with rebel Aquitainian nobles, they captured and sacked Charles's stronghold of Poitiers. Outside Charles's kingdom a Viking force sacked Dorestad and ravaged Batavia. It is likely that Dorestad was still in Roric's hands and that this attack was by a rival Viking group.

At the start of 858 Charles recruited a new Viking leader Bjorn and his warband. Another Viking gang kidnapped Charles's cousin, Abbot Louis of St Denis, and got a vast ransom for him. Charles marched, presumably with Bjorn, to attack the Vikings at Oissel but suffered a sudden threefold disaster, from disaffected nobles, from sickness and from his brother Louis the German, whose forces invaded, swept through and took over much of the kingdom. We may remember 833, when Charles's brothers captured and imprisoned their father and put him quietly out of the way in a monastery; or look forward and compare this abrupt change of fortune with King Alfred's sudden loss of Wessex in 878.

By January 859 Charles had recovered his throne as his 'most faithful' counts and abbots, and especially his bishops, mobilised their fighting men and forced Louis to withdraw to Germany, just as twenty years later Alfred recovered Wessex as his magnates loyally brought their warriors to beat Guthrum in 878. Only north-west France, where he had installed his son Louis the Stammerer as king, remained opposed to him, under the dissident leader Count Robert of Anjou. Another Viking band, having sailed into the Mediterranean, ravaged lands in the Rhone valley and seized an island base in the Camargue. Later in 859 a new Viking force burnt St Valery and Amiens in the north-east of France and a second attacked Noyon and Beauvais, killing the bishops of both places. A particularly worrying development caused the Frankish authorities extra trouble. Groups of peasants in north-west France began to form subversive groups sworn to take up arms and fight the Vikings, which they did quite effectively on the Seine, and had to be suppressed at once.

In 860 another force from the Somme, failing to raise three thousand pounds of silver in their district, crossed the Channel to invade Wessex. They marched inland and took Winchester, just after Alfred's second brother Ethelbald had died, to be succeeded by the third brother Ethelbert. Two veteran governors, Ethelwulf of Berkshire and Osric of Hampshire, 'drove the Danes in flight and held the killing ground'.

In 861 Bishop Prudentius died, Archbishop Hincmar rather cruelly commenting when he got hold of the *Annals of St Bertin* and began to continue them, 'still jotting down all these contradictions and heresies'.[7] The Viking warband defeated in England, now commanded by the previously unrecorded Weland, burnt Thérouanne in passing and invaded the Seine valley. Charles the Bald took him into his service, offering him first three thousand and then five thousand pounds of silver to attack the camp at Oissel. This force had done so well out of nearby towns and passing river-traders that they gave King Charles the Bald quite a surprise. Under severe pressure, they offered Weland six thousand pounds of silver to let them go free. Both groups went off downriver for an autumn cruise in the Seine estuary and then back inland past Paris. They split up into family or clan groups for the winter. Weland camped for the winter at Melun and his son and the Oissel group took over the abbey of St Maur as a comfortable base. The Vikings in the Mediterranean took and burnt Pisa.

In January 862 the second warband from St Maur sacked Meaux, on the Marne above Paris, possibly hoping that King Charles would approve as the bishop was known to be disaffected. But this was the beginning of the end of their 'salad days'. Charles pursued them and trapped their ships behind a pontoon bridge which he threw across the river, forcing them to give hostages and agree to leave the Seine. This treaty included Weland, some of whose ships had made for Meaux. They all left and some were hired by the Bretons to fight Count Robert of Angers, who captured and killed them all. Count Robert hired the others for a fee of six thousand pounds of silver to fight the Bretons. King Charles and his counts assembled at Pîtres near Rouen to plan a defence system, which eventually ended this casual free-for-all raiding. We will continue the story later as part of a widespread move towards organised defences in which Alfred played an important part.

This series of attacks and raids on France and the Low Countries lasted almost thirty years, from 834 to 862, without inflicting catastrophic or crippling damage. It was hardly more of a burden on the European economy overall than the normal processes of government, carried on as they always were with frequent campaigns abroad and endemic rebellion and civil war at home. The Church became both more of a soft target and also more vocal in complaint, but churches had always been looted and burnt in all the wars between Christian kings.

One of the most significant entries in the Frankish *Annals* notes the emergence of the peasantry, banding together in sworn associations against the Vikings, as a threat to the ruling classes:

> Some of the peasants farming between the Seine and the Loire formed unions sworn together on oath and boldly opposed the raiders in fighting along the Seine. The authorities disposed of these groups as unlawful . . .[8]

which indicates clearly that the Frankish counts, mostly of Germanic blood, did not depend on peasant levies for their armies, but suppressed them vigorously and kept arms and independence well away from these descendants of the Romanised Gallic tribesmen, originally of Celtic stock. There was no doubt a similar gulf between rulers and ruled in other countries.

7

865–872, Battles and Devastation: the start of Alfred's reign

———❦———

THE ONLY NARRATIVE OF EVENTS IN ENGLAND in the years when Alfred was growing to manhood and of 871, the *annus horribilis* when he found himself king of a weak kingdom under fearful threat, was written under Alfred's auspices less than twenty years later. The *Chronicle*'s account of the short reign of Alfred's fourth brother Ethelred is a masterpiece of Tacitean prose, tersely piling up threat on threat and disaster on disaster as the action covers the whole of England, moving relentlessly towards Wessex until we reach 871, the year of battles, when Alfred came to the throne.

Before we attempt any explanation or comment, we had better read this account, set down shortly before 890 by the first compiler of the *Chronicle*, who must have lived through the events he records. Later in this chapter we will see how kings regularly held court while on campaign and government was geared to war and disruption.

865
a. A Viking army camped on Thanet and agreed a cease-fire with the men of Kent, who promised payment to get peace. With the armistice in force while the cash was collected, the army went inland and pillaged all east Kent.

866
a. Ethelbert's brother Ethelred succeeded as king of Wessex.

b. A great pagan army invaded England and spent the winter in East Anglia, where they got horses. The East Anglians paid tribute.

867

a. The army moved into Northumbria, crossing the Humber mouth to York. King Osbert had been deposed in a civil war and replaced by a king, Ælla, with no royal blood. Late in the year the two factions united to oppose the invaders and attacked York with their combined forces. Some of them broke into the city. The Vikings slaughtered both kings and massacred the Northumbrians inside and outside the wall. The survivors sued for a cease-fire.

b. Ealhstan, bishop of Sherborne for fifty years [in fact forty-three], died and was buried in the churchyard there.

868

a. The Viking army moved to Nottingham in Mercia to spend the winter. King Burgred and the Mercian senators begged King Ethelred and his brother Alfred to help them oppose the army. They mobilised, advanced to Nottingham, found the enemy on the defensive and blockaded them. The Mercians agreed to peace-terms and there was no major battle.

869

a. The invading army returned to York for the year.

870

a. The Viking army crossed Mercia into East Anglia and camped for the winter at Thetford. That winter King Edmund [of East Anglia] fought the Vikings, who killed him and conquered his kingdom.

b. Archbishop Ceolnoth [833–870; a survivor when Canterbury was sacked in 851] died.

871

a. The army moved to Reading in Wessex.

b. Three days later two Danish earls pushed further inland. Governor Ethelwulf clashed with them at Englefield and won the fight, killing Earl Sidroc there.

c. Four days after this King Ethelred and Alfred his brother marched their main force to Reading and attacked. Heavy casualties on both sides included governor Ethelwulf killed. The Danes held the battlefield.

d. Four days later King Ethelred and his brother Alfred fought the entire Viking army at Ashdown. The Danes deployed in two brigades, one led by the two pagan kings Bagsecg and Healfdene and the other by the earls. King Ethelred faced the kings and Bagsecg was killed. His brother Alfred opposed the earls. Fatalities included Earl Sidroc the elder, Earl Sidroc the younger, Earl Osbearn, Earl Fraena and Earl Harold. Both enemy divisions were beaten in combat which went on till night.

e. Two weeks later King Ethelred and Alfred his brother fought the pagans at Basing and the Danes won.

f. Two months later Ethelred and Alfred fought the army again at Meretun [unidentified]. For most of the day they drove back the two divisions in which the Vikings were deployed, with heavy casualties, but the Danes held the battleground. Bishop Heahmund [of Sherborne 868–871] and many senior officers fell there.

g. Later, after Easter, King Ethelred died after a reign of five years and was buried at Wimborne minster.

h. His brother Alfred, son of Ethelwulf, succeeded to the kingdom of Wessex.

i. A month later King Alfred, with a small detachment, fought the whole heathen army at Wilton and drove it back late in the day, but the Danes held the battlefield.

j. During the year, the Danish army had to fight nine full-scale battles south of the Thames, excluding skirmishes on patrols on which Alfred, as the king's brother, and single governors and ministers often rode. Enemy casualties included nine earls and a king.

k. Wessex made peace with the Vikings.

872
The army left Reading for London, where they settled for the winter. The Mercians also asked for an armistice.

Ethelred, King Ethelwulf's fourth son, was the nearest in age and the closest to Alfred of all his brothers. They were brought up together; they repeatedly appear together in witness-lists, indicating that they stood side by side at court ceremonies; and, as young men in 868, they campaigned together as far as Nottingham, well over 150km from home. This was an eventful march for social reasons too, as Alfred met, wooed and married his wife as a nineteen-year-old commander on active service.

Except for noting the deaths of kings and bishops, the *Chronicle*'s account of Ethelred's five-year reign, is entirely concerned, for dramatic effect, with the doings of the Viking host led by Ivar and Healfdene which landed in East Anglia in the autumn of 865; we must remember that the *Chronicle*'s year at this time begins in September. Numbering hundreds, rather than thousands as was once thought, this particular army formed such an effective military force that within four years they had destroyed the kingdoms of Northumbria in 867 and East Anglia in 870, their killer instinct better developed than it had been in France in the 850s. Northern evidence gives a date of 21 March 867 for the attack on York by the combined troops of the two rival Anglian kings of Northumbria, who were defeated and killed with no fewer than eight of their governors and no doubt a great number of warriors.[1]

In the fifth year of the invasion the Vikings began their onslaught on Wessex. Viking policy was to plunder year-round from defended bases, taking over weak provinces and kingdoms without too much fighting. Of course the slaughter of the ruling classes and their henchmen, as happened to Northumbria and East Anglia, released the farming community from the burden of supporting these consumers (who contributed little or nothing to production), at least until the invaders imposed their own burdens. That there was a monetary economy fully understood and used every market-day by the peasants of most European kingdoms is evident from the large number of coinage-issues and the vast number of, in England, silver pennies that must have been in regular circulation. The peasants produced the regular income, other than loot from campaigns against the Welsh and any other enemies, which the nobles and warriors lived on and spent. Small coin-hoards, which are found regularly, are as likely to be the savings of the more prosperous farmers as they are to be merchants' purses or warriors' pay or loot.

When their brother-in-law King Burgred of Mercia appealed for help in 868, Ethelred and his youngest and only surviving brother, the nineteen-year-old Alfred, marched to bring support and confront the Vikings dug in at Nottingham, but they refused battle and sensibly stayed put. This gratuitous reinforcement may well have been the incentive for the Vikings' seizure, late in 870, of Reading, a very defensible royal hall at the confluence of the Kennet and the Thames. Such pre-emptive strikes had long been a characteristic of Danish strategy and the Viking high command was no doubt determined to put Wessex out of the fight before returning to obliterate Mercia.

Late in 870 the Viking leaders began a determined and ferocious attack on Wessex, from their base at Reading. At one battle, at Ashdown, while his brother the king was still at prayer, Alfred personally led their army forward to attack. Asser tells us:

> The Christian battle-plan was for Ethelred and the royal guards to attack the heathen kings while Alfred, with the other [shire] contingents, tried his hand against the Viking earls' combined forces. When the forces had been deployed and the Vikings were advancing fully prepared, the king remained deep in prayer. Alfred, in command as deputy head of state, could not hold his ground without either retreating or going into action without his brother. Before the king appeared he ordered the Christian army forward against the enemy as planned, with the line closed up shield-to-shield, unhesitatingly leading the charge 'like a wild boar', sustained by his own courage and by 'divine resolution and the wisdom of the Holy Spirit'.[2]

Asser had been shown the lonely hawthorn tree which stood at the central focus of the fight and told how the cheering armies clashed and the men of Wessex cut their way uphill to the higher ground, which the Vikings had picked to give them an advantage. After furious and sustained hand-to-hand fighting, the Vikings broke, failing for once to make their retreat in good order. The English pursued the routed enemy, cutting down the fugitives through the night and all the next day until they reached their fortified base-camp at, we must infer, Reading.[3]

Here they were safe behind a new stockade put up when they arrived not long before.[4] Four days earlier, as soon as they could muster their main forces, Ethelred and Alfred had tried to storm the base and been driven off after bitter fighting around the gates. The courageous old governor Ethelwulf of Berkshire fell here at the head of his local forces, which he had led for well over a generation, since long before Alfred's birth, which he may conceivably have attended as governor of the shire.[5]

At the height of the crisis Ethelred died on 15 April 871 and was buried at Wimborne in Dorset, his favourite shire, to judge from the courts recorded in his charters. Alfred, now aged twenty-two, succeeded him as king, presumably by pre-arranged invitation by the royal council. Despite further bitter fighting, he was finally forced to pay the Vikings to go away.[6] In these circumstances, which constantly arose all over Europe, the recipients no doubt liked to think that the money was tribute paid by their new subjects, while the giver looked on it as straightforward extortion without strings.

The compiler of the *Chronicle* and all later commentators have failed to solve one editorial problem. It records that three earls called Sidroc were killed near Reading over a period of eight days, one at Englefield and two in the next-but-one battle at Ashdown. This seems rather too many. We may tentatively recognise the elder Earl Sidroc who fell at Ashdown as the Sidroc who raided along the Seine valley for some years from 852. No doubt the compiler got conflicting reports and for once trained memories failed and no one could recall quite which Sidroc they had slain when or exactly where. It may be more realistic to lay the blame for the confusion on a feckless early scribe, the copyist who displaced all the dates by two or three years in the A-text at Corpus Christi College, Cambridge. He may have skipped a line or two and begun to write about Sidroc's death, and then gone off for dinner; coming back in a merry state he continued the text, casually leaving in the first reference to Sidroc, to save scraping it out. Of course all manuscript sources are vulnerable to such hazards.

Before we go on to see Alfred narrowly survive his first round of trouble, we should examine the flexible and adaptable institutions of government that permitted him to keep his kingdom ticking over. There were no ministries with files; no TV or radio stations or offices to be raided or seized; and the only civil servants were part-timers, the governors, ministers and reeves who led their men joyfully into action and the bishops and their priests who rode beside them, perhaps with some qualms, into battle.

That Alfred's brother Ethelred and his court were not exclusively concerned with military affairs we can see from some eleven property transactions recorded among all the troubles of his short reign, as he carried on with 'business as usual'. We can follow him on a few of his endless moves around the kingdom, from Micheldever in Hampshire in 862 to Dorchester in Dorset for Christmas 863, (and then perhaps west to Devon and Cornwall,) back to Sherborne, in Dorset again, for Easter 864. In 867 we can trace him in Canterbury, and then in Dorchester again in 868, perhaps for Easter, before mustering an army to march north to Nottingham to Burgred's aid, and then home again. We find him last at Woodyates in the wooded north-east corner of Dorset. On almost every occasion, we find Alfred at his brother's side, except for meetings in Kent, the province in which Alfred had been left 'all my bookland' by their father King Ethelwulf. Perhaps he took time off from royal business to inspect his estates and check that his reeves were looking after them properly.

We will continue the detailed selection of royal assemblies, as before paying more attention to the circumstances and composition of the gatherings than to the transaction through which we happen to know about it:

10. In 860 King Ethelbert, Alfred's third brother, summoned an assembly to meet at an unknown place; it comprised the archbishop, four bishops, ten governors, his younger brothers Ethelred and Alfred, who was then thirteen, and their personal staff, with two recorded ministers and no doubt many more who were not listed.

Of the ten governors, Aldred, this particular Ethelred and Humbearht held office for only a very few years, if we can tell from their appearance as witnesses to other charters; they may not even have lived into their thirties. Five of them survived longer, despite the grave dangers of the time and their prominent, responsible and exposed posts. Dryhtwald held office for at least eight years, perhaps into his forties; another kept his province for over twenty years and may well have lived into his fifties; Osric, a kinsman of the king's mother, governed two counties within sixteen years; Wulfhere abandoned his responsibilities, when nearly sixty after more than twenty-four years in office, to die in disgrace and exile; Eanwulf governed Somerset for thirty-four years; Ethelwulf governed the province of Berkshire for something over thirty-five

Dorchester-on–Thames

Hereford developed around an early church. The medieval town wall can be seen curving in the distance from the castle-site on the park to the right. Alfred's fort included the cathedral and the area to the left

Alfred's sister, queen Ethelswith of Mercia at the court of
their brother, Ethelred of Wessex, in AD 868 (top) as seen
by a thirteenth-century scribe and (bottom) Alfred's daughter
Ethelfleda, as governor of south-west Mercia. Alfred appears
as the fourth witness at the top of the second column

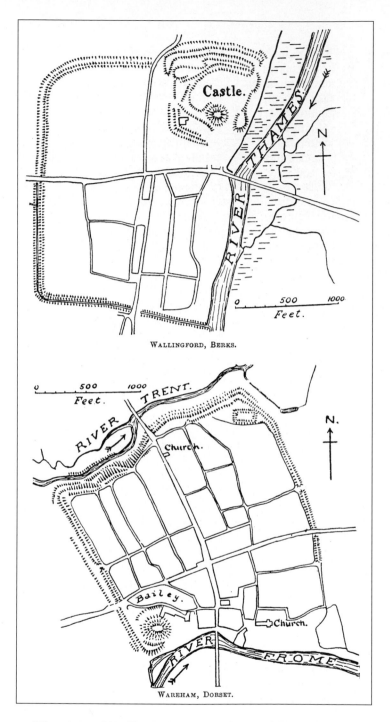

Castle.

RIVER THAMES

N

0   500   1000
Feet.

WALLINGFORD, BERKS.

0   500   1000
Feet.

RIVER TRENT.

Church.

N.

Bailey.

Church.

RIVER FROME

WAREHAM, DORSET.

The plans of Wallingford and Wareham published in 1912
which gave rise to the idea that Alfred's main forts were
planned on a regular grid and were fully developed towns

Wallingford began as one of Alfred's forts. From the castle earthworks in the background a grass bank, thought to be the rampart of Alfred's fort, runs west, then south (to the bottom left) and then east to the Thames

Portchester, a Roman coastal-defence reused by Alfred, lacks a street-plan. A rampart is visible in the foreground and to the right. The church and castle were built in Norman times

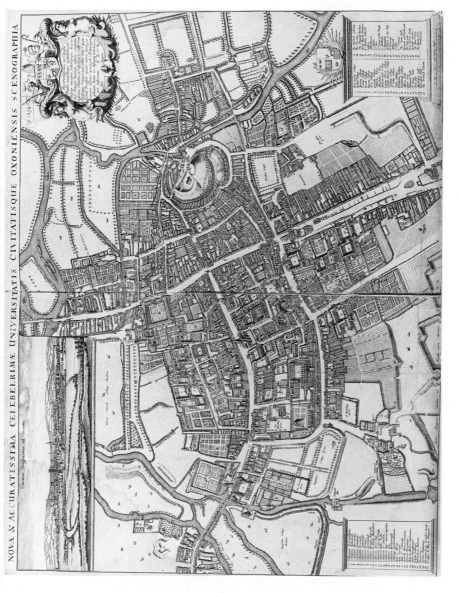

Oxford grew from a fort made by Alfred circa AD 895. Here it is seen from the north in a bird's eye plan of 1675. For early changes, see pp. 186 and 190

Gold 'pointer', uninscribed, smaller and simpler than the Alfred Jewel, but of much the same date and purpose, found in 1860 at Minster Lovell, Oxfordshire

Bronze disc with inset enamel decoration, found in Oxford in 1896. The date has shifted from '12th century' in the 1950s to 10th or even 9th century

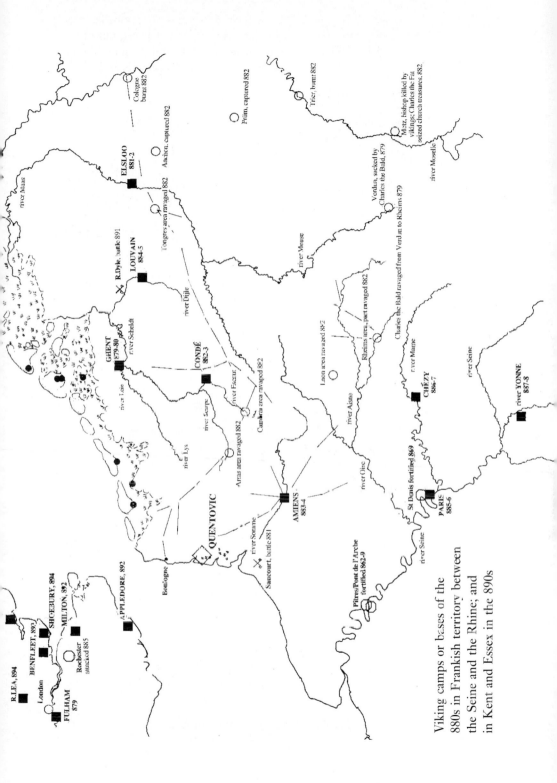

Viking camps or bases of the
880s in Frankish territory between
the Seine and the Rhine; and
in Kent and Essex in the 890s

R.LEA, 894

BENFLEET, 893

SHOEBURY, 894

MILTON, 892

London

Rochester
attacked 885

FULHAM
879

APPLEDORE, 892

Boulogne

QUENTOVIC

river Somme

Saucourt, battle 881

Pîtres/Pont de l'Arche
fortified 862-9

AMIENS
883-4

river Oise

St Denis fortified 869

PARIS
885-6

river Seine

river Seine

CHÉZY
886-7

river Marne

river Yonne
887-8

river Aisne

Laon area ravaged 882

Rheims area, part ravaged 882

Charles the Bald ravaged from Verdun to Rheims 879

Verdun, sacked by
Charles the Bald, 879

Metz, bishop killed by
vikings; Charles the Fat
seized church treasures, 882

river Moselle

river Marne

Arras area ravaged 882

river Scarpe

Cambrai area ravaged 882

river Escaut

CONDÉ
882-3

river Lys

river Lys

river Lys

GHENT
879-80

river Scheldt

river Dijle

LOUVAIN
884-5

R.Dyle, battle 891

Tongres area ravaged 882

river Meuse

ELSLOO
881-2

river Maas

Aachen, captured 882

Prüm, captured 882

Cologne
burnt 882

Trier, burnt 882

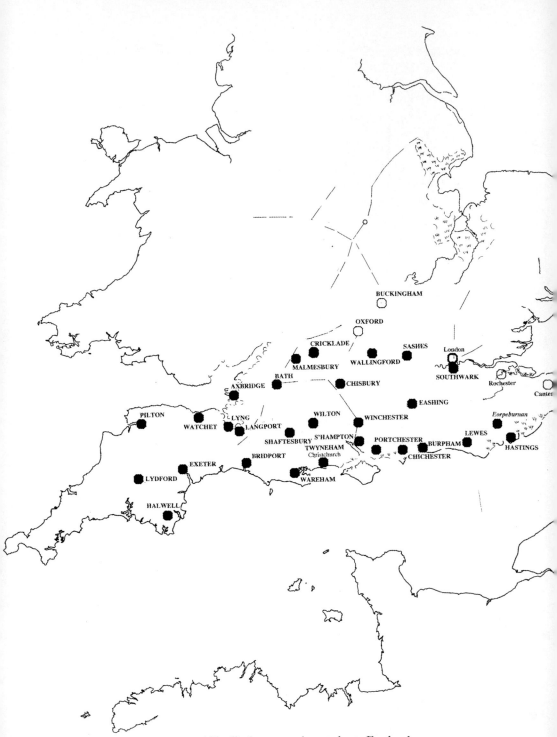

BUCKINGHAM

OXFORD

CRICKLADE

SASHES

WALLINGFORD

London

MALMESBURY

BATH

AXBRIDGE

CHISBURY

SOUTHWARK

Rochester

Canter

EASHING

Eorpeburnan

PILTON

LYNG

WILTON

WINCHESTER

WATCHET

LANGPORT

LEWES

SHAFTESBURY

S'HAMPTON

PORTCHESTER

BURPHAM

TWYNEHAM

HASTINGS

EXETER

BRIDPORT

Christchurch

CHICHESTER

LYDFORD

WAREHAM

HALWELL

Alfred's fortresses in southern England

Side views of the Alfred Jewel

Interior of Deerhurst parish church,
Gloucestershire, 9th century

A stone wolf's head as a door stop
in Deerhurst parish church

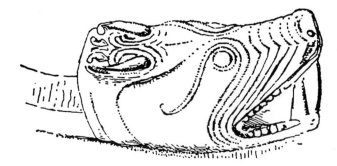

years, despite its transfer from one kingdom to another; as we have just read, he was killed at the gates of Reading trying to storm the Viking-held royal hall that was his responsibility. There are two difficult governors: was this Biorhtwulf the Brihtwulf of Essex who died in 893/6; and can this Wullaf be the one who witnessed charters in 882 and 898? If so they were governors for thirty-six and forty-six years respectively, not at all impossible if they were appointed in their twenties. In fact we can accept Brihtwulf but there were probably two Wullafs.

The actual business that we know they dealt with was Kentish. For fifteen pounds and thirty mancuses, the king sold Bishop Wærmund land in and near Rochester, described as 'eighty acres of the city of Hrob [Rochester], half a lane [or perhaps half a village] and one marsh.' The wording survives in three old versions: an original ninth-century vellum charter in the British Library, the twelfth-century property book still at Rochester cathedral and a back-up copy of this, the fourteenth-century *Liber Temporalium* or 'Book of Earthly Resources' in the bishops' records. In all of them the date has somehow become DCCXC for 790, not DCCCLX for 860.[7]

Like the charter that gave us our fifth court, this has lately been denounced as a 'crude forgery'.[8] In 1904 W. H. Stevenson, most austere and fastidious of scholars, pronounced it 'clearly genuine' as it certainly is.[9]

Churchmen	Governors	Princes' household	Ministers
archbishop CEOLNOTH	EANUULF	ÆTHELRED kings son	Uuerenberht
833–870	O[S]RIC	ÆLFRÆD kings son	Ciolmund
bishop EALHSTAN	UULFHERE	abbot UULLAF	
of Sherborne 824–867	ÆTHÆLUULF	abbot UUERFERTH	
bishop SWITHUN	HUMBEARHT	priest Uulfhelm	
of Winchester 852–862	UULLAF		
bishop GUTHHEARD	ALDRED		
of Selsey 839/45–860/901	ÆTHÆLRED		
bishop DIORUUL	DRYHTWALD		
of London 845/62–860/98	BIORHTUULF		
[bishop CUTHW]ULF			
of Rochester 862/8–868/80			

11a. At Dorchester in Dorset on the day after Christmas 863 King Ethelbert, Alfred's middle brother, again held court, with one bishop, two governors, the princes Ethelred and Alfred, who was now fourteen, two superior ministers, an abbot, a priest and a reeve or provost and nineteen ordinary ministers.

The business that we know they carried out was a royal grant exempting the vast estates of Sherborne minster, 28km to the north, from normal taxation, as the burial place three years before of the king's immediate predecessor and older brother, Ethelbald of Wessex. The estates, reckoned at 140 hides, may have amounted to nearly 7000ha.

The names are printed in three columns as they appear in the twelfth-century Sherborne property book, now in the British Library.[10]

Bishops, governors etc.	*Ministers*	*Ministers, continued*
bishop ALHSTAN	Cyma	Æthelwulf
governor EANWULF	Beocca	Wynsige
governor ÆLFSTAN	Æthelmod	Goda
ÆTHELRED kings son	Beorhtnoth	Coenwald
ÆLFRED kings son	Denegils	Æthelric
Osmund	Wulfred	Wulfhelm
Wulfhere	Ecgbreht	Hunred
abbot ALHHARD	Monnel	Ecgulf
priest HEAHMUND	Eadwulf	Ælfhere
provost HWITA	Wistan	

11b. In Sherborne minster, princely old Bishop Ealhstan's cathedral for the last forty years, King Ethelbert solemnly laid the charter on the high altar two days before Easter 864 to put into effect his grant of exemption. The ceremony was witnessed by the bishop and the two princes, Alfred and Ethelred, and seven priests, a deacon provost and two deacons and the unprecedented number of thirty-four ministers. No governors were present on this occasion, so it may not have constituted a proper court. Perhaps all the governors in the royal entourage were sitting as a high court, or took the day off hunting; or perhaps they did not approve of the grant to Sherborne because it would unbalance the budget.

We will compare the two lists of witnesses as we examine the standing and careers of ministers in Alfred's world, as these two lists give us by far the largest group of ministers recorded since the great church synods at Acleah, Chelsea and Clofesho in the early years of the century. In both these lists the order of names runs down each column successively.

The description of the second ceremony is given, like the body of the charter itself, in Old English from the same volume in the British Library and was printed with the last charter.

First column	*Second column*	*Third column*
king ÆTHELBREHT	priest Æthelheah	Herewulf
bishop ALHSTAN	priest Oswuulf	Ærcmund
ÆTHELRED kings son	priest Wistan	Ceolred
ÆLFRED kings son	deacon Ceolmund	Burhgred
priest Heahmund	Luhha	Wulfric
Osmund	deacon Beorhtwulf	Cyrred
Beorhtmund	Ceolred	Æthelwulf
Cyma	Eanwulf	Ceolhelm
Ecgbreht	Ealhferth	Eadulf
Babba	Ceolwulf	Ealhstan
Mucel	Cynemund	Ecgstan
Cynelaf	Ealhstan	Heorhtric
deacon provost Torhthelm	Æthelmund	Ceolheah
priest Burghelm	Ceofa	Wulfheah
priest Heoteman	Duda	Eardulf
priest Rædnoth	Wulfheard	Cuthred

12. Some time, perhaps at Easter, in 868 King Ethelred, Alfred's nearest brother, held court again at Dorchester, where their brother Ethelbert had held his Easter court four years before. His son or nephew Oswald, soon to die young, was given a high place in the assembly, as was Queen Wulfthryth, Ethelred's queen or perhaps sister-in-law, who is otherwise quite unrecorded; her appearance as a woman in a Wessex charter is almost unprecedented. With them were the two bishops of Wessex, Alfred, now nineteen, five governors and thirteen ministers.

The business that led to a record of this court surviving is the king's grant to his minister Hunsige of an estate (5 hides) at Worthy, a group of villages north-east of Winchester in Hampshire. It has been identified from the bounds given in Old English in the charter as Martyr Worthy, 4.5km from Winchester. The property was not necessarily the king's to give away, but may have been a property of the bishops or the church of Winchester; the transaction was perhaps confirmation of a church lease, or the conversion of a tenancy into a lease after a dispute between landlord and tenant. We can never tell when a charter is a court judgement.

The charter survives in the great Winchester property book in the British Library, in the main twelfth-century text, not among the assorted later additions. The recipient's name may be a scribal error for Wynsige, one of the ministers present at Dorchester in 863, though it is hard to see how this could have happened as the letters are very different. In the original charter the act of witness of the king and the bishop of Winchester may have run across both columns; the order of the names runs across the columns, although the twelfth-century scribe may have misplaced the right-hand names up by two places.[11]

Left column	Right column
king ETHELRED	OSWALD kings son
bishop ALHFERTH of Winchester 862/8–871/7	queen WULFTHRYTH
bishop HEAHMUND of Sherborne 868–871	governor WULFHERE
ÆLFRED kings son	governor EADWULF
governor WIGSTAN	Kynelaf
governor MUCEL	Æthelheah
governor ÆLFSTAN	Forthred
Ægbreht	Beorhtnoth
Beorhtmund	Goda
Milred	Æthelred
Æthelstan	Torhtred
Mucel	Mannel

13. In 868, probably while on campaign against a Viking force camped at Nottingham in Mercia, King Ethelred held a council for Wessex. Ethelred and Alfred, who was nineteen, had marched an army from Wessex to help their brother-in-law deal with the entrenched Viking army, bringing six of their governors, a bishop and an abbot and three named ministers. As the business to be done involved an estate of their sister Ethelswith, queen of Mercia, she and her husband Burgred, king of their host kingdom, also attended.

They witnessed their sister grant her Lockinge estate (15 hides) to 'the most faithful minister Cuthwulf'; King Burgred and Ethelswith herself witnessed the charter in fifteenth and sixteenth places, after the Wessex ministers. Cuthwulf may have been on the queen's personal staff, but does not seem to appear in any records of this time from Wessex or Mercia, apart from the wealthy purchaser in the next court that we examine.

The text survives in the two thirteenth-century property books of Abingdon abbey, both among the founding collections of the British Library. The medieval monks claimed that Cuthwulf had given the estate to Abingdon, but they are not the most reliable of witnesses and its later history may well be more complicated.[12]

Churchmen	Governors	An abbot	Ministers etc.
bishop ÆLHFERTH	WLFHERE	abbot ALHHARD	Æthelferth
of Winchester	EADWLF		Ægberht
862/8–871/7	WIGSTAN		Forthred
	MUCEL		BURG king
	ALFRED kings		ÆTHELSUTH
	son		queen
	OSWALD kings		
	son		
	ÆTHELWLF		
	ÆLFSTAN		

14. Between 872 and 874 or earlier, King Burgred and Queen Ethelswith held a court somewhere in Mercia at which Burgred sold the property of Marlcliffe in Cleeve Prior, Worcestershire (10 hides) to a man named Cered for a thousand shekels. The charter was looted and carried off in a Viking raid. After Cered's death when his widow Werthryth decided to sell the property to minister Cuthulf, a kinsman of her husband, and travel to Rome, she had to get it replaced. She made a sworn deposition 'that the book of the forementioned land had been seized by the pagans' and governor Ethelred of Mercia replaced or confirmed the lost charter in a form partially quoted in this memorandum. A likely time for the theft is 877–880 during the major Viking attack on Wessex and the time the army remained at Cirencester.

Cuthulf later gave the property to Worcester cathedral and a memorandum recording all this survives in the late eleventh-century part of the Worcester property book in the British Library.

It evidently quotes from Ethelred's replacement, but there are all sorts of problems, not least the witness-list headed by King Burgred and Queen Ethelswith, as though the witnesses were all of a time before 874, when they fled the kingdom. The rest of the names are not those of any of Burgred's officials remembered by widow Werthryth but must represent a later assembly of some date after 888, when Eadnoth was still a minister, and before 911, when governor Ethelred died;[13] we give the dates of their appearance in other charters.

Churchmen	*Governors*	*Ministers*
bishop WERFERTH of Worcester 872–915	AETHELRED (883–911d)	Wulfsige (901)
	ALHHELM (884–888)	Wifrith (888)
	EADNOTH (minister 883–888, not listed as governor elsewhere)	
	AELFRED (916)	

15. In 875 King Ceolwulf of Mercia, the 'silly minister' set up by the Vikings in 874 to rule Mercia for them and still active in 877, when they 'shared out some of the land, leaving part to Ceolwulf', held a court somewhere in his realm, attended by two Mercian bishops, four of his governors and eight ministers. Long gone were the days when the archbishop and all the bishops of the south flocked to the Mercian court, to meet as many as sixteen governors.

Among other business (perhaps discussing how to hoodwink and evade their Viking masters, as eventually some of these witnesses did), the assembly witnessed the king's grant, at Bishop Werferth's request, 'to the monks serving God in the monastery [or minster] of Worcester which was built to the honour of the holy and eternal mother and virgin Mary' the estate of Overbredon or Overbury (6 hides) with the hamlets of Conderton and Pendock, all in Worcestershire, with the consent of 'all my bishops. May almighty God see fit to watch over it,' added this nominee of a gang of pagan raiders who were busy wiping out the bishoprics of Leicester and Lindsey and all the monasteries of eastern England.

The text survives, like the one above, in the late eleventh-century part of the great Worcester property book in the British Library and was first published in 1723. It may have been altered or 'improved' by the monk who copied it out in early Norman times.[14]

Churchmen	Governors	Ministers
bishop WERFRYTH	BEORNOTH	Kyred
of Worcester 872–	ATHELHUN	Wulfsige
915	ATHELUUOLD	Heahstan
bishop EADBERHT	ALHFERHT	Eanulf
of Lichfield *c.*869–		Ecgberht
875		Beornfyrht
		Eadbald
		Turhtred

16. At Epsom in 882, King Alfred, now aged thirty-three, summoned an assembly, comprising eight of his governors, including Hampshire and Somerset, and fourteen ministers. They were 'on campaign',[15] no doubt 'against the enemy in London',[16] and we may presume not only that they had mustered and marched a large army to that spot but also that the governors and ministers named as witnesses were the senior commanders of this force.

To judge from the governors not present, there were two other armies converging on London in a pincer movement, a detachment from Surrey and Kent under Alfred of Surrey, and a force from the Mercian province under Ethelred, Beornnoth, Ethelferth and Ethelwulf.

The drum-head council, if they were in fact in camp rather than in Epsom church, witnessed Alfred's sale, for thirty mancuses, that is nine hundred silver pennies, of Creech and Stoke (St Mary) near Taunton in Somerset to his minister Athelstan. Did he have to produce the sacks of silver from a pack-horse then and there, we wonder, or did Alfred take IOUs?

Churchmen	Governors	Ministers
archbishop	ÆTHELNOD	Osric
ÆTHERED	WLFRED	Eggwulf
bishop DENEWULF	ORDDULF	Æthelm
Winchester 879–909	BUCCA	Witbrord

ÆTHELWALD	Deormod
WULLAF	Acca
GARRULF	Ælfhere
BYRHTNOD	Wullaf
	Babba
	Ealdwulf
	Æthelstan
	Tata
	Burlaf
	Æffa

17. At (Princes) Risborough in Buckinghamshire in 884, governor Ethelred summoned the provincial court of south-west Mercia, now part of Alfred's kingdom, comprising the three remaining Mercian bishops, six governors, including the steadfast old Beornnoth with thirty years' service behind him before he agreed with them to join forces with Alfred, and five ministers, two of them, Alfred and Eadnoth, future governors, to judge from the confirmation of the looted charter of Court 14.

King Alfred sometimes presided over the provincial court. In his absence Ethelred chaired the assembly, at first on his own and, after his marriage to Alfred's daughter, jointly with Ethelfleda; after his death, as we shall see, she summoned the court herself, just as she led the men of her province on campaign.

This gathering witnessed governor Ethelred's grant of Himbleton, Worcestershire (5 hides) to governor Ethelferth, the king's brother-in-law.[17] These Mercian nobles are notable for continuity; Ethelferth's family had held the office of governor continuously since his great-grandfather in King Offa's near-imperial days in the 790s, when Beornnoth's grandfather and namesake also appears as a governor.

Churchmen	Governors	Ministers
bishop WULFRED	ÆTHELRED	Eardwulf
of Lichfield 880–	ÆTHELWALD	Elfwald
889	ÆTHULF	Eadnoth
bishop WERFRITH	(=ÆTHELWULF)	Aelfred
of Worcester 872–	BEORNATH	Aethelmund
915		

bishop DEORLAF   ÆTHELFERTH
  of Hereford 857/   ALHHELM
66–887/8

18. At Woolmer in Hampshire, good hunting country on the border with Surrey, King Alfred held a court, his last to be recorded by a surviving charter, in 898 with his son Edward, now (we must infer) junior king in Kent. There were three governors, four senior ministers, a priest and three junior ministers. Rather surprisingly, no bishops attended; this is true of two of the other three courts that we know about in the 890s, so that bishops were evidently busier in their dioceses, less interested in public affairs or less popular at court. It was a select and informal affair, as we will discuss later.

Some of the business in hand was presumably King Edward's report to his father on affairs in Kent. As well as this, Alfred granted his faithful governor Sigelm a small property at Farleigh (1 hide) on the River Medway in Kent.

The original charter or a fairly early copy on parchment survives at Canterbury; the wording and the writing have both been criticised by different experts as later or foreign, so that its authenticity is not yet fully established.[18]

First column	*Second column*
governor ORDLAF	
governor SIGULF	minister Eadweald
governor WULLAF	priest Æthelstan
minister Beorhtsige	minister Cuthulf
minister Osferth	minister Ecgferth
minister Wulfhere	minister Eadhelm

Courts could be held almost anywhere the king happened to be, in his own country or the next kingdom. They could be of any size and composition and could advise the king or his deputy on any matter. The neighbouring king and queen could attend if the matter to be dealt with concerned them. The royal courts could act as councils of war, as courts of final appeal, as political cabinets, as taxing authorities. During the ninth century they gradually lost their ecclesiastical side and during the 890s bishops seem to have lost influence. Some of the governors who attended them were men of vast experience in war and the law and finance; others were very young. Some of the ministers were men of great knowledge and close to the king; some were his personal staff; while others had a local authority in the shire where the court was held. The gatherings were completely aristocratic, except for guards and perhaps servants taking refreshments around; ordinary people were not represented. Victorian notions of a national 'Witan' are crazy dreams without foundation, myths of a 'democratic parliament' that never was.

Kings held court while they waited for an enemy move; the priests wrote out any necessary 'paperwork' on vellum sheets wherever they happened to find themselves, as they always had in their completely itinerant ruling society. If the records of a rich church were burnt when the church was torched, all that was lost was a few chests or pigeon-holes full of stacks of folded documents. If a nobleman lost all his charters when a residence was fired he lost the same. They could be replaced. What mattered was the memory of those who had witnessed the ceremonies by which the grants had been made. A senior priest should be able to recite the possessions of his church and the donors without hesitation. If he had been a scribe writing charters, he should be able unhesitatingly to recall every transaction he had recorded. Surviving witnesses, even if they had been young children at the time, could recall the essential details, allowing the charters to be replaced.

These assemblies served a vital social function which held the kingdom together, by forging the local administrators and officials who attended them, for the day, into the central organism of the state, which was the king and his court.

8

872–877, England
under Viking Domination

IN THE LATE 860S AND THROUGHOUT THE 870S England was
continuously overrun by a powerful Viking force determined to
break up and take over the existing social order of the four kingdoms, as the Vikings had overrun Frisia in the 830s and 840s and
done their best, as their ambitions grew, to exploit and dismantle
northern and western France in the 850s and early 860s. The
main text of the *Chronicle* for the years 872–877 recounts the
movements of the principal Viking army and omits all events not
immediately related:

872
a. The army left Reading for London and settled there for the winter.
The Mercians negotiated a cease-fire.

873
a. The Viking army ravaged Northumbria and wintered at Torksey in
Lindsey. The Mercians negotiated a truce.

874
a. The army moved from Lindsey to Repton and camped for the
winter.
b. They drove King Burgred abroad, after a reign of twenty-two years,
and conquered all his kingdom. He retired to Rome and is buried in
the English church of St Mary.

c. As king of Mercia, the Vikings chose the foolish minister Ceolwulf. He swore solemn oaths and gave hostages, promising to hand back the kingdom on demand and aid the enemy with his men.

875

a. The Vikings evacuated Repton.

b. Healfdene returned to Northumbria with a wing of the army and camped for the winter on the River Tyne. They subjugated the region and pillaged the Picts and the Britons of Strathclyde.

c. The kings Guthrum, Oscytel and Anwend took a strong division to Cambridge for the year.

d. That summer Alfred took a squadron to sea, attacked a fleet of seven ships, captured one and put the rest to flight.

876

a. Evading our outposts, the Vikings seized Wareham.

b. The king agreed to an armistice with them, taking hostages from the most senior leaders after their king. They swore on the holy ring to leave the kingdom at once, which they had never done for anyone.

c. This was a ruse; the mounted Vikings eluded the English forces and rode for Exeter.

d. In Northumbria Healfdene shared out the land and his warriors took up farming for a livelihood.

877

a. The Vikings captured Exeter by land.

b. Sailing west along the south coast, their fleet lost a hundred and twenty ships at Swanage in a great storm.

c. King Alfred and his troops pursued the land army, but could not overtake them before they reached the strong fortress.

d. The Vikings swore great oaths and agreed to give all the hostages he demanded. They kept the cease-fire and rode off into Mercia at harvest-time; they shared out some of this land, leaving part to Ceolwulf.

878

a. In midwinter, after Twelfth Night, the Viking army struck secretly at Chippenham and took over almost the whole kingdom of Wessex.

In 872 Alfred's brother-in-law King Burgred and his councillors negotiated peace with the Viking force based in London since the previous autumn, paying them a great tribute. This expensive humiliation is confirmed by a charter of Bishop Werferth of Worcester dated 872, by which he sold the lease of an estate of the ancient minster of Stratford-on-Avon, which he controlled, to the king's minister Eanwulf to raise cash 'for the immense tribute to the barbarians in the year that the pagans were settled in London'.[1]

After being drawn north in 873 into Yorkshire by a rising against them in the old kingdom of Northumbria, as we learn from northern sources,[2] the Vikings suppressed the rebellion and returned south to camp for the winter at Torksey in Lindsey. Although the Mercians again sued for peace and paid tribute, the following year saw the destruction of Mercia as an independent kingdom, but not its final break-up, which was delayed for another three years.

In 874, among all the Viking troubles, Alfred's brother-in-law left his kingdom and sought sanctuary and exile in Rome. Our knowledge of the event is not complicated, as it is in Frankish lands with more detailed annals, by any knowledge of constant feuds and rival factions hiring Viking mercenaries to fight for them. Ceolwulf, a minister not documented in any charter before this date, was picked by the Vikings to keep the kingdom warm for them, that is to say to continue to draw the revenues from royal lands and all the assorted other dues, until they were ready to complete their takeover with a share-out of royal, ecclesiastical and aristocratic estates among the Viking kings, earls and holds, with the likely division of lesser estates among junior officers and the assignment of some farms to veteran warriors. All active fighting men would be needed for security duties by the new regimes and it is most unlikely that they would be given farms and farmland on any scale.

With Mercia out of action, the Viking army split at the end of 874 or early in 875. Healfdene led one division into Northumbria, while the three kings Guthrum, Oscytel and Anwend took the other wing, a powerful force, to Cambridge, where they stayed for a year, perhaps exploring ways of taking over and dividing East Anglia. During the summer Alfred took his ships to sea and attacked a squadron of seven Viking ships, capturing one of them. In the face of this repeated threat, the three kings in Cambridge planned another invasion of Wessex. We see something of the condition of Mercia at this time in the charter by which the puppet-king Ceolwulf granted land at Overbury.

In 876 Guthrum led his 'great army' from its current base in Cambridge to Dorset on the south coast of Wessex and seized Wareham, where a large Anglo-Saxon church stood on the site of a British monastery. Although Alfred paid tribute, hoping that the Vikings would leave Wessex in peace, they moved on westward and occupied Exeter in Devon (the Roman Isca Dumnoniorum) where, within the Roman walls, there was perhaps a church by a spring and a handful of inhabitants, many of them Britons apparently not fully assimilated to their English overlords; Alfred's grandson Athelstan deported the Britons from Exeter sixty years later, or so William of Malmesbury recorded in the twelfth century.[3]

Paid yet again to go away, the Danes left in 877 to divide up part of Mercia. This probably marks the beginning of the extensive Scandinavian occupation of the country round Derby, Leicester, Lincoln, Nottingham and Stamford. We may imagine that many of the peasants, originally Romanised Britons, then Anglicised in the fifth and sixth centuries to conform to new overlords, could quite equably face conforming to their Danish lords and their warriors. The remaining 'rump' of Mercia, the south-western half of the kingdom, somehow maintained its integrity as a separate territory to become, within five years, a vast extra province of Alfred's kingdom.

Wherever we look in Europe, we find that the very greatest men below the kings, never more than a handful, were exceptionally powerful magnates: a Byzantine *doukos* set over a group of *strategoi*; a *markgraf* in the Frankish marches responsible for a whole group of *comites*, or his equivalent in central Italy, the pope with his local *rectores* and *consules*; and in England by the early 880s the great *ealdorman* Ethelred of Mercia governing the 'rump' of Mercia for King Alfred through his lesser governors. Each of these very great men was in charge of a dangerous frontier region where sudden emergencies could blow up. In somewhat more peaceful regions, a great provincial lord, the *strategos* in the Byzantine Empire, the *comes* in Frankish and Asturian lands and the *ealdorman* in England, whom we refer to as governor, answered direct to the king for every aspect of government in his district.

As we can see from the painstaking construction of their biographies, some governors appear only briefly in the record and, presumably or certainly, died young after only a few years in office. Other names appear in documents so consistently over periods of thirty or even forty years that we can be certain that they lived, sure-footed survivors in intrigue and battle, into their sixties or perhaps even their seventies. This allows us to say that some governors were appointed young, perhaps in their early twenties, because of royal blood or high connections; others were promoted at a more mature age from among the experienced junior officials, the ministers, through a fairly regular system of promotion in government ranks, judging from the evidence to be set out below.

These wealthy nobles, often of royal blood, spent some of their time governing their provinces with the help of local assemblies, and some of it assembled in the king's court to form the royal government of each kingdom. Their administrative, financial, legal and military roles were inseparable. Each of them governed his province, collected the king's revenues, judged civil and criminal cases and trained and led the warriors of his province to war. This was no job for the fearful; the surviving record, far from complete, tells us of nine Wessex governors killed in battle at the head of their men between 802 and 903. In this period the same record of events in Wessex, the *Chronicle*, casually refers to the violent deaths of six governors of the next-door kingdom of Mercia. Most of a governor's public duties took place at one of a number of royal halls in his shire; meetings on general business were also the times for payment of taxes and dues, for serious trials and for mustering, inspecting and training the warriors who accompanied each of the ministers and lesser officials and minor landowners.

In the next chapter we will see what we can find out about the lesser office-holding nobles, *thegns* in Old English or *ministri* in Latin; here we call them ministers as they are also known as *ministri* in Frankish lands. Below them again were lesser local officials, such as reeves.

In the last chapter we studied Alfred's magnates collectively in royal courts and assemblies. To come closer to them as individuals we must first assemble the names of all Wessex governors documented during Alfred's life with the dates when they are recorded. Such a systematic listing seems never to have been attempted before, although the bulk of the evidence has been available to scholars since the early seventeenth century in Sir Robert Cotton's library in Westminster, the earliest of the three founding collections of the British Museum, and now part of the British Library. A systematic listing of places, documents, people or finds is the only way to proceed in any historical or archaeological field.

We can find the names of just under fifty governors of provinces ruled by the kings of Wessex in Alfred's lifetime, 849–899, six of whom (Ceorl, Ealhhere, the two Eanwulfs, Ethelwulf of Berkshire and Osric) were active before 849. The precise number is not clear because of problems of identity; Eadred might be a slip for Aldred, or vice versa (I leave them separate), while Ordlaf and Ordulf (whom I merge into one) could be two individuals, and so on. Several governors, as we have just noted, can be identified as ministers earlier in their careers. Several quite well-documented ministers who appear as governors just after Alfred's death may well have been promoted governor by Alfred during the none-too-well documented 890s. Of the fifty or so governors, fifteen, or just under one-third, appear in both the *Chronicle* and charters, while only eight are documented as governor in a single source (compared to thirteen out of thirty-four documented Wessex governors of the previous half-century); the eight are not necessarily totally obscure. Dates given in **bold** are from the *Chronicle*.

Name	Dates recorded in charters, Chronicle etc.
ALDRED	860,862
ALFRED	863,867,871
ALFSTAN	862,867,868,868
ALFSTAN ii	868
BEOCCA	*c.*877,882,**888 to Rome**
BEORNNOTH, Mercia	844/5,855,855,857,862,866,866,875, 875,884
BIORHTWULF of Essex	860,867,**d.893/6.**
BYRHTNOTH	882
CEOLMUND of Kent	**d.893/6.**
CEORL of Devon	841,844,**851**

CUTHRED   871/7
DRYHTWALD   860,863,867,868
  862 given Bromley, Kent by King Ethelbert[4]
EADRED   855,855,868
EADWALD   888 (perhaps Ethelwold of Mercia)
EADWULF   850,868
EALHELM, Mercia   884,888
EALHHERE of Kent   841,842,843,845,850,**851,k.873**
EANWULF of Somerset   833,838,838,841,844,**845**,850,854,
                          c.855,856,860
  842 given Dicheat, Somerset by King Ethelwulf[5]
EANULF ii   844, & see above,854,c.855,**c.877**
EASTMUND (pedesecus)   858,867,867
ETHELBALD   850,854,c.855
ETHELBERT   854,c.855,856
ETHELFERTH, Mercia   875,883,884,888,901,903,903,904,904,916
ETHELHELM of Wiltshire   c.878,**887,893,d.897**
  892 given North Newnton by King Alfred[6]
ETHELMOD in Kent   (minister 841–5) 853,855,858,859
ETHELNOTH of   **878**,c.877,c.878,879,882,c.886,**893**
Somerset
ETHELRED in Kent   858,860,862,863
  863 given Mersham, Kent by King Ethelbert[7]
ETHELRED of Mercia   883,884,**886,887,888,893**,900,901,**d.911**
ETHELRED of Devon   892,**d.899**
ETHELRIC   855,855
ETHELWOLD in Kent   c.877,882,**d.888**
ETHELWOLD, Mercia   875,883,884
ETHELWULF of   836 (in Mercia), 838,839,841,841,842,
Berkshire   843,844,844,**860**,860,863,867,**871,k.871**
  '862' given Wittenham, now Oxon by King Ethelred, reigned 866–
  871[8]
ETHELWULF, Mercia   872/4, 871/7(in Wessex),c.877(in
                         Wessex),884,888,896,897,**d.901**
GARRULF   862,863,867,882
HUDA of Surrey   850,**k.853**
HUMBEARHT   860
LULLEDE   854,855,855,c.855,856,
MUCEL   867,868

ODDA of Devon	**878, only in Ethelward's** *Chronicon*[9]
ORDLAF (or Ordulf)	879,882,*c*.889,898,900,901,901,903, 903,904,904,904,909,909
OSRIC of Dorset/	841,844,**845**,847,850,854,c.855,856,**860**,860,860
Hampshire	
SIGERIC	854
SIGEWULF in Kent	898,901,**k.903**
WERFRED	867
WIGSTAN	868,868
WULFHERE of Hampshire	854,*c.*855,856,860,862,867,868,871/7

    863 given Buttermere, Wilts by King 'Ethelred', perhaps Ethelbert, reigned 860–866[10]

WULFRED of Hampshire	867,879,882,892,**d.893/6**
WULLAF	i – (845,*c.*853,858),860; ii – 882,898

    as minister in 858 given Wassingwell, Kent by King Ethelbert of Kent[11]

From this preliminary list we can extract for special scrutiny the nineteen governors of shires in Wessex during Alfred's reign (leaving until later five of the six Mercian governors of Alfred's regime there, but assuming that an Ethelwulf[12] was his brother-in-law briefly in charge of a Wessex shire), and list them alphabetically in a table which also shows the order in which they appear in the witness-lists of his charters. In all kinds of repeated lists of names the order can tell us a good deal, about where people lived in seventeenth-century parish poor-tax lists, for example, or here about how senior they were and how they stood during court ceremonies; and this order of names can also help us to date charters, as we shall soon see. Here is the rough data, with the poorly dated charters on the right:

Birch, *Cart. Sax.*	**531–2**	**549**	**550**	**567**	**576**	**565**	**581**	**568**	**740**
Date:	871/7	879	882	892	898	879/99	892/9	871/99	871/99
ALFRED of Surrey, left will									
BEOCCA or Bucca	–	–	4	–	–	–	–	–	4
BYRHTNOTH	–	–	8	–	–	–	–	–	–
BEORHTWULF of Essex d.893/6									
CEOLMUND of Kent d.893/6									
CUTHRED	3	–	–	–	–	–	–	–	–

EANWULF ii	-	-	-	-	-	-	-	-	1
ETHELHELM of Wiltshire	-	-	-	-	-	-	-	1	-
ETHELNOTH of Somerset	-	1	1	-	-	-	-	2	3
ETHELRED Devon d.899	-	-	-	2	-	-	-	-	-
ETHELWOLD	-	-	5	-	-	-	-	-	5
ETHELWULF, d.901	2	-	-	-	-	-	-	-	2
GARRULF	-	-	7	-	-	-	-	-	-
ODDA of Devon (d.878 in Ethelward)									
ORDULF (or Ordlaf)	-	3	3	-	1	1	-	-	-
SIGEWULF	-	-	-	-	2	-	-	-	-
WULFHERE	1	-	-	-	-	-	-	-	-
WULFRED Hants d.893/6	-	2	2	1		-	-	-	-
WULLAF	-	-	6	-	3	-	-	-	-

We can extend this table back a few years, refine the dates of the charters by making seriation-tables of ministers (see Chapter 9), and rearrange it to see whether we can establish any pattern, such as a regular hierarchical rank by seniority, among the fifteen of the governors who appear in witness-lists. This does not seem to be true for earlier reigns in Wessex but from 840 a rigid hierarchy is evident both among the governors of Mercia and also here in Wessex. This increasing social rigidity and the ceremonial that went with it are evident in the table below from the way the numbers run, even when we have added fourteen more governors by looking back over the five years before Alfred came to the throne. The brief notes remind us that we are dealing with people, not just playing with numbers.

Two further points also emerge from a study of the table. One is that we can assign reasonably close dates to undated charters, such as B740 and B568, on the basis of the order of the governors' names (and find later that a further study of the order of ministers' names confirms this). The other is that there are no obvious objections to identifying as the same man Ordulf, Orlaf and Ordlaf,[13] as together they fit the same pattern of rising seniority, indicated by the numbers of order in the lists running from right to left. This reduces the number of governors appearing in witness-lists

Birch, Cart Sax	1210. 867i	519 867ii	520 868	539 875	543 c.875	532 c.876	740 c.877	568 c.878	549 879	550 882	581 c.892	567 892	565 890s	576 898
ETHELWULF	1	1	–	–	–	–	–	–						
WULFHERE	–	–	1	–	1	1	1	1						
BEORHTWULF	2	–	–	–	–	–	–	–						
WIGSTAN	–	–	2	–	–	–	–	–						
ATHELSTAN	–	–	–	–	2	–	–	–						
EADWULF	–	2	3	–	3	–	–	–						
DRYHTWALD	3	–	–	a	–	–	–	–						
MUCEL	4	3	4	–	–	–	–	–						
EASTMUND	5	–	–	–	–	–	–	–						
ETHELRIC	–	–	–	1	–	–	–	–						
EALHRED	–	–	–	2	–	–	–	–						
ETHELBALD	–	–	–	b	–	–	–	–						
EANULF(1)	–	–	–	–	–	–	1	–						
ETHELWULF(2)	6	–	–	3	–	2	2	–	1	–	x	–	–	–
ALFRED(3)	7	–	–	–	–	–	–	–	–	–	x	–	–	–
ETHELHELM(4)	–	–	–	–	–	–	–	1	–	–	x	–	–	–
ETHELNOTH(5)	–	–	–	–	–	–	3	2	1	1	x	–	–	–
WULFRED(6)	9	–	–	–	4	–	–	–	2	2	x	–	–	–
ORDULF(7)	–	–	–	–	5	–	–	–	3	3	x	1	–	1
ALFSTAN	8	–	5	–	–	–	–	–	–	–	x	–	–	–
WERFRED	10	–	–	–	–	–	–	–	–	–	x	–	–	–
CUTHRED	–	–	–	–	6	3	4	–	–	4	x	–	–	–
BEOCCA(8)	–	–	–	–	–	–	5	–	–	5	z	–	–	–
ETHELWOLD(9)	–	–	–	–	–	–	–	–	–	–	x	–	–	–

SIGEWULF(10)	–	–	–	–	–	–	–	–	–	–	x	–	–	2
WULLAF(11)	–	–	–	–	–	–	–	–	–	6	x	–	–	3
GARRULF(12)	–	–	–	–	–	–	–	–	–	7	x	–	–	–
BYRHTNOTH(13)	–	–	–	–	–	–	–	–	–	8	x	–	–	–
ETHELRED(14)	–	–	–	–	–	–	–	–	–	–	x	2	–	–
Birch	1210	519	520	539	543	532	740	568	549	550	581	567	565	576
	867i	867ii	868	875	c.875	c.876	c.877	c.878	879	882	c.892	892	890s	898

Notes

1. Not Eanwulf of Somerset, active from 833, who died in 867, but a namesake.
2. This second Ethelwulf may be Alfred's brother-in-law from Mercia.
3. Alfred of Surrey, active 863–871, who may have died soon after 871.
4. Ethelhelm of Wiltshire, active 887–897, perhaps Alfred's nephew.
5. Ethelnoth of Somerset, active 879–894, bravest of Alfred's governors.
6. Wulfred of Hampshire, active 878–896.
7. Ordlaf, grandson of Eanwulf and father of Ordwold.
8. Beocca, active 882–909, who went to Rome in 888.
9. Ethelwold, active 877–888, perhaps son of Alfred of Surrey.
10. Sigewulf, Alfred's butler in 892 as a minister, then governor of Kent.
11. Wullaf, a minister in 845–858 and a governor by 862; a namesake was governor in 898.
12. Garrulf, a minister in the 860s, appears this once as governor in 882.
13. Byrhtnoth appears as a minister in the 860s and as governor in 882.
14. Ethelred of Devon, who died before King Alfred in 899.

of Alfred's reign to fifteen and the total who can be identified during the reign to nineteen. Having listed the governors and moved them around in tables, we should try and see them as people and do our best to produce some short biographies from this scanty evidence. We begin with a minor member of the royal family.

Oswald, a young prince active 868–875

Born in about 860, the son of one of Alfred's elder brothers and named presumably as a compliment to his grandmother Osburh, Oswald must have been a cousin or brother of Alfred's nephews Ethelhelm and Ethelwold who had, like them, had been passed over for the throne in 871. He was evidently dead by the early 880s, when Alfred made no mention of him in his draft 'will'.

Oswald appears as a *filius regis* or 'king's son' on witness-lists of three charters of the 860s and 870s.[14] The first, of 868, lists King Ethelred, two bishops and Alfred, then aged about eighteen, with Oswald in fifth place, followed by the otherwise quite undocumented Queen Wulfthryth, presumably the wife of one of Alfred's elder brothers, attending our Court 12 at Dorchester.

The second, also of 868, records an occasion when the kings of Mercia and Wessex met, probably at Nottingham, and lists King Ethelred, a bishop and four governors, then Alfred seventh and Oswald eighth.

The third charter, concerning some kind of private settlement or lawsuit to do with land at Ham in Kent, made before Alfred in 875, lists Oswald third, after King Alfred and Archbishop Ethelred, and before two governors, twelve ministers and a priest-abbot. Oswald may have died at about the age of fifteen.

Alfred of Surrey, active 863–871

Born perhaps about 830–840, this Alfred is nowhere recorded as a minister before he became governor, probably of Surrey, for at least eight years. He may have been appointed young because of high noble birth, or his early career may simply have escaped documentation. He witnessed two charters, in 863 and 867.[15] He came to an agreement with Archbishop Ethelred that he would bequeath to him his smaller but very productive property at Chartham in Kent in exchange for a life-tenancy of the archbishop's great Croydon estate, which was not so highly developed.[16]

With his wife Werburh he bought a magnificent illuminated book from the Vikings, who had looted it from some Kentish monastery, and gave it to Canterbury. Now one of the great treasures of the National Library of Sweden, it is known as the 'Stockholm Golden Gospels'.

Alfred died between 871 and 889, somewhere between his thirties and his fifties, leaving a will which survives as an original ninth-century parchment document in the British Library.[17] In it he left six fully stocked estates in Surrey and Kent and two thousand pigs to his wife Werburh and daughter Ealthryth. A son, Ethelwold, was to get two smaller estates in Surrey and a hundred pigs, while lesser bequests were to go to three kinsmen, Brihtsige, Sigewulf and Eadred.

It is not clear whether this son was illegitimate and thus to be excluded from the main family estates or whether he was already set up for life with estates of his own. He may have been the governor Ethelwold active in Wessex in 877–888, not to be confused with the Mercian governor of this name.

Beocca (a minister in 864), active 882–909
The fourth governor to witness at Epsom in 882 was Bucca,[18] presumably the same as Beocca who led the annual embassy to Rome in 888, an onerous and dangerous duty that the great nobles probably took in turn, and no doubt the governor Beocca in a witness-list of *c.*900–909.[19]

Byrhtnod of Essex (a minister in 864), active 882
Governor Byrhtnod, the eighth and most junior of the governors at Epsom in 882, had, like Garrulf, a background outside Wessex. The celebrated governor Byrhtnoth of Essex, whose death in battle a century later in 991 inspired the well-known heroic poem *The Battle of Maldon*, was almost certainly a great-grandson named for this man, very likely a princeling of some former royal house of eastern Mercia or East Anglia, who had taken refuge in Wessex and gone into Alfred's service.

Eadred, active 855–868, perhaps identical with *Aldred*, active 860–862

Born about 830, governor Eadred appears in an original ninth-century parchment charter in the British Library which bears the date DCCLV for 855, but has long been thought for various reasons to be of 853, or DCCLIII.[20] His name comes immediately before the four-year-old (or perhaps six-year-old) Alfred, who was not with his brother Ethelred and his usual staff, the minister Esne and abbots Wullaf and Werferth. In the twelfth-century Rochester property book another charter, more certainly of 855, lists Eadred just after the six-year-old Alfred,[21] while a third which survives copied into the two thirteenth-century Abingdon property books in the British Library lists governor Aldred just after Alfred in 862, when Alfred was thirteen.[22]

This conjunction must raise a suspicion that governor Eadred took special care of Alfred on occasion and that the two governors may be tentatively identified as the same man appearing in different dialect-forms, transcribed by different medieval scribes. But both names also appear in charters in the Rochester property book, Aldred in 860 and Eadred in 868.[23]

Ethelhelm of Wiltshire, active 887–897
Born in the 850s or '60s, this governor may have been a son of Alfred's next older brother King Ethelred, passed over for succession to the throne in the crises of 871. He was not recorded as a minister in the 870s and 880s but makes his appearance as a governor leading the annual mission to Rome in 887.

In 893 early in the Viking war of the mid-890s, while King Alfred with the main army was relieving Exeter, under attack by one Viking army, Ethelhelm, with governor Ethelred of Mercia and governor Ethelnoth of Somerset and a powerful army from west-central Wessex, the Cotswolds and the Severn valley, pursued three groups of Viking raiders, which had combined, up the Thames, across to the Severn and up the Severn until they overtook and blockaded them at Buttington. Eventually, as we read in the *Chronicle*, the Danes cut their way out with heavy casualties and fled.

Unusually, Ethelhelm is better documented in the *Chronicle* than in the charters, appearing three times in the former and only twice in the latter.[24] He died perhaps in his late thirties in 897, the year after the war ended. His daughter Elfleda married King Edward, Alfred's son, as the second of his three wives. If he was indeed King Ethelred's son, his brother Ethelwold rebelled against King Edward, was accepted as king in the North, led his Viking subjects to plunder Mercia and the upper Thames valley and was killed in the battle of the Holme in 903.

Ethelnoth of Somerset, active 879–894

Listed as the senior governor at Epsom in 882, Ethelnoth had shown himself the most steadfast and reliable of all Alfred's governors, distinguished for his great courage in the terrible crisis of four years earlier, when Guthrum's Vikings had overrun the kingdom in midwinter. While the king and his immediate retinue had fled from Wiltshire and taken refuge in the marshes at Athelney, an outlying part of the great royal estate of Somerton, Ethelnoth had, so Ethelward tells us in his *Chronicon*, mustered some of his warriors and 'stayed with his small force in a certain wood'.[25] This was doubtless near Somerton, a few miles east of Athelney, well placed to cover Alfred from Viking attack and to gather the fighting men of his shire as they straggled in to their usual rendezvous.

Ethelnoth retained his bold courage for many more years. In 893, eleven years later, he was one of three governors who led their men in hot pursuit of a Viking force far from Wessex to Buttington-on-Severn, where they trapped and blockaded them. The following year, in 894, he repeated his long-range strike tactics and attacked the new Viking kingdom of York, 300km north of Somerset, from which we must assume the bulk of his men came.[26]

Ethelred, probably in Kent, active 858–863

An Ethelred who appears in the reign of Alfred's elder brother King Ethelberht, as a minister in 858 and as governor in 860, 862 and 863,[27] must have been born in the early 830s. His interests seem to have been entirely in Kent and he probably died in his thirties. He must not be confused with the rather younger governor Ethelred of Mercia who became Alfred's son-in-law or with governor Ethelred of Devon who died in 899.

Ethelwold, perhaps of a south-eastern province, active 877–888?
A governor Ethelwold, perhaps the son of governor Alfred of
Surrey, witnessed Alfred's agreement with Archbishop Ethelred
of Canterbury about Chartham and Croydon and appears in witness-lists in about 877 and, with the army at Epsom, in fifth place
in 882;[28] he may be the governor Ethelwold who, the *Chronicle*
tells us, died in 888. At this time there was an equally poorly
documented governor of the same name in Alfred's Mercian province so we must be cautious about them.

Ethelwulf of Berkshire in Mercia; then in Wessex, active 836–871
Born in about 800–810, perhaps to a noble family in north-east
Mercia, this is the only governor of the ninth century whose biography has been examined in full detail. F. M. Stenton concluded
from the evidence that we give below that Berkshire became part
of Wessex in the late 840s; he cited a charter of 844 by which
King Berhtwulf of Mercia granted to Ethelwulf an estate at Pangbourne in central Berkshire as evidence that the entire county was
then in the kingdom of Mercia and Alfred's birth in 849 at Wantage
(in part of the county transferred to Oxfordshire in 1973) as proof
that the whole shire had by then become part of Wessex.[29] Given
an underlying assumption that shires were unified blocks of territory, part of a single centralised kingdom within which no other
king could sell or dispose of land, this conclusion is reasonable.
But the assumption itself is patently unsound; in 868 Queen
Ethelswith of Mercia sold or granted land at Lockinge in her
brother's kingdom of Wessex, in fact in the same county of Berkshire (in the part transferred to Oxfordshire in 1973).[30]

The evidence tells us only that a Mercian king had acquired the
patronage of a minster, at Pangbourne within present-day Berkshire, some time before 843/4, when he disposed of it. As well as
having ruled an area, there are plenty of other explanations for a
king's ownership of a church in a particular territory, whether in
his own kingdom or in an adjoining one: (i) his grandmother,
mother or wife (or almost any other relative) may have brought it
as dowry (like Lockinge) into another ruling family, or inherited
it later; (ii) he may have foreclosed on a loan for which some priest
or noble had used it as security; or (iii) a former tutor may have
become priest or provost of the church and left it to the king.

Nonetheless the main drift of Stenton's claim that Ethelwulf and his shire were transferred from Mercia to Wessex is perfectly acceptable, even if presented in much too simplistic a way. There is no reason to think that Berkshire was a homogeneous territory more or less identical with the modern county; or that the entire territory must belong only to one kingdom; or that any grant made by a king must be to one of his own subjects; though it may be true that a governor could owe allegiance only to one king at a time.

We could argue that Berkshire was split into several districts transferred from one kingdom to another at different times, that governor Ethelwulf did indeed move from Mercia to Wessex but for some quite other reason, such as marriage to an heiress, or an offer of a better governorship, and on a different occasion from the cession of territory. Or, of course, there may have been not two but three people of this name at the same time. We may cautiously accept Stenton's basic claim, but not his date. The transfer was probably made in about 837; the governor Ethelwulf who witnessed a Mercian charter of 836 may well have been one of the two governors named Ethelwulf who attested a Wessex charter of 838 dealing with Kentish business.

We could assert that the 838 charter was carelessly copied, with the name accidentally written twice, but in this particular case it is fair to conclude that the Mercian governor had gone over to Wessex between 836 and 838 for one of a number of different reasons: (i) having rebelled and fled and been given a new job; (ii) having rebelled and taken his whole province over to a new master; (iii) having been mortgaged and traded with his province for financial reasons; (iv) having married an heiress and changed jobs and countries; (v) having applied for and been offered a better paid post in the next-door country; or even (vi) having been head-hunted for some special skills as an administrator or warrior to induce him to move, and then having persuaded a financially strapped king to trade his county along with him.

The *Chronicle* tells us some of the main events of Ethelwulf's later life; he beat the Vikings in two battles, in 860 near Winchester and in 871 at Englefield, and must have been well into his sixties when he fell in an attack on the Viking camp at Reading just before Alfred came to the throne in 871, having governed the shire for well over thirty years. His body was 'secretly recovered and taken for burial into Mercia to the place called Northworthy, now Derby in Danish'[31].

We can thus follow earlier scholars in assembling a long and fascinating career of Ethelwulf, but something eludes us. Who did he marry? What happened to his children? And, almost our biggest problem, who was he and what was his background? Here we have to speculate, something that we have been trying to avoid as we have pieced together our tale of King Alfred and his family and their whole social world from scraps of evidence. Perhaps he was a brother of the Mercian governor Ethelred Mucil whose daughter Ealhswith married the nineteen-year-old Alfred in 868. And perhaps the great governor Ethelred of Mercia was his nephew and Ealhswith's cousin. Such a family link would explain a great deal, especially if it was just one of several marriages between closely linked families.

Ethelwulf, Alfred's brother-in-law, active about 875–897
Ethelwulf, son of Ethelred Mucil of Mercia and thus brother of Alfred's Queen Ealhswith, seems to have governed a county in Wessex in the 870s[32] and then to have transferred back to his homeland in the early 880s to take over a shire of Alfred's new Mercian province; we discuss him at greater length in that context.

Garrulf, active 862–882
Born *c.*830–840, Garrulf served as a senior royal minister in the 860s; his career in the 870s is not documented. By 882 he had become a governor, perhaps of Dorset or Somerset, and brought his fighting men to Epsom for Alfred's first major campaign against London. After that he disappears from the record; he must have lived at least into his forties.

Humbearht, active about 860
Not documented as a minister, governor Humbearht appears just once, in a Rochester charter dated 790, which is evidently meant for, or corrected from, 860. Although this has been denounced as 'a crude forgery', we have discussed it as good evidence for a court meeting in 860, and the denunciation was not so much over-hasty as irresponsible; no forger could ever have concocted such a wit-

ness-list with a vast majority of names well attested at the time and others, such as Humbearht, based on no existing list. It is clearly based on authentic material and the charter itself is conspicuously genuine. We can surmise that Humbearht was born about 820–830, became a governor in his twenties or thirties and, for all we know, died, rebelled or fled into exile soon after.

Orddulf or *Ordlaf*, active 883–909
The third governor to witness at Epsom in 882 was 'Orddulf', who can be identified as governor Ordlaf, perhaps of Wiltshire, who was, much later, the beneficiary of four royal charters between 900 and 903. Most unusually, we can reconstruct an outline of four generations of his family, from governor Eanwulf, Ordlaf's grandfather,[33] to Ordwold, his son[34]; the family and their estates would repay a detailed study, in the charters and on the ground.

Wulfhere of Hampshire, active 854–878; disgraced
Probably a grandson of governor Wulfhard who died in 840 and a brother or cousin of Queen Wulfthryth, who appears in a single charter and must have been the wife of one of Alfred's elder brothers, governor Wulfhere appears in eight charters between 854 and about 876, as the senior governor from 867.[35] Wulfhere abandoned his county and his responsibilities and fled into exile when the Vikings seized the kingdom in January 878, just as King Burgred had fled from his kingdom of Mercia in 874 and retired to Rome. We learn from a later charter that some, perhaps all, of his estates were declared forfeit.[36]

Wulfred of Hampshire (a minister 867–878), active 878–893/6
When governor Wulfhere had brought disgrace on his shire in 878, by leaving his post of honour and danger and fleeing abroad, Hampshire had failed to send its full contingent at Alfred's summons. Some warriors, 'the men of Hampshire who had not sailed overseas in terror of the Vikings',[37] answered Alfred's call to mobilise and joined him at 'Egbert's Stone', to fight and win at Edington.

In 879 a new governor of Hampshire appears, evidently a kinsman of Wulfhere, from his name, Wulfred.[38] We could assume that he had done his utmost to muster a fighting force in the absence of the governor and that he had brought the warriors into battle at Alfred's side, being rewarded with his absent kinsman's post, but for one scrap of evidence: a badly scrambled copy of a charter to St Paul's cathedral in London in 867 lists a governor Wulfred ten or eleven years before 878,[39] so we cannot be at all confident that he was promoted on the field of battle. Or we must assume that he was a different, slightly older, man of the same name. Or, of course, we could assert that the charter was a muddle or a forgery and ignore it, as was done to far too many charters for most of this century. Wulfred appears in only two more charters, of 882 and 892,[40] and died, the *Chronicle* tells us, between 893 and 896.

Wullaf (a minister 845–858), active 860 and 882–898

Governor Wullaf is a fascinating question of probabilities: was he one man, or two, or even three? We will choose the middle path and say two. One or more of them may have been related to Archbishop Wulfred (805–832) or to the Wulf– family of Hampshire (see Wulfhere and Wulfred above). He appears in the witness-list of a Canterbury charter of 845 and in another Kentish charter of about 853.[41] In 858, still as a minister, he exchanged his Mersham estate in Kent with Alfred's middle brother Ethelbert, then junior king in Kent, for land at Wassingwell.[42] He appears as governor in 860 in a Rochester charter that survives as an original[43] and we may assume that he was promoted and perhaps died not long after, as no governor of this name is recorded in the next twenty years until 882.

A governor Wullaf was at Epsom in 882 in a relatively junior position, ranking sixth of eight governors; and, by then rather more senior, at Woolmer in 898.[44] Had he been a grand old man, the minister of 845 still on his feet well into his seventies, he must have ranked higher than third of three governors in seniority. We must therefore interpret our evidence to present two Wullafs.

9

878–880, The Kingdom
Lost and Won

THE *Chronicle* RELATES THE MOST DRAMATIC EPISODE of English history in restrained and dignified language. This is the climax of the whole work, for which the author contrived and gradually built up the underlying tensions.

878

a. In midwinter, after Twelfth Night, the Viking army struck secretly at Chippenham and took over almost the whole kingdom of Wessex.

b. They drove many people into exile abroad and subjugated most of the others.

c. While they submitted, King Alfred did not. With a small personal bodyguard he trudged through forest and marshland with great hardship.

d. That winter a Viking chief, the brother of Ivar and Healfdene, invaded Wessex, landing in Devon with twenty-three ships. He was slaughtered with eight hundred and forty of his men and his Raven Banner was captured.

e. Afterwards, at Easter, King Alfred and his small force fortified Athelney. With the fighting men of the nearest part of Somerset he kept up an offensive against the Vikings.

f. In the seventh week after Easter he rode east of Selwood to the Egbert Stone, where all the warriors of Somerset and Wiltshire and Hampshire that side of the sea were mustering. Alfred's presence raised their morale high.

g. Next day they rode from base to Iley and the day after to Edington, where they fought and defeated the entire Viking army. They pursued them to their base, which they blockaded for two weeks.

h. The enemy surrendered hostages and gave the most solemn undertakings to quit the kingdom. They also promised that their commander-in-chief would turn Christian, a promise that they kept.

i. Three weeks later King Guthrum and thirty Viking leaders came for baptism to Athelney, with Alfred as godfather.

j. The ceremony of taking off the white robes [eight days later] was at Wedmore. Guthrum spent twelve days with Alfred, who gave rich gifts to him and his companions.

879

a. The Vikings moved from Chippenham to Cirencester and stayed there for a year.

b. A new Viking force mustered in a camp at Fulham on the Thames.

c. There was a one-hour eclipse.

880

a. The Viking army moved from Cirencester to East Anglia, which they colonised and divided.

b. The army from Fulham crossed the Channel to Ghent in Frankish territory and spent a year there.

At the start of 878, early in January, a Viking force led by King Guthrum, one of the many nephews of King Horic of Denmark and a failed candidate for a share of the Danish throne in 850, suddenly went into action and invaded Wessex from the East Midlands, which they had been sharing out. Their plan was to make a direct attack on Alfred in person, to eliminate him and cripple his government, just as they had disabled Northumbria in 867, East Anglia in 870 and Mercia in 874 by killing or driving out the rulers.

The timing may have been related to a particular pagan feast-day on which the sacrifice of Alfred, the last available English Christian king, was specially desirable. In their midwinter attack the Vikings almost caught Alfred unawares at the end of his Twelfth Night festivities. The enemy army came stealthily to Chippenham, where Alfred and his staff and bodyguards were perhaps holding the

Christmas feasts and ceremonies with the magnates of the district, occupied the kingdom and set about sharing it out. Or at least that is a quite reasonable interpretation of this passage in the *Chronicle*.

Alfred fled west to Somerset and eventually took refuge at Athelney among the impenetrable marshes of Sedgemoor, which he knew well, we have already suggested, from hunting there as a boy with governor Eanwulf and old Bishop Ealhstan. The Danes began to share out Wessex; one of Alfred's greatest noblemen, governor Wulfhere of Hampshire, fled abroad, as we learn from a much later charter, when one of his forfeited estates changed hands again.[1] Some nobles and officials fled abroad, as this passage in the *Chronicle* tells us; others were conquered and the people of Wessex submitted. At least we really should compare the words of the *Chronicle* with Asser's:

> . . . and took over almost the whole kingdom of Wessex. They forced many people into exile abroad and subjugated most of the others.[2]

> With their overpowering force they drove many of the inhabitants beyond the seas through terror and hardship and nearly all the people gave in to them.[3]

Our authors are referring to a fairly small minority of the population, the greater and lesser lords and their officials, henchmen and warriors. The peasants themselves may hardly have noticed the difference between one bunch of oppressive overlords and another, except for the chance of escaping having to pay rent and dues in the break between them.

Alfred kept his head and stayed on the move through woods and marshes that he knew with his personal attendants, a small retinue and no doubt a substantial force of royal guards. Asser relates how they seized their supplies from the Vikings and from his own people who had given in to them:

> The only provisions they got came from ambushing Viking patrols and from the straightforward plunder of his own Christian subjects who had come under Viking rule.[4]

Some of the great men of the kingdom remained steadfast and rallied their warriors; governor Odda of Devon, which may have been the only part of the country to escape attention from the Vikings based at Chippenham (if indeed they made their base there), crushed and slaughtered a second Viking force closing in on Alfred from the west. The *Chronicle* notes, but does not locate, the battle and is followed in this by Ethelward. Asser places the fight at Cynuit, which figures as 'Kenwith' in several of the Georgian dramas on the theme of Alfred (see Chapter 15); this has been identified as Countisbury in north Devon.

This is 25km west of Carhampton where, on low rolling ground at the mouth of the little River Avill, both King Egbert and King Ethelwulf had been defeated by earlier Viking forces landing on the broad muddy beach of Blue Anchor Bay. At Countisbury the medieval church and village lie on the shoulder of a stupendous hill that rises from the shingle beach of Lynmouth and above a large fort formed by digging a great bank and ditch right across the peninsula from the East Lyn river to the cliffs above the Bristol Channel. Asser had himself seen the dramatic and rugged hills and adds a great deal to the *Chronicle*'s bare account.

The local ministers and their men had taken refuge in the fort. The Vikings, aware that there was no fresh water supply within the defences, confidently blockaded it on the east or landward side away from their ships and the little harbour. In a fierce dawn attack the men of Devon overwhelmed and cut down the enemy and their king.[5] Only the later chronicler Ethelward adds that governor Odda, otherwise quite unknown, was blockaded with his men. He tells of eight hundred Viking fatalities but records a final hard-fought Danish victory.[6] Asser gives twelve hundred casualties and a Viking defeat, which we can compare with the *Chronicle*'s more precise eight hundred and forty dead in the defeat; its earliest version, the A-text, makes no mention of the war-banner. All in all, this incident has more than its share of problems and uncertainties, even for the ninth century.

After ten weeks on the run, the king and his men went to ground in a fortified base at Athelney in the middle of the great Somerset marshland of Sedgemoor; this need have been no more than a short stockade across the narrow tongue of low ground rising above the brackish marshes that were occasionally covered by the highest tides. Ethelward adds that governor Ethelnoth of Somerset 'was remaining in a certain wood with a small brigade'.[7] No doubt they chose the two positions in consultation so that Ethelnoth covered Alfred's base against the main Viking army while the royal guards at Athelney were in a position to reinforce the Somerset fighting men. Ethelnoth may have spread his scouts between Street and Ilminster, to guard against any approach from the Fosse Way, the great Roman road that runs from north-east to south-west, and kept his reserve closed up at Somerton or Langport.

Seven weeks after Easter, as the regular campaigning season started in early May, Alfred came out of his refuge to hit back. He summoned the fighting men of three counties and mustered them at 'Egbert's Stone'. Then he led them, without a break, a day's march north to the lost 'Iley Oak' near Warminster and then another 9–10km north to fall unhesitatingly on King Guthrum at Edington where at last he defeated and broke the 'Great Army'. Instead of being sacrificed, the fate he may have faced if captured, Alfred imposed compulsory baptism and twelve days of peaceful feasting, defying the ruthless pagan gods, from whom he claimed descent, with his own more powerful Christian magic.

This action all took place across north and west Wiltshire and central and eastern Somerset. Athelney lies 70km south-east of Chippenham and Edington is 20km south of Chippenham. Asser adds, as he had for the battle of Ashdown, that Alfred's battle-line was formed 'in close order shield-to-shield'.[8]

The *Chronicle*'s bare outline can only fuel speculation about all the details. Some writers have claimed that the beaten Vikings fled to Chippenham, others that it was to Bratton Castle, the great hill-fort 2km west of Edington. This view was well established by the 1840s when Samuel Lewis wrote of 'the figure of a horse, cut out, as tradition relates, by the troops of Alfred in memory of the victory . . . several fragments of military weapons have been dug up in the vicinity.'[9] Without being able to produce these, or early drawings of them, as securely dated Viking or late Saxon spearheads or swords from a reasonable provenance, we must maintain an agnostic view; whether speculation, suggestion or working hypothesis, we cannot say very much for or against any of this until much more detailed topographical work is done across the whole area

In the ninth century and throughout the Middle Ages (and to some extent even into this century), war was a major and really the primary occupation of all noblemen and landowners; their regular pastime of hunting was simply a training for war. This attitude was so widely accepted that, in emergencies, bishops, who were often of royal or noble blood, led their men into battle. Bishop Ealhstan of Sherborne had shown himself a valiant commander. His successor Heahmund fell in battle at Meretun in 871. Bishop Udalrich of Augsburg, the future St Ülrich, saved the German empire of Otto I in 927 by a dramatic intervention at the head of his armed retainers. Around Rome throughout the ninth century the popes combined their leadership of the Western Church with acting as margraves of a great threatened frontier province, as they planned and built fortresses, manning them by drafting whole populations.

In England the king and every great lord governed their people by presiding at council and court in peace. In war they mustered their fighting men, rode at their head in search of the enemy and led them into battle, marching in the centre of the line. No fewer than nine of the great provincial governors of the small kingdom of Wessex are recorded as having fallen in battle between 802 and 903.

Alfred himself was involved in at least sixteen major confrontations with hostile Viking forces, according to our major narrative source, the *Chronicle*, a reliable and precise, though taciturn, source. Half the time the enemy evaded battle, or Alfred obtained his objective by manoeuvre. But at least eight times the confrontation resulted in close-quarter fighting from which he emerged safe every time, while enemy fatalities included five named earls at Ashdown in 871 and two complete ships' crews slaughtered in 882, to induce two more crews to surrender.

Some writers have disparaged Alfred's military skills. Our favourable source, the *Chronicle*, admits that he was on the losing side in four of the eight battles which it mentions. However, three of these took place while Alfred was a prince in his early twenties, before he succeeded to the throne, and the fourth immediately afterwards, when he was still young and inexperienced. At Ashdown in 871, as a prince and deputy commander of his brother's army, he took the initiative and led the English battle-line forward to victory 'like a wild boar', as Asser graphically puts it.[10] At his last major battle, Edington in 878, after three months on the run, he mobilised his warriors and led them to sudden and overwhelming victory over the Viking army that had practically destroyed his kingdom by its midwinter assault. Alfred's tactical skill and high courage on the battlefield cannot really be faulted. But it is as an expert on defences, sieges and the relief of forts that we should judge him.

In the defensive situation, under attack or awaiting attack, in which Alfred was almost always placed, a knowledge of the enemy's whereabouts and intentions was of paramount importance. In all the crises that he faced he must have been forced to rely more and more on coastal observers and patrols along his land frontiers. When his son and daughter went over to a sustained offensive in the 910s they will have reduced the settled Danes to the state of hesitant and uneasy defence that the English kingdoms had been in during the 850s, 860s and 870s.

Alfred must have learnt early in his reign the need for reliable intelligence from within the enemy camps. The ancient legend that he penetrated a Viking camp in 878 disguised as a minstrel may be based on such an achievement by one of his retainers. As the chain of new forts around his territories reached completion in the 880s, Alfred and his staff and governors must have realised their value in gathering and assessing intelligence more systematically than hitherto, as well as in planning operations from permanently staffed bases.

All European societies, literate and illiterate, Christian and pagan, were broadly similar in that they could be described as 'heroic'. Every ruler in Europe in the ninth century was in an almost permanent state of war and faced the expectation that his realm might be wiped out at any time. Invading or being invaded was the most normal state of things. Threats often came from far-distant countries, as well as from nearby. Empires were broken up as a matter of course among jealous neighbours or the heirs of the great warrior rulers who had formed them a few generations before, rather like shuffling and redealing a pack of cards.

Warfare was endemic, fighting an important and exciting part of everyday life. Death in battle against great odds was something to be sought out, not avoided. Raiding, burning and looting were normal everyday behaviour, to be practised not only against an enemy but also on any local people who were slow with their taxes or needed to be overawed and kept in order for any reason.

In Scandinavia and the rest of Europe as well as in Britain the fighting men so constantly at work were not local peasants hastily summoned, but professional warriors in the pay of the rulers and nobles. The princeling Cynehard had an armed retinue of eighty-four men with him when he caught King Cynewulf of Wessex in bed with a girlfriend in 786 and assassinated him while the king's personal attendants fought to the death around them. When Cynehard barricaded himself into the 'stronghold' and tried to bribe his way out, the rest of the royal guards and governor Osric and minister Wigfrith, who had been in attendance on the king, broke in and slaughtered every man of the eighty-four, except one. A badly wounded British hostage survived the first slaughter, while governor Osric managed to save a godson, badly injured, from the second.[11]

These warriors must also have been sent with messages, serving as a combined telephone and postal service. They no doubt helped collect taxes and acted, in a rough and ready way, as a police force. While they did not form a standing army in the sense of being instantly available for the king's use, they all made up a permanent warrior class. It is not likely that there was much to choose between them and their opposite numbers among the Viking 'rank and file'.

The royal guards of Wessex were evidently an élite. No king of Alfred's line ever fell in battle in spite of their exposed position in the centre of the shield-line which they personally set into motion. In all Alfred's defeats we can only imagine the guards grimly closing up in furious hand-to-hand combat as they steadily gave ground, holding their shield-wall around the king while the horses were brought up and the royal party rode away, leaving the guards to continue their sullen retreat. They had ridden to Rome and back in 853 with their young prince safe amongst them, and two years later they escorted King Ethelwulf and the same young prince on the same long journey through a disintegrating world again.

Through the winter of 878 a main group of guards remained loyal and accepted grave hardships at their king's side and then, no doubt, formed the spearhead of the attack at Edington. They played a central role in Alfred's recovery of his kingdom, as no doubt Charles the Bald's guards did when he lost and recovered his west Frankish kingdom in the winter of 858–859. We can probably say the same for the Mercian royal guards when King Wiglaf lost his kingdom to Alfred's grandfather Egbert in 829 and regained it in 830.

Most of Alfred's available soldiers were the retainers and body-guards of his greater and lesser landowners, who could be mobil-ised at fairly short notice. The persistent old belief that peasants and small farmers gathered to form a national army or *fyrd* is a strange delusion dreamt up by antiquarians in the late eighteenth or early nineteenth centuries to justify universal military conscrip-tion. No more than a ridiculous fantasy, it has obsessed scholars who have dissected the *fyrd* in endless futile debates. The pro-fessional warriors of the ninth century were not, of course, full-time soldiers in a Victorian and modern sense, with endless drills and parades. But they may have been just as obsessed with polishing weapons and trying on parade gear as their more recent successors.

They practised for war as huntsmen, grooms, storekeepers and bodyguards. They must often have acted in some way as police, messengers, sometimes as thugs, 'heavies' or 'gofers', and were probably as well used to collecting rents from the recalcitrant tenants of their lords as to buying luxury goods for them at distant fairs. Axe-fighting, sword-play and target-practice with spears and arrows may have been their everyday diversions, enjoyed against local game animals and the rival gangs of bodyguards of neighbour-ing lords, and could be used as threats against unfortunate peasants behind with the rent.

We should not think of the warriors as being in any way 'aristo-cratic'; they were a particular group, almost a 'caste' of henchmen and dependants, not the sort of people you would fancy meeting on a dark night. They no doubt looked on themselves as 'Saxons', 'Jutes' or 'Angles', depending on the traditions of their lords, what-ever their actual ancestry. Their ambitions were loot and reward, ultimately in land, a small farm or so, allowing them to pose as minor landowners and support a group of sons and henchmen themselves; in old age they may have continued to spend their time at their lord's hall, giving unwanted advice about tactics and boring the youngsters with tales of bloodshed long ago.

With a few weeks' notice to mobilise at a certain spot, such men could fairly easily be mustered for an attack or a raid, by the king ordering his lords to assemble for campaign. He could issue the order at a convenient feast or great court assembly when many of his magnates came together. But for a long-term defensive role against sudden attack they had drawbacks; they were scattered at the country residences of their lords and elsewhere and not instantly available, away on all kinds of errands besides purely military work.

The forts that Alfred constructed in the 880s will soon have become the major centres for mobilisation and must thus have come to house military stores of all kinds. He may well have sought a different kind of person to draft into his fort-garrisons, more reliable than his nobles' thugs. The *Chronicle*'s long-winded account of the invasions of 892–896 seems to indicate that Alfred and his staff had developed a defence system that incorporated, in a rough and ready way, effective arrangements for reconnaissance and early warning, rapid mobilisation and response to threats as well as forces capable of sustaining co-ordinated campaigns up to 300km from base, far beyond Alfred's personal control.

Numbers involved in military operations must have been small for all kinds of reasons, logistical and operational. Command on campaign and in battle was exercised, as in all heroic societies, by the king in person, or by the senior nobleman present. This meant that there was a strict limit to the size of the force which they could handle. The laws of King Ine (688–726), as edited under Alfred's reforms in the 880s, gave a clear definition of numbers of rioters and troublemakers: 'thieves are up to seven in number; a gang is from seven to thirty-five; more than thirty-five is an army.'[12]

The Viking force defeated in north Devon in 878 may have numbered nine hundred or a thousand men. The *Chronicle* reported eight hundred and forty dead from twenty-three ships; if sixty men survived and got away in two or three of the ships, there were thirty-nine men in each ship. But all these figures are really boasts rather than statistics. None can be relied on.

The strategy and tactics of Alfred's wars generally consisted of simple and direct responses to Viking raids and invasions. Battles, as briefly recorded in the documents and interpreted by biographers and historians, amounted to two opposed lines of well-armed warriors trudging towards each other on foot until they clashed, and then fought ferociously until one line began to give way and either successfully retreated and disengaged or broke and fled. Operational command can only have been rudimentary, although the tactical importance of the unbroken line of the 'shield-wall' may well have been over-emphasised in this country by writers vividly aware of the British army's constant reliance on line over column in all its late eighteenth- and nineteenth-century wars. We might even suspect that mounted cavalry played a much greater part in battles than hitherto suspected, as they did on the Continent.

Our knowledge of tactical detail is minimal. Fights may sometimes have been quite involved affairs. Asser's account of the battle of Ashdown, a few months before Alfred came to the throne in 871, tells us that he had inspected the battlefield and been shown its central focus, the small and isolated thorn-tree. His words imply that Alfred told him something of the battle and that he discussed it further with other veterans who had been there.[13] But we know nothing of the impact that King Ethelred's personal guards made on the battle when he finished praying and they finally joined the fray.

In an attempt to come nearer to the realities of warfare and the daily running of the kingdom, we must examine the evidence for the next rank below the governors, the lesser office-holders known as *ministri* or *thegns* in Old English, whom we call ministers. They were not of course remotely 'middle class' but noble and even so obscure; the best we can do is to scan through the large number of their names and fit together skimpy outlines of the lives of a few of them. We can recognise some individuals over quite long periods in the documents, but it is difficult to be reasonably sure that we are not dealing with several different people.

We can name almost a hundred ministers listed in Alfred's charters and other sources dating from his reign. Most of them, nearly two-thirds of the total number, are named only once. All those listed or documented in other sources more than once can be used in a dating technique for historical and archaeological material evolved by the Egyptologist Sir Flinders Petrie (1852–

1942), now known as seriation, by which groups of artefacts or names can be placed in series and dated relative to each other. It was clear while we were studying lists of governors that several undated charters must belong to early in Alfred's reign and not later, from the presence of some names and the absence of others.

A meticulous study of ministers' names and the rearrangement of the witness-lists until they form a matching series confirms the dating proposed then and allows it to be expanded and refined, giving us relative dates. The lists themselves – before 'seriation'; during the process while inconsistencies are encountered and resolved by adjusting their overall position; and at the end when a 'best fit' has been achieved – are too long to include here. We will instead include a few short 'Lives' of Alfred's ministers; the dates of their appearance in charters are those given by the charter or worked out by other scholars and are given as plain dates, while the new relative dates are given as 'about . . .'.

Acca, active 867–882 and perhaps later; and his son Eadwald
Born perhaps about 840–845, Acca entered royal service in the 860s, appearing fifth of nine ministers in 867 and sixth in the much larger gathering of fourteen ministers (and their warriors) waiting to attack London at Epsom in 882.[14] We should not identify him with 'Ocea' who was listed eleventh of twelfth ministers in 892 and first of five in 901;[15] his position in 892 indicates that he was then too junior to be the man who was ranked fifth in 867, while his high rank in 901 tells us that the new King Edward had chosen him for special office. Acca, however, was sufficiently well remembered at this time for the death of his son Eadwald in battle at the Holme as one of the dilatory Kentish division to be noted under 903 in the *Chronicle*.

Alfred, active 867–about 892 and later promoted governor
Born probably in the early 840s, some years before King Alfred, minister Alfred entered royal service at much the same time as or a little after Acca. He appears eighth of nine ministers in 867, sixth of twenty in about 877 and again sixth of seven in 879.[16] He was not recorded among the large gathering fully mobilised for war at Epsom in 882, when he may have been absent on some special duty. But he remained close to Alfred and was listed as

third of eight ministers in about 892.[17] This number of listings and the steady upward progression in seniority inspires us with some confidence that we are dealing with one man.

He is very likely the Alfred who renewed his parents' lease from the bishops of Winchester of Alresford in Hampshire, a very large estate of 40 hides, for the very high rent of three pounds a year. After his wife left him he lived openly with a girlfriend between duty periods at court. After King Alfred's death, Bishop Denewulf (879–909) considered he set a bad example, brought a charge of adultery and had his property seized by the crown.[18] It is hard to see why such a drastic penalty was enforced, as the usual fine for moral offences ranged from one thousand four hundred and forty silver pennies for adultery with a nobleman's wife down to thirty pence for seducing a third-class slave-girl. It cost the bishop a great deal more, three thousand six hundred silver pennies, to recover Alresford for the Church from the new king Edward.[19]

Alfred's misdemeanour seems soon to have been forgotten and he became a governor in Wessex in 900–901, or perhaps in Mercia in about 905–916. But the confiscation caused trouble for a very long time. In 956 minister Alfred's son Elfric persuaded King Edwy, King Alfred's great-grandson, to grant him Alresford outright. But after Edwy died in 959 King Edgar, his brother and successor, expropriated Alresford again and handed it back to the bishop.

Deormod, active *c.*877–903

Born perhaps about 850 and possibly related to Bishop Deorlaf of Hereford (*c.*860–888), Deormod appears in about 877 as fourteenth of fifteen ministers. He rose rapidly at court and was listed second of eight ministers, perhaps as a royal steward, in about 878 and first of seven ministers in 879. On campaign at Epsom in 882, with the court on a war footing, he was outranked by several veterans and was listed merely fifth among the ministers.[20]

At peace again he appears in about 892 as second of eight ministers and in 892 as first of twelve, now with the title *cellarius* or steward.[21] In 898 he acquired Appleford in modern Oxfordshire (formerly Berkshire) from King Alfred, who described him as 'my faithful Deormod', in exchange for his land at Horn Down nearby, both being close to the great royal manor of Sutton Courtenay.[22]

He lived on into the next reign and regularly appears as a high-ranking minister and, on occasion, perhaps through scribal error, as a governor.

He seems to have married off a daughter, Deorswith, to a man named Ethelwulf who gave her, as her 'morning-gift' after marriage, an estate at Wylye in Hampshire.[23] Deormund, listed first of twenty-one ministers at the court of King Alfred's son Edward in 909, may be a son who succeeded Deormod in his high court office.[24]

Ecgwulf, active 854–893/6
Born perhaps in the 830s, Ecgwulf first appears at court in 854 and in 878 was listed eighth of eight ministers in a charter that later reached the archives of Malmesbury. He perhaps rose to command one of the guards regiments, and appears as the second of fourteen ministers at Epsom, ready for an assault on London, in 882.[25] We know nothing else about him until his death at some time during the third great crisis of Alfred's reign, the Viking invasion of 893–896, when, in his sixties, he features in the *Chronicle* among the list of principal casualties as 'Ecgwulf the king's marshal'.

Osric, active about 876–882
Born perhaps about 850, Osric was almost certainly one of the king's closest relatives on his mother Osburh's side. He first appears as the third of five ministers in about 876, and as the first of fourteen when the court was at Epsom on campaign in 882.[26] He may have been commander-in-chief of the household guards, or chief-of-staff to the king.

We may note that men of the Os– family, or at least men with Os– names, regularly appear first or second among the ministers, from Osmund in 863 and 864 to Osferth in 898.[27] A military rank commanding the royal guards regiments seems quite a likely role for reliable kinsmen in a kingdom that we have to consider as something of a family business.

Wihtbrord, active 882–909
Born perhaps in the late 850s, Wihtbrord first appears as fourth of fourteen ministers on campaign at Epsom in 882 and, soon after

King Alfred's death, as second of nine and second of twelve in 900.[28] In 901 Alfred's son Edward granted him an estate at Fovant in Wiltshire.[29] He remained high in favour, perhaps like Osric as a senior guards officer, being listed second of twenty-one ministers in 909.[30]

It is very likely that in the ninth century almost all noblemen were descended from several of the ancient royal families that had established themselves in England in the 400s and 500s and that each of them could lay some claim to any kingdom that happened to be vacant before and during the devastating Viking invasions of the 860s and 870s. Despite our scanty evidence, we have been able to identify a few individuals from lists of mere names and assign them roles in the royal household, without making too many wild assumptions.

Every English nobleman must have known almost without thinking who was descended from whom and who was related to whom, so there was no real need for written genealogical records of society and none seem to have been kept. Except for the evidence of the few surviving wills, which give a little incidental information, we can reconstruct families at this time only very tentatively from chance later references to fathers and grandfathers and by constructing genealogies based on name-forms, like the Wulf–s and the Byrht–s above, with links sometimes from local connections.

10

Expansion and Consolidation

THE TWELVE YEARS FROM 880 that followed the narrow midwinter escape and dramatic and overwhelming victory may be seen as the relatively peaceful long central period of the reign when Alfred laid the foundations of the future kingdom of all England, a time of steady preparation, while he overhauled and reorganised every detail of government, from finance and tax-assessment to defence. For this period we lack a continuous narrative of events in England since the *Chronicle*'s compiler devotes more than two-thirds of its entries to foreign affairs.

Despite this change of emphasis in a record that we have come to depend on, we can extract and piece together a surprising amount of information, either from explicit statements in charters and other sources such as Alfred's 'will', or deduced from the documents, rather more than most scholars (always more prone to read each others' writings than the actual evidence) have noticed and made use of. Before turning to Alfred's settlement of national and family assets, we will see how, in the years 882 to 886, Alfred enlarged his kingdom by nearly half as much again.

The Vikings camped at Cirencester had direct military control of the whole of south-west Mercia in 879–880. The *Chronicle* tells us of Ceolwulf, whom they had installed as a puppet-king of Mercia in 874. He appears as king of Mercia in two charters of 875, both preserved in the eleventh-century Worcester property book. In the first Ceolwulf is 'with God's grace granting his blessings King of the Mercians', a formula used by his legitimate predecessor Burgred with the words in a different order. The witness-list, which must have been abbreviated by the eleventh-century scribe whose copy alone survives, lists Ceolwulf with three bishops and only two governors.[1] The second charter uses the same royal formula and has a fuller list of witnesses: Ceolwulf as king, two bishops, four governors and eight others, presumably ministers.[2] Ceolwulf last appears in the record in 877, when the Viking army which had withdrawn by negotiation from Exeter 'shared out some of the land and left the rest to Ceolwulf'.[3]

In 883, or shortly before, Alfred took over the Cotswolds and Severn valley and perhaps also the upper Thames valley in what seems to have been a peaceful deal; we can deduce the annexation only from charter evidence. Alfred entrusted his newly added province to governor Ethelred, a man who will play a large role through the following pages, and who may already have succeeded or displaced Ceolwulf. It would be exciting to think that Ethelred raised a group of anti-Viking governors in rebellion and invited Alfred to be their king. This might be so. At least we can say without hesitation that a number of Ceolwulf's governors, including one or two survivors from King Burgred's time, continued in their posts after the change. We may conclude that they did not oppose any conquest by Alfred and are that much more likely to have acted together in joining him.

Can we identify this governor Ethelred further? He does not seem to have any connection with his namesake in Kentish charters of between 858 and 863 who must have been born in the 830s. Ethelred of Mercia was probably born in the late 850s and can first be identified in 883 in a charter in the Worcester property book, acquiring an estate from Berkeley abbey and granting a lease for three lives to Cynulf son of Ceoluht, to revert to the bishops of Worcester.[4] We cannot doubt that Ethelred of Mercia was a great nobleman, no doubt descended from the ruling princes of a tribe absorbed by Mercia, such as the Hwicce. He may well have been related to both Alfred and his wife Ealhswith through marriage and intermarriage long before. As kingdoms were such close-knit family businesses at this time we may suggest that he was a first cousin of Ealhswith. He may even have been her brother, but no source even hints at such a close relationship, which is explicitly noted, just once in the *Chronicle*, for governor Ethelwulf whose career we come to shortly. A few years later, Ethelred married

King Alfred's daughter Ethelfleda and from then on shared with her his authority as governor over south-west Mercia.

Some writers have confused Ethelred's position, and write as though his Mercian territory was autonomous and distinct from Wessex. The charter evidence makes it clear that Alfred, by then the only remaining English monarch, was king and that Ethelred, first on his own and later jointly with his wife, governed a great frontier-province far larger than any of the old shires of Wessex, with the help of four or five subordinate governors, whose careers we will examine.

After Ethelred's death, Ethelfleda continued to govern much of the province under the royal authority of her brother Edward, who had succeeded Alfred. Such an arrangement was standard all over Europe and in the Byzantine Empire for dangerous frontier regions and recently annexed territories. Alfred's grandfather Egbert had set his son Ethelwulf up as junior king over Kent and the newly annexed south-eastern provinces and Alfred's father Ethelwulf put in three of his sons there in succession.

There are no indications that any 'separatist' tendencies developed in the new province; indeed, with Alfred's daughter and son-in-law Ethelred in overall charge and his brother-in-law Ethelwulf as one of the governors, the atmosphere of an expanded family business was as firmly maintained as it must have been in the small early kingdoms such as Kent or Essex in the seventh and eighth centuries. Indeed, the veterans such as governor Beornnoth (see below), with well over thirty-five years' service under Mercian kings before he led his shire over to Alfred, added ripe experience and stability to the realm, while the immense contribution that the Mercians made to the new kingdom of England as Alfred's son and grandsons established it was out of all proportion to their numbers, as we can see from a glance at the careers of governor Ethelferth's sons and grandsons.

Beornnoth of a province in Mercia, active 845–884
Born about 820, he was no doubt a grandson of the Mercian governor Beornnoth (*c.*798–825), and a kinsman of the unfortunate King Beornwulf of Mercia (823–825). He served as a minister in the 840s and was perhaps a protégé and supporter of governor Burgred.

He appears as governor about the time Burgred became king of Mercia and may have been promoted as a reward for his support. He witnessed most of Burgred's surviving charters and remained governor for thirty years through the Viking invasions and the break-up of the kingdom. He witnessed both surviving charters of the Vikings' puppet-king Ceolwulf as senior governor of whatever was left of the Mercian kingdom.

He must have agreed to King Alfred of Wessex taking over south-west Mercia's provinces and the appointment of Ethelred as a superior governor, but was left with diminished status, to judge from his position at his last appearance, in his sixties. He was called 'Atheling' or prince when his son died.

Ethelferth of a Mercian province, active 875–916
Born about 850 and never recorded as a minister, he appears as a governor in King Ceolwulf's Viking-dominated kingdom of Mercia, keeping his position when south-west Mercia acceded to Wessex soon after 880, a move which he must have supported.

It is not at all clear where his province was; his property included two very large estates: Monks Risborough, Buckinghamshire, in Mercia, which he got by marriage to Ethelgyth, daughter of Alfred's brother-in-law governor Ethelwulf, and Wrington in Somerset, in Wessex, which he may have inherited from a kinsman. He was governor under King Ceolwulf, under governor Ethelred and his lady Ethelfleda, Alfred's daughter, and under Ethelfleda on her own for at least forty-one years, and must have lived well into his sixties.

The descendants of Ethelferth and Ethelgyth have been worked out in detail to the end of the next century.[5] They had four sons who all became governors, Elfstan (active 930–934), Athelstan 'Half-King' (of south-east Mercia and East Anglia, active 932–956), Ethelwold (active 931–946) and Eadric (932–949). Athelstan in turn had four sons whose careers have been traced: Ethelwold (governor of Kent and the south-east 949–956 and of East Anglia 956–962), Elfwold, Ethelsige (chamberlain to King Edgar 958–987) and Ethelwine 'God's friend', or *Dei Amicus* (governor of East Anglia 962–992), the main patron of the religious reforms of Bishops Dunstan and Ethelwold.

Ethelwulf, Alfred's brother-in-law, active about 875–897
Born in about 850 to Eadburh, of Mercian royal blood, and her
husband Ethelred Mucil, governor of the Gaini in Mercia, who
appears in only one Mercian charter, of 872/4.[6] His grandfather
Mucel was a governor for forty-one years from 814 and evidently
lived well into his sixties, ranking as the most senior Mercian
governor for over a quarter of a century, from 840 to 866.

In 868 King Ethelred and his brother Alfred with six governors
brought an army from Wessex to confront the Vikings at Nottingham. Alfred, then nineteen, met and married Ethelwulf's sister
Ealhswith. When Burgred abandoned his kingdom of Mercia in
874 and fled abroad, he may have joined Alfred, now king of
Wessex, and been given a shire to govern. From the early 880s he
was a governor under the great governor Ethelred of Mercia, who
governed Alfred's vast new frontier province and married his
daughter. No hint or clue helps us locate his shire, which can
scarcely have been Worcestershire, where he owned property, as
he never appears in a close relationship with the well-documented
Bishop Werferth. Ethelwulf also owned land in Buckinghamshire:
a daughter Ethelgyth, no doubt with his Monks Risborough estate
as dowry, married his fellow governor Ethelferth, who lost his
charters in a fire.[7]

Ethelwulf seems to have been able to read; he may have been
influenced by Alfred's insistence in the 880s that his younger son
Ethelward and all the young nobles could read and write.[8] In 897,
late in life, he undertook research in history, or at least legal history,
in the Mercian royal archives at Winchcombe.[9] After a varied
career as a great nobleman of Mercia and Wessex, he died in 901
aged about fifty; his sister Ealhswith of Wessex died at much the
same age in 903.

A large area north and east of London was under the control of
Wessex in the 860s; a charter of Alfred's brother King Ethelred
in 867 records his gift to St Paul's minister or cathedral, at the
request of Bishop Deorwulf (*c.*855–875) and governor Eldred, of
an estate at Navestock (15 hides), just south of Ongar. The *Chronicle* tells us of the loss of London at the start of Alfred's reign,
when the Vikings seized it as their winter base for 871–872.

An abortive campaign against London in 882 in which Alfred was joined by almost all of his governors and their fighting men, no doubt in conjunction with Ethelred, his new ally, subject and governor, is well documented by two mutually supporting sources. Many commentators have puzzled over it unnecessarily. The *Chronicle* tells of a mission sent into western Asia by a decision reached at Alfred's court, probably in the summer of 882:

883

c. Sigelm and Athelstan took the offerings to Rome and went on to the shrine of St Thomas and St Bartholomew in India, while the English campaigned against the Viking force in London. Thanks be to God that their prayers were answered.

This circumstantial reference to an attempt to winkle the Vikings out of London as quite incidental to a fantastic 8000km round trip by a diplomatic and religious mission shows how vast the gaps in our knowledge are. Did the writer mention India simply as a routine destination? – or because this was a unique enterprise? The mission went, not to what we think of as India, but almost certainly to Edessa in Mesopotamia, now known as Urfa in modern Turkey, an ancient city and later a Roman colony (as Colonia Marcia Edessenorum). The relics of St Thomas, long reputed to have spread the Gospel in India, were moved there in 394. Later the city was a major nerve centre of the Byzantine frontier, captured by the Arabs in 638.

The far-travelled Sigelm or Sigehelm, who must have ridden right across the Byzantine Empire, acquiring an excellent knowledge of their army and defensive strategy as he travelled across the border into Arab-held lands, can readily be identified. He came from an old princely family in Kent or Essex where names in Sige– were generally used. With his brother or cousin Sigewulf he appears in 875 as a royal minister, listed before eleven other ministers.[10] He was killed in battle late in 902 or in 903 as a governor of one of the provinces of Kent, largely through his own fault in delaying a retreat ordered by King Edward. Sigewulf, also a governor by then, fell in the same battle at the Holme. It is not so easy to identify this Athelstan, as Alfred had a chaplain and two ministers of that name in the 880s; we might presume without any real certainty that he was the chaplain.

Our other source for this attempt on London is a charter, of special importance in that it documents the largest known assembly of Alfred's reign, which we have already examined as giving us an example of a court meeting not just in wartime, but on the march. The 'Epsom' charter, barely noted in print and never discussed in detail, which records the failed attack on London is a key document for understanding administration and government in ninth-century England. The main forces of Wessex had come together *in expeditione in loco qui Hebbesham appelatur*, 'on the expeditionary force at Epsom', an episode that must be related to 'while the English campaigned against the Viking force in London'. The twenty-five men present on this occasion held most of the military commands and, at the same time, most of the civil administration of the kingdom.

Alfred's court, seldom more than a couple of bishops, two or three governors and seven to ten ministers, was a small and very informal assembly, a personal and intimate group which provided the stimulus and setting where he wrote or supervised the translation and adaptation from Latin of a series of prose works into his own tongue, one of the outstanding intellectual achievements of Dark Age Europe. We have suggested elsewhere that by custom the king's most personal attendants, although noble, and perhaps also chaplains, were not included among the witnesses of charters.

This list of twenty-five witnesses, including eight governors, is unique in Alfred's reign. The gathering is a remarkable contrast to his grandson's court: King Athelstan could summon an almost imperial assembly of fifty-nine great men, including three subordinate kings.

The document does not tell us that the assembly was a council of war, nor that it met in the open air, leaving such details to our imagination. It does tell us that Alfred himself made the sign of the Cross to mark his gift, presumably after the document, 'written out' on the occasion, had been read out. This was his part of the formal ceremony of witness that he had taken part in countless times (and committed to memory) since he was a small boy.

Archbishop Ethelred of Canterbury (870–889) and Bishop Denewulf of Winchester (879-909) followed suit. They were there both as spiritual leaders and, on this occasion, as warlords with their armed retinues. The archbishop's act of witness was described: *'Ego Æthered archiepiscopus manum adpono'*, 'I Archbishop Ethelred place my hand', clearly on the charter itself as it lay on the altar round which they all stood, whether on a temporary trestle-altar in camp, in Epsom church or in the lord's manor there.

We have already gone through the individual careers of the governors present: the bold and steadfast Ethelnoth of Somerset; Wulfred of Hampshire, a hero of Edington who had brought into battle some of the warriors of his shire, mustered in the absence of his kinsman Wulfhere, then governor; Ordlaf of Wiltshire who survived well into the next reign; Beocca or Bucca who led the mission to Rome in 888, also surviving into the next reign; with Ethelwold, Wullaf, Garrulf probably from modern Hertfordshire which the Vikings had seized with London in 872, and Byrhtnoth from Essex or nearby.

Alfred continued his campaigns and recovered London, no doubt with the whole region, in around 886:

886
a. The Danish division which had struck east turned west and went up the Seine to camp for the winter at Paris.
b. King Alfred occupied London and all the English free of Danish rule gave him their loyalty. He entrusted the city to governor Ethelred.

Asser adds some extra detail, presumably from his own first-hand observation, as he was with Alfred for most of the year 886:

King Alfred recovered the city of London gloriously, with the burning of many towns and the slaughter of many people, and committed it to governor Ethelred.[11]

ROYAL ESTATES: KING ALFRED'S 'WILL'

While he was involved in winning this great new frontier province, Alfred was also concerned to make a sensible disposition of the various assets that he found in his possession when he came to the throne. His so-called will is a draft settlement of the royal family's assets for his successor on the throne and for the rest of the family, drawn up soon after 880, perhaps as late as 882–883. The earliest copy, in the British Library, is in an early eleventh-century volume of assorted items collected at Hyde abbey just north of Winchester, successor to the New Minster that Alfred ordered to be founded beside the cathedral.[12]

The document is a major source of evidence about royal manors throughout the kingdom, but not in its Mercian province. It may well exclude all the most important of them, the estates considered inalienably royal and always kept in the king's hands as head of state, to serve as the principal source of crown revenue and also as major centres of government, never to be given away, and thus exempt from consideration in a settlement such as this. Here, it seems, we are told of more casually held private royal lands.

Alfred's 'will' leads on from one that his father made. King Ethelwulf had been rather prone to making grand gestures without much consideration of practicalities. His disposal of his personal assets among his four surviving sons in 855 was singularly lacking in foresight. Alfred, the youngest son, had to sort out the inevitable disagreements and satisfy his council and the claims of his relatives and his father's intended beneficiaries, where they had not yet received his bequests.

Alfred's eldest son Edward was to get, in addition to the crown and its resources, six great estates in Cornwall, Devon and Somerset, six more in Wiltshire, Hampshire and Surrey (no doubt as dowries for daughters and to endow younger sons) and one thousand five hundred pounds in cash. The younger son, Ethelward, whose loyal support was essential for the future running of the kingdom as a family enterprise, was to have one thousand five hundred pounds and a truly princely grant of seventeen great estates well spread across the kingdom, two in Somerset, one in Dorset, two in Wiltshire, one in Hampshire, one in the Isle of Wight and one in Sussex; so far Alfred ensured that Ethelward's power-base would not be so concentrated as to let him think of establishing a kingdom for himself, but give him places where he could stay and interests throughout Wessex. The nine remaining estates were all in Devon, a shire distinguished for its loyalty when the kingdom so nearly went under in 878. In the far west were Whitchurch and Lifton, which had a great lordship over south-east Cornwall; in the east of the county were Axmouth, Branscombe and Exminister and Luton; but the nucleus of the young prince's land lay in mid-Devon around Collumpton, Tiverton and Milborne or Silverton. These three properties may together have amounted to 15,000ha and included much of the richest farmland in the south-west, stretching 20km from Bampton Down in the north to the River Culm near Killerton in the south by 18km from Cruwys Morchard nearly to Uffculme.

Alfred's elder brothers had left three sons, who were passed over for the throne in the crisis-ridden days of 871. Oswald, named only in charters, must already have died young; of Ethelred's two sons, Ethelhelm was to have eight large estates in Hampshire, Surrey and Sussex, while the younger, Ethelwold, got three very large and wealthy estates, Godalming and Guildford in Surrey and Steyning in Sussex. Ethelhelm seems to have become the governor of Wiltshire active from 887 to 897; this is not certain and he may instead have been the archbishop of Canterbury of this name shortly afterwards. Ethelwold, not to be fobbed off with his pittance, rose in revolt on Alfred's death. Osferth, the closest to Alfred of his mother's family, was to receive seven estates in Sussex, where Alfred evidently intended him to maintain a loyal body of supporters and perhaps succeed as governor. The three were each to receive a hundred mancuses, or three thousand silver pennies.

Alfred's daughters did not do so well, but may already have been well provided for by their mother, Ealhswith, who was of Mercian royal blood. Ethelfleda was to have the palace or manor-house at Wellow in Somerset; she was soon to marry governor Ethelred of Mercia and govern the province jointly with him. Ethelgifu, the middle daughter, was perhaps disabled in some way and had already been lavishly provided for with a new nunnery at Shaftesbury in Dorset, of which she was to be at least nominally abbess, endowed with seven estates in Dorset and Wiltshire.[13] The youngest, Elfthryth, was to have Chippenham, where the Danes so nearly captured Alfred and his family in 878, and another Wiltshire property with one in the Isle of Wight. When, in the mid-890s, she married Count Baldwin II of Flanders, the son of Alfred's flighty stepmother Judith by her runaway third marriage, the dowry was no doubt paid up in cash. Each of the girls was to have a hundred pounds in cash, as was their mother Ealhswith who was to retain two great Berkshire estates, Lambourn and Wantage, where Alfred had been born, and Edington in Wiltshire, where he won his great victory in 878.

Each of Alfred's governors was to have a hundred mancuses or three thousand silver pennies, while governor Ethelred was to get a sword of the same value; it is not clear whether he and the other Mercian aristocrats had yet decided to combine with Alfred. There are bequests to bishops, to priests and to the poor. Alfred's old tutor, Bishop Werferth of Worcester in Mercia, was to have the same as each of his governors; as with governor Ethelred his position is not clear and he may at this time have been active in persuading all Mercians free of direct Viking control to come over to Alfred.

KING ALFRED'S CHARTERS

Throughout his life, from the moment he ceased to be a toddler, Alfred was constantly aware of and involved in property deals and transfers by which whole villages and sometimes groups of villages, fully stocked with the bailiff and his slave farm-hands on the big home-farm and all the peasant farmers with their oxen, cattle, sheep and pigs, were bought and sold for investment, given away as rewards for royal service or granted to endow churches and monasteries. The other main form of 'investment' at the time was plunder, the booty brought home on raiding expeditions, but we know much more about land because of the chance survival of a fair number of charters.

The ceremonial grants of land which have so constantly formed our only evidence for royal assemblies combined two traditions of legal grants and echoed both the written conveyances of the late Roman Empire and the barbarian chieftain's spoken gift before his assembled warband of a whole tribe or tract of country to a great warrior, in the hope that he would refrain, for another few months, from ambushing him and hacking him to death. The parchment charter itself, and sometimes an actual turf from the land, represented the estate as the king handed it to the recipient or laid it on the high altar of the church to which he was making the gift. Then one by one in order of office or seniority the great men of the kingdom gave witness by word of mouth, perhaps by laying their hands on the turf or charter on to which a scribe then wrote their names.

From the age of nine Alfred was a substantial property owner; we can infer that his father left him properties in Hampshire and Wiltshire and a swath of estates across Kent, perhaps intending him for the Church and setting him up with land handy for Canterbury. Ethelwulf had no doubt acquired this batch of Kentish lands when he was junior king there between about 827 and 839. He had left a large group of family properties, as opposed to royal estates, to his three younger sons jointly, to go to any survivor. When he came to the throne of Wessex in 860 the eldest, Alfred's middle brother Ethelbert, took them all over to run in trust for the two younger brothers.

For the rest of his life, especially while king from 871 to 899, Alfred gave judgements on, managed and dealt in property. This gave him an intimate knowledge of his kingdom, as he rode over every part of his realm, inspecting his own and the royal family's lands and holding court. How far this personal knowledge was supported by lists of districts and townships is not clear. Since the 1640s scholars have from time to time suggested that Alfred compiled a complete new survey of all estates in the kingdom on the lines followed in 1086 by William the Conqueror when he ordered Domesday Book to be made.

Alfred's surviving charters are very varied. One survives as an original vellum document, ineptly written by a scribe who must have been senile or drunk,[14] and several have been so badly copied that we have them in a distinctly scrambled form. He granted land to bishops, abbeys, ministers and other individuals, sometimes as endowments for rewards and services, sometimes no doubt as judgements or settlements in court cases; some grants are evidently royal acts to establish fortresses or consolidate their territories. Alfred did not rule as an arbitrary despot; exchange and consensus appear regularly.

Glancing at some examples in chronological order, we see that in 873 Alfred and the archbishop of Canterbury jointly sold a 'little farm' to the otherwise quite unknown Liaba, son of Birgwin;[15] in about 876 he endowed his daughter Ethelgifu's abbey at Shaftesbury with seven large estates in Dorset and Wiltshire;[16] in about 878, with the consent of the monks of Malmesbury, he gave his minister Dudi their property of Chelworth in Wiltshire on lease for four lives;[17] in 878 (wrongly copied as 852) he endowed the new abbey at Athelney, the 'isle of princes', with an estate in Somerset;[18] in 879 (wrongly copied as 979), he gave the bishop of Winchester a Somerset property which was to form the nucleus of their great estate around Taunton;[19] while on campaign against London in 882 he sold his minister Athelstan two Somerset properties that the bishops of Winchester later added to their great Taunton estate;[20] in 883 governor Ethelred of Mercia granted privileges to Berkeley abbey 'with Alfred's permission and the witness of all the Mercian Council' in exchange for an estate in Gloucestershire which he then passed on, as a lease for three lives, to Cynulf, son of Ceoluht, who cannot be identified elsewhere.[21] From the late 880's two grants to the bishop of Worcester survive: in 887 (wrongly copied as 880), in Alfred's presence, governor Ethelred gave to the 'episcopal seat' two estates of a minster church in present day Oxfordshire[22] and in 889 Alfred and Ethelred jointly gave bishop Werferth a large plot of land in London.[23]

11

Reconstruction and Defence

WE MUST CONTINUE OUR INVESTIGATION into the 880s and very early 890s, just over a decade of relative peace, with the *Chronicle*. This section, which may be an addition to the original text, remains our only narrative account, albeit one that tells us little of Alfred himself and is more in the nature of a backdrop. For Alfred's achievements during these years, when he was vigorously expanding, consolidating, overhauling and defending his kingdom, there are two important sources not in a narrative form, the *Burghal Hidage* and the final sections of Asser's *Life*.

The *Chronicle* mentions events in England only occasionally during these years; it gives us three summaries, two in 885 and one in 887, of the succession crises that resulted in the final break-up of the Frankish Empire; and it has most interesting information on Alfred's diplomatic and religious links with Rome and the Near East. These details are simply inserted into the main theme of this section of the *Chronicle*, a first-hand account of Viking plundering up and down Europe. Most historians have speculated that this interest in the Continental adventures of the Viking army came from Frankish clergy who had suffered from the army's attentions or feared that they were at risk.

But it is far more likely that the author or compiler is simply quoting the words of a Viking commander, very likely a Danish earl or king who took service with Alfred as a military adviser or had been driven to seek sanctuary at his court to escape a blood-feud. He might even have had a genuine change of heart or decided that it was time to retire and live on his ill-gotten booty. A Viking leader who had undergone baptism, perhaps as the king's godson, will have been able to claim all kinds of privileges. This one was no doubt illiterate but able to chant an endless series of both traditional epics about heroes and royal ancestors of long ago, fairly intelligible to the English nobles, and also new ones praising his fellow Vikings and himself. The text of the *Chronicle* may be in part the summary of a list or programme of the new epics of a bloodstained life.

The Viking's story may have been intended to give the *Chronicle* a tense introductory build-up to the account of the fierce Viking invasion of 892–896, which follows. But as drama, if not as history, it is inferior to the section of the original *Chronicle* for the years 865 to 877, just as the next section, a prosy and long-winded journal of the invasion of the mid-890s, falls far short of the few terse sentences that tell of the fearful, but in the end triumphant, climax of 878.

880
a. The Viking army moved from Cirencester to East Anglia, which they colonised and divided.
b. The army from Fulham crossed the Channel to Ghent in Frankish territory and spent a year there.

881
a. The new army moved on inland. The Frankish army assembled and fought them.
b. After the battle the Danes rounded up horses to ride.

882
a. The army moved even further inland on the Maas [to Elsloo] and spent the year there.
b. Alfred took a fleet out to sea, attacked four Danish ships and took two of them, killing the crews. The other two ships surrendered after heavy losses in killed and wounded.

883
a. The Viking army moved up the River Scheldt to Condé [a nunnery] and spent the year there.

b. Pope Marinus [see 885g] sent Alfred a fragment of wood from the Cross.

c. Sigelm and Athelstan took the offerings to Rome and went on to the shrine of St Thomas and St Bartholomew in India [Edessa in Turkey], while the English campaigned against the Viking force in London. Thanks be to God that their prayers were answered.

884

a. The army went up the River Somme to Amiens and camped for a year there.

885

a. The Viking army split in two. One division went east into Europe; the other came and laid siege to Rochester, building themselves defensive works. The garrison held out until King Alfred brought up the army. The enemy took to their ships, abandoned their camp and horses, and sailed back across the Channel.

[885h should probably be read here]

b. King Alfred sent a fleet from Kent to East Anglia. In the mouth of the Stour they attacked and took sixteen Viking ships, killing the crews.

c. On their return voyage they were intercepted and defeated by a large Danish fleet.

d. Just before Christmas King Charles of France was killed by a boar; a year earlier his brother the king [Louis] in the west had died. Both were sons of King Louis [the Stammerer] who died in the year of the eclipse (879), son of King Charles [the Bald] whose daughter married our King Ethelwulf.

c. Charles [the Fat; soon deposed, see 887b] succeeded as king in the west from the Mediterranean to the Channel, as his great-grandfather [the Emperor Charlemagne] had ruled, except for Brittany. Charles was son of Louis [the German], brother of Charles [the Bald] the father of Judith, whom our King Ethelwulf married. They were sons of Louis [the Pious], son of old Charles [Charlemagne], son of Pippin.

f. A large Viking fleet, assembled in Lower Saxony [around Bremen or Hamburg], lost two great naval battles with the [German] Saxons and their Frisian allies.

g. The excellent Pope Marinus died. At King Alfred's request he had exempted the English quarter from tax and had also sent lavish gifts, including a fragment of the Cross on which Christ died.

h. The Danish army of East Anglia broke the peace with King Alfred.

886

a. The Danish division that had gone east turned west and went up the Seine to make winter camp at Paris.

b. King Alfred occupied London and entrusted the city to governor Ethelred.

c. All the English free from Danish rule gave Alfred their loyalty.

887

a. The Danish army went up the Seine above the bridge at Paris and on up the Marne to Chézy, spending two winters there and on the Yonne.

b. King Charles [the Fat, see 885f] of France died six weeks after being deposed by his nephew Arnulf. His kingdom was divided and five new kings were crowned with Arnulf's consent. He was the only one of royal blood through his father and grandfather. He ruled [Germany] east of the Rhine; Rudolph [count of Upper Burgundy] had the Middle Kingdom; Odo [count of Paris] the Western Kingdom [France]; Berengar [margrave of Friuli] and Guido [duke of Spoleto] divided up Lombardy and the lands over the Alps. This pair argued, fought two major battles [in 888–889], expelled each other and devastated the land.

c. Governor Ethelhelm [of Wiltshire] took the offerings of Alfred and his people to Rome.

888

a. Governor Beocca went to Rome with the offerings of the people of Wessex and of King Alfred.

b. Queen Ethelswith, Alfred's sister, died and was buried in Pavia.

c. Archbishop Ethelred [of Canterbury, 870–890] and governor Ethelwold [of Kent] died in the same month.

889

a. The mission to Rome did not take place; King Alfred sent two envoys with letters.

890

a. Abbot Beornhelm took the offerings of the people of Wessex and King Alfred to Rome.

b. King Guthrum the Viking, baptised as Alfred's godson with the name Athelstan, died. He was the first Dane to settle in East Anglia, where he remained.

c. The Danish army in Europe moved from the Seine valley to the Breton border at St Lô. The Bretons attacked and beat them, forcing them into a river where many drowned.

d. God and his people elected Plegmund archbishop of Canterbury [890–914].

891

a. The Danish army pushed on eastward. King Arnulf and the East-Frankish [German] army, with Old Saxon and Bavarian reinforcements, fought and defeated their mounted force before the ships came up.

b. Three Scots [Irish], Dubslane, Macbethu and Maelinmum, came in a boat without paddles. They had set off in secret, determined to roam abroad for the love of God, without caring where, with seven days' rations in a boat sewn from two and a half ox-skins. After seven days they landed in Cornwall and went straight to King Alfred. The most learned scholar of the Scots [Irish], Swifnch [Suibhne of Clonmacnoise], died.

c. At the end of April the star called [Halley's] Comet appeared. Some call it the 'long-haired star', as a long ray shines around it or on one side.

892

a. The great Danish army which had ravaged the Continent for twelve years left Germany and assembled at Boulogne.

b. They found enough ships for a single crossing with all their horses and gear and arrived in east Kent at the mouth of the River Lympne . . .

During Alfred's lifetime, we can identify a much larger number of fortified places than before, partly because the chronicles and other documentary sources are more abundant and more detailed, and so name more places likely to have been fortified. The pioneer study of the forts that Alfred organised, improvised or constructed, made more than eighty years ago and a notable achievement by the Liverpool-born wife of a Nonconformist minister in Leeds, is still of value today and has sometimes been drawn on without acknowledgement.[1]

This increase is found throughout Europe, where fortified local centres for defence and administration are everywhere distinctive of the late ninth and tenth centuries. This period saw a marked change from loosely controlled tribal forts and market centres to military bases linked to form a network or system within a recognisably bureaucratic organisation. At the same time there was a gradual change from essentially unstable empires and kingdoms to more durable states. We could well argue that the new forts, their garrisons and the organisation needed to make them effective were the vital element that brought stability to the areas that they protected and were thus crucial for the developing nations. Every European monarch or governor of a frontier province faced very similar problems with the same traditions and broadly comparable resources.

In their developed form these forts had three essential elements: defences; a local organisation for manning and maintenance and for assembling a field army; and a place in an overall national defence plan. Before the end of his reign in 899, Alfred had organised a regular defence system, adapting or constructing more than thirty strongholds in a circuit around his kingdom of Wessex, and introduced systematic arrangements for manning them. Each had a specified standard number of defenders, provided and supported by the main landowners and estates of the district, the length of stockade, rampart or wall being calculated by a simple equation based on common farm and taxation measures familiar to everyone.

Such an arrangement was universal in the ninth century, a legacy from the late Roman Empire as an obligation on land and landowners. In 808 when King Godfrid built a great rampart right across the Jutland peninsula to define and protect his kingdom, he 'divided the work up among his commanders'. In the 850s Pope Leo built the Leonine City around St Peter's at Rome in just the same way, as the surviving inscriptions show. In 868 King Charles the Bald 'measured the defences' of his twin forts at Pîtres or Pont de l'Arche and 'divided them into sections so many feet long, assigning responsibility for them to his magnates'.[2] No doubt, once Charles realised the problems and got things organised, all Frankish fortresses were built and maintained in a similar way and manned by forces supported by the local landowners on a regular system.

We can be sure that Alfred did exactly the same and that each of his forts was sited at his personal direction for construction, or for repair if the site was an ancient Roman city or earlier hill-fort, while the work was carried out by sizeable labour forces, mostly no doubt peasants drafted from all the great estates in the district assigned to each fort, working on their particular length. In the next reign the new author of the *Chronicle* tells us several times that King Edward remained in the area for four weeks while a fort was made.[3]

When each fort was put into service, sometimes after no more than a month's hectic work, we may be sure that it was blessed solemnly by the senior churchman available and very likely inaugurated with the sort of processional service with which Leo blessed his new defence work at Rome in 852. Public relations no doubt followed the same precedent. We must expect that every gate carried, carved in stone or painted on boards, a grandiloquent inscription in rather poor Latin, as at Rome, and that monograms of the fort's name and the monarch's name were freely dotted around on commemorative coins and door-jambs. We must stretch our imaginations to see the war-banners fluttering over the gates in the shape of or bearing images of the birds and beasts that had been adopted as family and personal totems. Did Alfred's father Ethelwulf, the 'Noble Wolf', ever adopt a wolf's head as his own or as one of a number of family emblems? Is the head on the Alfred Jewel at Oxford just this? Was the 'Bull Stake' at Oxford by the original Ox-ford a local or tribal totem?

What other examples were there for Alfred to follow? The English evidence has often been considered in too much of a vacuum as parallels can be found throughout Europe. Defence works, often accompanied by transfers of population, are well documented in every European kingdom and country with any sort of documented history; countries without annals or charters have plenty of archaeological evidence for defence works. We can glance at a few.

These systems of fortification may all have been inspired by the work of Pope Leo IV in and around Rome in the 850s which itself, as noted above, was only part of a gradual process which extended throughout the ninth century. On the southern frontier of the Frankish Empire, exposed to constant attack by Arab regular and piratical forces, the popes never lost their territorial power within the Carolingian Empire and the later kingdom of Italy. In their exposed position on the southern frontier of what was then becoming the Western world, they were among the most active and influential fortress builders of the day. Successive popes carried out at least ten defence schemes between the 840s and the 880s, all of them well documented because of their growing role as the centre of the Western Church. Seven of the projects were on new sites or among the ruins of towns and three involved the restoration of ancient Roman town walls.[4]

As Alfred himself saw as a small boy, the main new fortress at Rome protected St Peter's and the quarter of Rome most familiar and most dear to the English, as it also included the church of the Holy Spirit founded in the early 700s by Alfred's forebear, King Ine of Wessex, and the attached *schola* or hostel for English pilgrims. Close beside church and hostel, one of the three main gates of the fortress, the Porta Saxonum, the Saxon Gate, was no doubt manned by residents, diplomats and pilgrims from the English and other northern kingdoms. Early in Alfred's reign Pope John VIII (872–882) built another outlying fort around the basilica of St Paul outside the walls, naming it Johannipolis, 'John's City', which has produced fragments of dedication inscriptions with fine bold lettering.[5]

In France, at a royal assembly at Pîtres near Rouen in June 862, King Charles the Bald and his great nobles initiated a vigorous new defence policy by planning a defence system for the Seine. At Pont de l'Arche, above Rouen, they began two forts, each about 250m broad and 200m deep with timber-laced ramparts, linked by a pontoon or trestle bridge across the confluence of the Seine and the Eure, to stop Viking raids upriver. This worked, until the Vikings contrived to capture and hold the forts in 865–866. It took some time to recapture them and the whole operation was a fearful shambles until Charles realised he had to collect data on the resources of local estates, make regulations and enforce fortress-duty as an extra burden and make all necessary arrangements for manning them and the other similar twin river-forts that he planned. In 869 his council discussed making bishops responsible for defence while the counts enjoyed their traditional offensive role. Fortress-building continued in France, with at least nineteen documented forts being built by 900.

In 868 Charles had Angoulême, which had been sacked in 863, refortified and from 869 a steady programme of defence works appears in the records, with walled defences at Le Mans, Tours, Dijon and around the monastery of St Denis outside Paris, which had suffered in the sudden Viking attack of October 865.[6]

One direct result of Charles's new and in the end effective defence policy was the arrival in England of a Viking force, which landed on Thanet in 865, followed in 866 by the 'great army' which invaded East Anglia and was eventually to overrun and settle three of the four English kingdoms by 880. Other warbands tried to establish permanent footholds in France and in 872 a Viking force occupied and settled down to hold Angers, from which the residents had fled.

Over the last thirty years a group of circular fortresses has been recognised along the north coast of France, Belgium and Holland. Nine of them had been identified by the late 1980s and we can suspect that more remain to be discovered. They are not very large, 140m across the ramparts being the norm; so far a number of excavations, some on a very large scale, have not succeeded in establishing a precise date for any of them.[7] They have been hailed as constructions of the Emperor Louis the Pious in the 830s, but might equally be Danish forts run up by King Harald or his sons at some date between the 840s and the 880s, or the work of Louis' great-grandson Charles the Fat, who briefly united most parts of Charlemagne's empire in 885–887.

The Czech tribe took over other small Slavonic tribes and constructed a dramatic new central fort on the Hrad, still the focus of Bohemian aspirations. In the reign of Alfred's grandson Athelstan, the East-Frankish king applied a systematic plan of fortification to much of former West Germany and extended his kingdom to the River Elbe in 928–929 with many new forts.

The Asturian kings had expanded their realm in a long series of campaigns. We have briefly examined the campaigns of the 850s when they consolidated new territory with forts and farm-colonists.

While Alfred's son and daughter were extending the English kingdom northward with forts, the Asturians expanded to the south with twenty forts by 910 and some thirty by 915.

As we have seen, the *Chronicle* records numerous places where the Vikings established a camp for the winter and improvised or constructed defences for a stay of some duration. It notes the winter-camps on Thanet (851/2) and Sheppey (855/6), on Thanet again (865/6), somewhere in East Anglia (866/7), their base in York (867) and winter-camp at Nottingham (868/9) and in York again (869/70) and Thetford (870/1). These were the main bases for the elimination of three English kingdoms.

During the long attempt to bring down Wessex in the 870s, the *Chronicle* mentions the Viking camps at Reading (871/2), London (872/3), Torksey (873/4), Repton (874/5), Cambridge (875/6), Wareham (876), Exeter (876/7) and Gloucester (877/8). At Fulham (879) a new army mustered but was induced to move to France. In later campaigns it records their fortified base for the siege of Rochester (885) and camps at Appledore in south-east Kent (893), Milton and Benfleet on the Thames estuary in Kent and Essex respectively (both in 893), Shoebury in Essex (893), Mersea (894), Buttington on Severn (895), on the River Lea 30km above London (896) and at Bridgnorth on the Severn (895). These sites have all proved rather elusive to the archaeologist, or at least only Repton has been the object of determined campaigns of excavations.[8]

We may ask, what did the Vikings actually do in their numerous, and frequently changed, winter-camps, forts or bases? How far were these commercial enterprises with a range of goods on display, where governor Alfred of Surrey and his wife could pick and choose among the luxury gospel-books or perhaps find a slave skilled as a pastrycook, where bishops called in regularly to ransom a priest or two, while merchants and other outsiders brought goods to sell, and local peasants sold their ale and grain to the invaders for a good price? Or did the Vikings prepare grimly for foraging patrols, looking forward to feasting and revelry when they had brought in supplies for another few weeks? Most likely the atmosphere was not so very different from the times when a provincial governor was staying in the same centre.

And what were these camps like? How big were they? The one

at Repton was only 200m wide by 110m deep from the River
Trent. Only after a long programme of research and excavation of
royal and monastic sites, when scanty traces of brief Viking occupation and perhaps minor changes to the defences will eventually be
recognised on a whole series of sites, will we be able to discuss
such things more comprehensively.

That Alfred's arrangements for his forts were workmanlike and
effective is clear from the *Chronicle*'s account of the unsuccessful
Viking attack on Rochester in 885 by one wing of the great army
that had been terrorising north-east France and the Low Countries
and decided on a sudden cross-Channel strike. This is the first
record of any defended place in Alfred's realm being held successfully against a Viking attack and allows us to conclude that Alfred
had evolved a defence strategy for his kingdom and firmly imposed
new and rigorous obligations on his magnates to construct and
maintain fortresses and also man them permanently. He had begun
the work and also completed the most exposed defences well
enough to be tenable. That his strategy succeeded for another
generation is clear from the many recorded attacks on forts, some
of them new, in the 910s.

The *Burghal Hidage*, which may perhaps be described as our
earliest surviving administrative document of central government,
may be an updated version, made in the 910s, of a summary of
the defences of Alfred's kingdom drawn up in the early 880s when
the system was planned.[9] It lists thirty places (some texts give
thirty-three) with the number of hides, or land-assessment units
(perhaps of about 45ha) attached to each. It continues with a table
of lengths in poles and furlongs, which all landowners, farm-bailiffs
and peasant-farmers knew and used for measuring fields. A final
sentence then explains that a hundred and sixty men are needed
for every furlong of defence and every pole requires four men:

Eorpeburnan	324 hides
Hastings	500 hides
Lewes	1200 hides
Burpham	720 hides
Chichester	1500 hides
Portchester	500 hides
Southampton	150 hides

Winchester	2400 hides
Wilton	1400 hides
Chisbury	500 hides
Twyneham	470 hides
Wareham	1600 hides
Bridport	760 hides
Exeter	734 hides
Halwell	300 hides
Lydford	140 hides
Pilton	360 hides
Watchet	513 hides
Axbridge	400 hides
Lyng	100 hides
Langport	600 hides
Bath	1000 hides
Malmesbury	1200 hides
Cricklade	1400 hides
Oxford	1500 hides
Wallingford	2400 hides
Buckingham	1600 hides
Shaftsey	1000 hides
Eashing	600 hides
Southwark	1800 hides

To keep up and defend an acre's breadth of wall, 16 hides are needed. If one man comes from each hide, every pole of wall will be furnished with four men.

Thus 20 poles need 80 hides.

A furlong needs 160 hides by this reckoning.

Two furlongs need 320 hides;

Three furlongs take 480 hides;

Four furlongs need 640 hides.

Five furlongs of defence take 800 hides,

Six furlongs 960 hides,

Seven furlongs 1120 hides,

Eight furlongs 1280 hides,

Nine furlongs 1440 hides,

Ten furlongs 1600 hides,

Eleven furlongs 1760 hides

and an enclosure of twelve furlongs need 1920 hides.
For a longer defence-line it is simple to work out the extra hidage, as a furlong always needs 160 men and each pole requires 4 men.

Several versions of the text add, after Chisbury:

Shaftesbury   700 hides

and after Southwark:

All these total 27,070 hides for the 30
forts in Wessex; also
Worcester   1200 hides
Warwick   2400 hides

It should therefore be possible to match the nominal defensive circuit of each of the places named with an actual length of Roman city wall, prehistoric rampart or at least an evident likely stockade-line visible on the ground and on a large-scale map. In several cases the nominal length corresponds very closely with the Roman and medieval city wall; in others, as at Exeter, it does not. The 2400 hides at Winchester indicate a defence-line of 9900 feet or 3016m; the Roman walls measure 3033m, a discrepancy of only 17m. It must be said at once, however, that Alfred and his works have proved, in solid form, to be singularly elusive. There have been hundreds of excavations at the places named in this list and in the other places where Alfred's interest is documented in the *Chronicle*, in charters and on coins. No detail of any defence or street or structure of any kind has yet been identified and investigated in such detail that it can be securely dated and categorically assigned to Alfred.

The *Burghal Hidage* almost invites us to conclude that Alfred ordered a fairly detailed land survey of his realm to be carried out as the logistical and practical basis for manning and maintaining his forts, as Charles the Bald was eventually driven to do. At Easter 869, seven years after embarking on his defence projects, Charles 'sent letters throughout the kingdom instructing the bishops, abbots and abbesses to prepare lists of their estates showing how

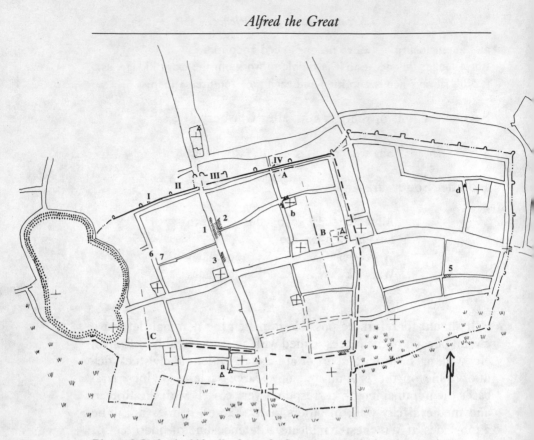

Plan of Oxford. Alfred's fort of *c.*895 must underlie the modern street plan. Ditch of stockade-trench or early fort: A to C. Turf rampart: I to IV. Late Saxon structures and roads: 1 to 3, see p. 190; 4, postholes, floors and pits; 5, pits; 6, occupation debris; 7, coin of Edward the Elder. Burials found under streets and buildings: a to d.

many "farms" [tax-assessment units] each of them contained, by the beginning of May. The royal tenants were to list the counts' estates while the counts listed those of their own tenants to report at the next assembly. A fighting man was to muster from every hundred "farms" and a two-ox cart from every thousand. The men were to finish and then garrison the stone-and-timber fort at Pîtres.'[10]

While preliminaries such as these were in motion, Alfred then had to ride across the general vicinity of a proposed stronghold,

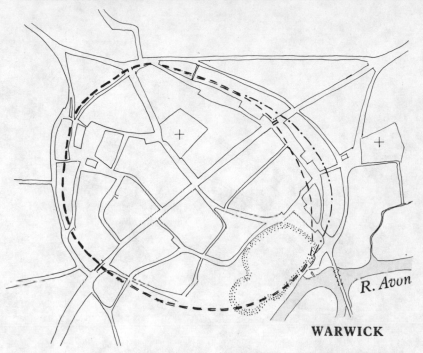

WARWICK

Plan of Warwick on a hill above the Avon. Alfred's daughter Ethelfleda built a fort here but it may already have been an important centre, perhaps a prehistoric hill-fort. The presumed rampart is indicated by dashes, the castle with dots and churches are shown by crosses.

as commanders and kings had done since time immemorial to choose the site, whether a former prehistoric hill-fort or river-fort with grass-grown rampart and ditch, a Roman town or fort with some surviving walls and ditch or a likely-looking defensible spot on a hill, at the confluence of two streams or in the bend of a river. After renting or buying the property, or simply evicting the owner with a promise of future compensation[11] and prayers to initiate the project, a labour force and raw materials had to be found. Thousands of peasants could be assembled, more or less willingly, by the king's order to the local governor, ministers and other landholders to assemble teams of woodsmen, carters, carpenters, shovel-men and basket-men, and quarrymen too if new stonework was intended. Organisation cannot have been a problem to

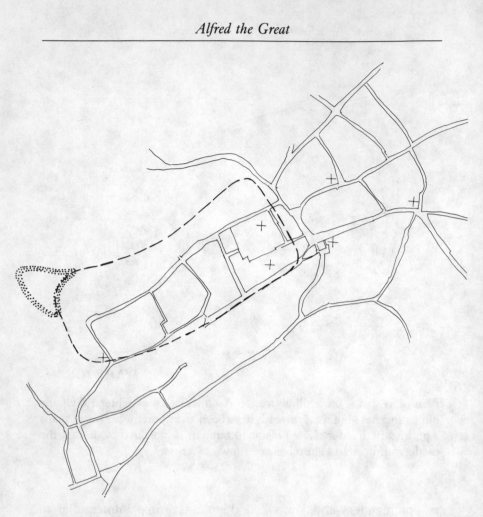

Plan of Shaftesbury on a spur rising 100m above the valleys to the top
left and bottom. The town lies outside Alfred's fort, which is marked by
dashes; medieval churches are indicated by crosses, the castle with dots.

governors and ministers accustomed to training the fighting men
of a district with the help of reeves and bailiffs used to mustering
their peasants for haymaking and harvest on the manor-farms.

A stockade was the first priority, requiring split timbers and a
post-trench, rather than a row of post-holes, for rapid construction.
A defensive ditch or ditches outside the stockade would provide
firstly turf for stacking behind the stockade and secondly subsoil

ÆLFRED REX HA
NC URBEM FECIT
ANNO DOMINIC
Æ INCARNATIO
NIS DCCCLXXX
REGNI SUI VIII

Drawing of a fragment of an inscribed stone found at Shaftesbury in 1902 and then lost, with missing parts of letters restored (shown by dashes), and (above) the full inscription restored, reading 'Alfred made this town in the year of (Christ's) incarnation 880 and the 8th of his reign'. Such inscriptions must have been carved on wood or stone at practically all forts of this time.

or rock that might be piled behind the stacked turf to form the beginnings of a rampart. A gate or gates for access completed the first stage of a fort, which could be defended during an emergency by the men assigned from the surrounding estates while they slept on the ground or lived in tents. For a longer occupation the new garrison required plots of land and buildings of some kind. As yet archaeology has provided no clear examples of reliably dated land divisions and primary buildings of any of Alfred's forts. Streets and something we might consider the outline of a town-plan may have been imposed much later across a fort. At least a third of the minor streets and back lanes of medieval Oxford are later changes, mostly of the early or mid-twelfth century, a pattern that may be broadly true of other places, while one of the main central streets, Cornmarket, seems to have been both reduced in width and shifted sideways in about the eleventh century. No element of the street plan can be assumed to have remained from the ninth century.[12]

The garrisons may have been second-line troops, rejects from the permanent military retinues of the great noblemen and lesser

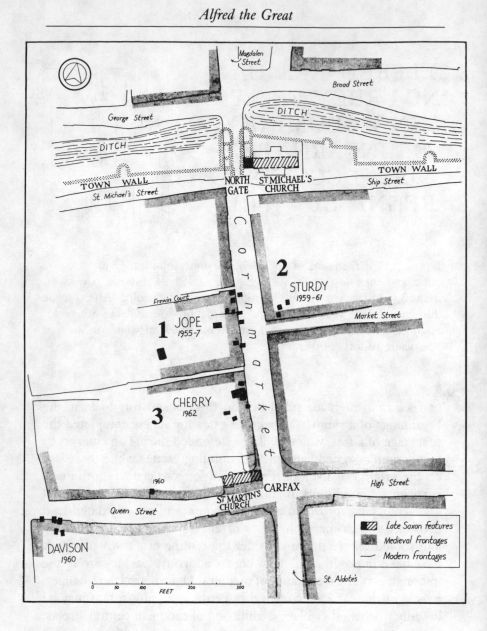

Late Saxon cellar-pits found in central Oxford. 1, pits taken to indicate that a narrow early street had been widened; 2, making it clear that a wide street had been narrowed; 3, showing the street was realigned when narrowed in the eleventh and twelfth centuries.

landowners. Or we can imagine that aged warriors no longer able to keep up on an arduous march were brought together from the governors' and ministers' firesides and concentrated in the forts. We might think of them, like all old soldiers, furtively selling off equipment, grain and iron from the garrison stores. Or perhaps Alfred imposed a great social change and peasants had to be recruited to fill up numbers. And we can wonder what chance single Danes or whole warbands stood of being taken on.

The great difference between forts of the late ninth century and earlier royal and church centres is that formerly they stood largely empty for much of the year and the magnates' retinues were constantly at their personal disposal. Alfred, like his fellow monarchs, made sure that his new or re-established forts were fully manned under a reeve or garrison commander personally responsible to him. As well as his own royal guards he thus had regional forces ready for use, a significant increase in power.

At the forts, no doubt initially outside the gates, serfs from the home-farms of nearby landowners and local peasants brought beasts, grain and other produce to sell in impromptu markets that, we can imagine, rapidly developed. Another germ of trade was the blacksmiths and other artisans to make and repair weapons and military equipment, craftsmen who may have been drafted to a fort and then attracted or developed some local business. Trade on any scale and the import of luxury goods from a distance were not relevant to a fort's main function, although no doubt a certain amount took place here and there, particularly in times of peace.

The notion, which began as a vague suggestion in the 1880s and gradually developed a life of its own, that Alfred established 'planned towns' with fully developed manufacturing and trading functions, with merchants, artisans and markets, is simply a myth.[13] Roads and lanes of various dates running off approximately at right angles to a spine road do not constitute 'planning' and no indisputable archaeological evidence for ninth-century trade or manufacture has yet been found at any of the places in the *Burghal Hidage*. The myth was further developed in the 1960s. On the basis of several broad sections meticulously excavated through one end of a single street at Winchester, we were assured that Alfred had planned nine kilometres of streets there and had eight thousand tonnes of cobbles dumped to form the road surfaces.[14]

Common sense tells us that a single example cannot sustain such sweeping conclusions and should never have been applied indiscriminately to twenty other streets and many other places.

During the two decades after his death, Alfred's son and daughter continued to build fortresses, so that in 925 his grandson Athelstan took over a kingdom, the nucleus of present-day England, very much larger than in Alfred's day and defended by over sixty forts, many of them large enough to serve as refuges for the local peasant-farmers and their herds and flocks.

We should probably envisage significant urban growth within and around some of the forts developing rather later in the tenth century, probably under continuing royal patronage in the hope of producing income, as commanders and kings had done since time immemorial. It is noticeable that in 1086 towns were much more lightly taxed in relation to their recorded population than country estates, allowing us to suspect that royal and noble patronage were still vital to the success of any town.

12

The Church and Culture

IN 893 ASSER GAVE US A TOUCHING PORTRAIT of the mature Alfred in peacetime at his books and at prayer, looking back over the eight years he had known him.[1] Alfred himself, hard at work on his personal literary project, an unparalleled attempt to put the knowledge and standards of the ancient world before the English of his own day, had been forced to set all this aside and prepare yet again for war.

Bishops had a vital role in the small English kingdoms of the ninth century. They were spiritual and cultural leaders and also territorial magnates with great estates. At court they advised the kings as active members of central government, providing, with their priests, necessary secretarial staff with many administrative skills. They were usually chosen from priests of royal, princely or noble blood, who moved naturally in court circles, and especially from those who had distinguished themselves in administration or other court duties.

When in their bishoprics, they rode round from property to property with large retinues of priests and the fighting men of their bodyguard, inspecting the work that their reeves were carrying out in exploiting natural resources and managing the peasants and their farms. Many of their estates had been well-endowed independent minster churches which, as charters make clear, fell increasingly into the bishops' control in this period. In their cathedral 'cities' they had to find time from meetings and paperwork to lead the worship in their cathedrals.

The bishops and their warriors played a key role in national and international politics. As landed magnates they counterbalanced the governors, who tended to accumulate property and power as well as authority in their own provinces. They also fought manfully in battle. We have read of Bishop Ealhstan of Sherborne (824–867) as a commander of Ethelwulf's expedition into Kent in about 827 and of his part in victory over the Vikings at the Parrett mouth in 845.

His short-lived successor Heahmund can be traced as a priest at court in 854, in 863 and in 864.[2] He may have been appointed bishop, as many medieval priests were, as a reward for skills in government, like being able to bring forward the right charter from a stack of files in a legal dispute or write a new charter in fifteen minutes. Administrative skills were not enough for a bishop in those violent days; he fell in battle at Meretun in 871.

The churchmen who assisted King Alfred in recreating learning and spiritual life are not much better documented than the noblemen, although they and their priests were literate and kept records.

We know most about Werferth, bishop of Worcester. King Burgred of Mercia nominated him to succeed Bishop Ealhun or Alhwine of Worcester who died in 872 after about twenty-five years in his see. Through the chances and vagaries of the survival of archives, Worcester is the best documented bishopric of the century overall. Except perhaps for Archbishop Wulfred of Canterbury (805–832), we know more about Werferth or Waerfrith of Worcester, one of King Alfred's closest associates, than about any other churchman of the ninth century.

We can say a surprising amount about Werferth and his household, always assuming that the same name in a series of documents quite close in date often represents one person while the same name over a broad range of dates may be father and son, uncle and nephew, godfather and godson, if not a rare long-lived individual. A relevant example is two bishops of Rochester, Wermund I (781/5–803/5) and Wermund II (845/62–860/8), presumably uncle and nephew or great-nephew. The practice, widespread in Saxon times, of alliterating the first letter or repeating the first element of the father's name for sons and the mother's more often for daughters, allows us to reconstruct families, however tentatively.

Born in about 830 to a noble family established in both Middlesex, which was still Mercian territory, and also Kent (which had been a kingdom, then a Mercian dependency until conquered by Wessex in about 827), Werferth was perhaps a son of Werenberht, governor perhaps of Middlesex and the Chilterns, who rose in seniority in the strict hierarchy of Mercian civil administrators from nineteenth place in 845 to third in 855;[3] he may have been a godson and nephew of Bishop Wernbeorht of Leicester (801/3–814/6). A younger Werenberht, who may have been Werferth's brother, appears as a minister in Mercian charters of 845–862.[4]

We may identify two Kentish abbots as close relatives in the Wer– family. Wernod of St Augustine's at Canterbury (*c.*833–845) and Werhard of Christ Church, Canterbury (*c.*838–845) may have been Werferth's uncles. As young priests they may have played some part in the deep-seated quarrel between King Coenwulf of Mercia (796–821) and their kinsman Archbishop Wulfred (805–832). They flourished after the conquest of Kent, when King Egbert of Wessex installed his son Ethelwulf as junior king in Kent; Werferth probably began his career in the Church at Canterbury, the obvious place for advancement, especially with relatives in high places. Another kinsman, the moneyer Werheard, no doubt named for the abbot, began his career in finance at Canterbury.

To set Werferth in a likely family background in rather more detail, we must examine three charters which bracket 830, the likely date, within five or ten years, of Werferth's birth. The first survives in three medieval copies of relatively late date, in thirteenth- and fourteenth-century property books. It tells us that in 826 Archbishop Wulfred and his *familia*, or religious household, at Minster, a wealthy nunnery in his special patronage, traded an estate at Doddingland for one at Ealdanford (both unidentified but no doubt in Kent) with Abbot Wernod and the *familia* of St Augustine's.[5]

The second document is a will, possibly of 833 and certainly of the 830s or '40s. Like most Anglo-Saxon charters, it survives as a copy, rather earlier than that of the exchange we have just noted, in a twelfth-century register of property deeds at Canterbury. Like many other charters that survive as copies, it has undergone some changes to the original wording. Here the monk or scribe who compiled the register at Canterbury took a document written in Old English and, for convenience and uniformity, translated it into Latin as he copied it out.[6] The priest Werhard bequeathed to the cathedral at Canterbury thirteen substantial estates, including 'Harrow or Hergas in Middlesex, where his kinsman Archbishop Wulfred had given him 104 hides'. Other sources tell us that Werhard was abbot of Christ Church, the cathedral at Canterbury, by 838 and was still in office, as this charter shows, in 845. He is presumably the Abbot Werhard who witnessed a charter of Mede-hamsted abbey (later Peterborough cathedral) in 852.[7] No doubt his kinsman Archbishop Wulfred had appointed him to head the cathedral when he imposed a more regular monastic rule on the hitherto lax clergy.

The third charter, of 845, is one of the rare documents of the time that survives in its original form in Latin as a single sheet of parchment in the British Library.[8] As the opening sentence tells us, it is a *vicissitudo agellorum*, an exchange of farms, between 'Uuer-hard priest and abbot' and 'the king's minister Werenberht'. In the main clause:

> I prefect Uuerenberht give land of one mower, to Abbot Vuerheard in exchange for other similar land which also lies in the middle of that field which is known by the local people as *Et Hroces Seadum* [Roxeth in Middlesex] with all the fields and woods and meadows and all conveniences rightly and properly belonging to it. This farm used formerly to belong to that celebrated village called *Et Grenan Forda* [Greenford, also in Middlesex]. I give it to be granted as an eternal inheritance for him to hold and possess and fruitfully enjoy with the same liberty which previously . . .

The charter is very precisely dated and located to Sunday 8 November 845 in the city of London, when there was clearly a major church event; Archbishop Ceolnoth of Canterbury (833–870) and nine other bishops make up the witness-list with the two prime agents. We could note in passing that Ceolnoth may well have been a Mercian prince, one of a group of rival royal clans, and closely related to the last king of Mercia, Ceolwulf II (874–*c.*881/2).

We must presume that Abbot Werhard and the 'prefect' Weren-berht were kinsmen, perhaps adjusting their shares of a bequest or joint investment. From this basis of a noble clan almost monopolising church posts in Canterbury and controlling vast estates of thousands of acres of their own and of church land, we can now turn back to their younger relative Werferth.

As an able priest trained at Canterbury and of noble blood, Werferth may have been given accelerated promotion, not in Mercia, but in Wessex, the kingdom which now held Kent and the whole south-east. An Abbot Werferth appears in the witness-lists of at least twelve charters of the kings of Wessex between 854 and 862: in the six relating to king Ethelwulf's special offerings to the Church or 'decimations' in 854, a group of gifts to Winchester cathedral also in 854, and three others about royal gifts, in 854 to Malmesbury abbey, in 856 to a *thegn* or 'minister' Aldred and in 860/2 to Bishop Wermund II of Rochester.[9]

While, of course, there may have been another priest of this name, there is a very good chance that the abbot, still perhaps in his twenties, was the future Bishop Werferth. In all the lists he appears beside Abbot Wullaf and very close to King Ethelwulf's two youngest sons, Ethelred and Alfred. Just after the two princes all the lists name minister Esne. These five names adjoin each other, in one order or another, so often that we cannot resist the belief that in successive court ceremonies they regularly stood next to each other in a group, the two abbots as tutors to the two young princes and Esne as their keeper or governor. This suggestion explains Werferth's 'special relationship with the king' shown in Alfred's 'will'.[10]

Wullaf was abbot of Malmesbury, to judge from the witness-lists of two charters about Malmesbury estates, of 844 and 850,[11] but there is no hint of the whereabouts of Werferth's abbey. Twenty and thirty years later there was a Bishop Esne, to whom King Alfred intended in his 'will' to leave a large cash bequest of a hundred mancuses and who leased three estates around Taunton to various *thegns*.[12] It is just possible that minister Esne became a priest in his later years and ultimately an assistant bishop. He did not have a regular bishopric and may have been, as Finberg suggested, in charge of Somerset as deputy to the bishops of Sherborne.

Werferth does not appear in any ecclesiastical manifestation in the fairly scanty historical record of the 860s. The abbot may, of course, have died and have been an entirely different person. He may have been away from court engaged in multifarious duties for his abbey, or in all kinds of financial and administrative work for the kings of Wessex, or equally Mercia.

Werferth was consecrated bishop of Worcester on 7 June 873, having been appointed some time the previous year by King Burgred and his council. It is tempting to suggest that he was recommended for the post by the young and newly crowned Alfred, his old pupil paying a great compliment. If this is so, Alfred may have been trying to bring Mercia into even closer relations than before, desperately anxious to keep and buttress an ally against the marauding Vikings. Werferth's name means 'Treaty of Peace' and if he was, as the evidence of his name suggests, of Mercian noble blood, though educated and trained in religion and government in Wessex, Alfred may have intended him for a special role in reconciliation.

By now probably in his early forties, Werferth knew that a bishop's life could be long, active and warlike or short and bloody, without very much in between. He must have known Bishop Eahlstan (824–867), who had marched to conquer Kent and the south-east for King Egbert of Wessex, and Bishop Heahmund (868–871), killed in battle by the Vikings a few weeks before Alfred came to the throne the year before. Werferth managed to avoid such a fate and held his bishopric for forty-two years, until he was probably well into his eighties.

Werferth was active in reorganising church life, badly shattered by the Viking raids, in the new province. One charter shows him making a fortress 'for the protection of all the people' at Worcester at the command of governor Ethelred and Alfred's daughter Ethelfleda.[13] Another shows him reorganising the property of an ancient minster church at Pyrton in the foothills of the Chilterns in Oxfordshire, moving his peasant-farmers or serfs around on his lands.[14] Two more, of 889 and 898, again show him involved, with Alfred and Ethelred, in the refounding and planning of London.[15]

Werferth's activities are quite well covered in charters of his time, which show him seven times witnessing charters at sessions of the council or court of Alfred's province of Mercia; four times engaged in organising cities and four times dealing with what were properly the estates of churches other than his own; three times leasing out the estates of his bishopric and three times being involved in final settlements after court cases about his estates;

once shifting an estate from his cathedral clergy to his own direct control, once selling an estate outright and only once acquiring a new estate, or rather group of estates.

Werferth's first recorded action as bishop was to sell off land on lease to raise cash to pay off the Vikings in 872 before his actual consecration as bishop; he sold a four-life lease of Nuthurst, a hamlet in Hampton-in-Arden, Warwickshire.[16]

In 899 he gave the priest Werwulf, perhaps a kinsman to judge from the Wer– in his name, a two-life lease of Ablington on Coln, a Gloucestershire property of the bishopric of 600 nominal acres. This was a special favour, 'because of our long-standing comrade-ship and his faithful love and obedience'. Werwulf may be identi-fied as the 'Wærulf presbyter' who was the eighth of nineteen witnesses to a charter by which King Alfred granted North Newn-ton, Wiltshire to governor Ethelhelm.[17] He is obviously the man referred to by the Welsh Bishop Asser when he writes of 'Æthelstan and Werwulf, priests and chaplains, Mercians by birth and learned men' whom Alfred summoned from Mercia to help in his writing projects.[18]

Six charters, of 872, 889, 892, 899, 904 and 899/904, have witness-lists that must list the bishop's priests and household retainers.[19] Altogether, so far as this evidence goes, he had on his staff at one time or another between 872 and 904 more than fifty men, twenty-one of them clergy and thirty-one laymen. Each list names between nine and thirty individuals, important enough to be considered fit witnesses of the bishop's property affairs and legal business; on average there were nineteen, seven clergy and twelve laymen, at any one time. We can suppose that some of these men themselves had lesser retinues, but we can merely guess that the priests often had two or three assistants, servants, escorts or grooms and that the laymen were *thegns* present on escort duty with as many as ten fighting men and perhaps as many servants and grooms.

It is thus quite likely that Bishop Werferth rode round the country, visited his estates and attended affairs of state with an ecclesiastical and secretarial staff of twenty or thirty and an escort or bodyguard of more than one hundred armed men with as many grooms and carters again.

13

892–899, The Third Crisis and Final Peace

THE VIKING ARMY WHICH HAD ASSEMBLED AT FULHAM in 879 and had devastated the Continent since 880, briefly returning to attack Rochester in 885, crossed back to Kent in 892, to begin a brutal four-year assault on Wessex helped by the Danes already settled in England.

Alfred's newly contrived defence system held firm; only one unfinished fort is recorded as having fallen in a war of raids and instant pursuits, sieges and sea-fights and very few battles on land. During the war, we can safely infer, some new forts, among them Oxford, were established to cover major strategic 'gateways' that turned out to be inadequately covered in this violent war of movement.

Our main, practically our only, evidence for these years of war is the *Chronicle* for 892 to 896, the first section to be added to the original 'standard' text. Its long and meticulously detailed account of each season's campaign differs in many respects from the terse dramatic prose of the years 835–878. The new section is a revised and improved version of a 'war diary'. We can speculate that it was dictated by a timid staff officer, a minister not really up to his job, to a bellicose priest acting as his scribe. After the event they, or their patron and commander, went through it adjusting details which had shown up their poor staff-work, to evade criticism. It has a distinct whiff of self-justification; the authors may have been consciously glossing over some of the truth. We must remember too that they took for granted a range of knowledge about military practice and the places and people involved. As before we will take the words of the *Chronicle* as our starting point.

892

a. The great Danish army which had ravaged the Continent for twelve years left Germany and assembled at Boulogne.

b. They found enough ships for a single crossing with all their horses and gear and arrived in east Kent at the mouth of the River Lympne, which flows out of the great forest of the Weald, which is a hundred and twenty miles east–west by thirty miles across. They rowed four miles inland to the forest edge, stormed an unfinished fort manned by a few rustics, and fortified a base-camp at Appledore.

c. Soon after, Haesten invaded the Thames mouth with eighty ships and built a fort at Milton.

893

a. A year after the Vikings constructed these strongholds, the Danes settled in Northumbria and East Anglia mobilised to fight with and for the invaders. They had sworn solemn undertakings to King Alfred and the latter had given six initial hostages.

b. Alfred assembled his main army and took up a strategic position midway between the two enemy camps, very handy for safeguarding wood and water.

c. The enemy sent out skirmishers and mounted patrols searching for gaps in the defence and almost every day we sent out daylight and night patrols from the army and the fortresses.

d. The king's army reforms kept half the warriors on duty and half in reserve, apart from the garrisons.

d. The Vikings came out of the base-camps twice, when they first arrived and when they left.

f. We caught them at Farnham, marching north with quantities of loot to join their ships on the Thames and cross to Essex. We defeated them and recovered the booty. The fleeing Vikings could not find a ford, crossed the Thames somehow and took refuge on an island in the River Colne.

g. We blockaded them there while rations lasted. Supplies and time ran out and our men dispersed while Alfred was bringing the reserves to continue the blockade, leaving the Vikings and their king who had been too badly wounded to be moved.

h. Launching several hundred ships, the Danes from Northumbria and East Anglia sailed up and down the south coast. A squadron of forty ships attacked a fort in north Devon and the main fleet attacked Exeter.

i. At this news, the king rode west for Exeter with the main army.

j. He left a small force to go on east to London. With the garrison and other English support they advanced to Benfleet, which Haesten had fortified with his army from Milton. The great army from Appledore on the Lympne had joined him.

k. Finding the army in camp and Haesten away on a raid, we attacked and stormed the base, capturing all the booty and the Vikings' women and children. We sent these to London, towed some ships to London and Rochester and smashed up or burnt all the rest.

l. The captives included Haesten's wife and two young sons, who had previously been baptised, with Alfred standing godfather to one and governor Ethelred to the other. At that time Haesten had sworn oaths and given hostages to Alfred, who had given princely gifts in return.

m. But as soon as he got to Benfleet and fortified it, Haesten had gone out to devastate the province governed by his own son's godfather, Ethelred, and was away on another raid when we took his base.

n. Despite this, our king sent back the woman and her boys.

o. Alfred reached Exeter to find that the attackers had retreated to their ships.

p. While he was occupied in the west with the army [of settled Danes], the other two armies [of plundering Vikings] had reformed and fortified a base at Shoeburyness in Essex. They set off on a pillaging raid up the Thames [and across the Cotswolds] to the Severn and up the river.

q. Three governors, Ethelred, Ethelhelm and Ethelnoth, and the off-duty ministers from all the king's forts [military districts] east of the River Parrett, from both sides of Selwood and from north of the Thames and west of the Severn, with Welsh support, concentrated to trap the raiders at Buttington on the banks of the Severn. We barricaded them in and maintained a blockade on both sides of the river for weeks, while the king was occupied with the Viking fleet in Devon.

r. Desperate from hunger with many dead of starvation and some surviving by eating nearly all the horses, they broke out east of the river. We won a savage battle, losing Ordheah and many others. Some Danes escaped, but their casualties from the slaughter were very heavy.

s. The survivors rallied back at their base in Essex and managed to recruit a strong force from Northumbria and East Anglia before winter. Sending their women, ships and booty to East Anglia for safety, they rode day and night to Chester, a deserted city in the Wirral.

t. Unable to halt them before they seized the fortress, our forces besieged the place for two days, drove off all cattle, burnt the crops or fed them to our horses and wiped out all the foraging parties we could catch.

THIS WAS JUST A YEAR AFTER THEY CROSSED THE CHANNEL

894

a. Driven from the Wirral by our scorched earth tactics, the Danes went west into Wales. On their way back with their loot, they crossed Danish territory in the north and Midlands to reach Mersea Island in Essex.

b. The other Danish force which had threatened Exeter ravaged Sussex on their return voyage. The Chichester garrison drove them off with hundreds of fatal casualties and captured some ships.

c. Early that winter the Danes from Mersea rowed into the Thames and up the Lea.

THIS WAS TWO YEARS AFTER THEY CROSSED THE CHANNEL

895

a. The Vikings on the Lea fortified a base twenty miles above London.

b. Most of the London garrison and other forces attacked them and were defeated, losing four royal officers.

c. In autumn the king camped close to the Viking stronghold, to protect the farmers at harvest and ensure that the Danes could not stop them.

d. Making a personal reconnaissance, riding along the river, the king found a spot to block the river and prevent them getting the ships out. With the barrier in place and two forts, either side of the river, begun, the enemy realised that their ships were trapped.

e. They abandoned them, checked that their women were safe in East Anglia, raided overland to Bridgnorth on the Severn and camped for the winter.

THIS WAS THREE YEARS SINCE THEY SAILED INTO THE LYMPNE

896

a. This summer the enemy dispersed. One group set off to East Anglia and another to Northumbria. Those who were still penniless scrounged some ships and went back to their old life across the Channel, raiding up and down the Seine.

b. By God's grace this invasion had not affected us too disastrously. Far more serious were the outbreaks of both cattle fever and the plague which had struck down many promising officials during those three years. Among the most distinguished of the fatalities were Bishop Swithwulf of Rochester (*c.*870–*c.*895), governor Ceolmund of Kent, governor Brihtwulf of Essex, governor Wulfred of Hampshire, Bishop Ealhheard of Dorchester (*c.*883–*c.*895), minister Eadwulf from Sussex, Beornwulf the reeve of Winchester and the king's marshal Ecgwulf.

c. The Danes of Northumbria and East Anglia endlessly raided the south coast with squadrons of ships, left from the old days.

d. To cope with them, King Alfred built a fleet of double-size ships, some with as many as sixty oars. They proved to be faster and more stable, as well as higher, than the others. This was a completely new design, owing nothing to Frisian and Danish models, worked out by the king as the optimum solution.

e. When a squadron of six Viking ships was ravaging the coast between the Isle of Wight and Devon, the king sent nine of his new ships after them.

f. They caught the enemy ships in an estuary, three afloat and the others beached, with the crews on shore. We boarded and captured two of the first three in the river mouth, killing the crews. Five survivors escaped on the third ship when our ships grounded on the ebb-tide. Three ran aground near the beached ships, the rest on the other side of the channel, each group unable to help the other. At low water, the Danes from the beached ships attacked our three on that side. In the combat we lost Lucuman the reeve, the three Frisians Wulfhard, Ebba and Ethelhere with Ethelferth the king's servant; in all sixty-two Frisians and English for a hundred and twenty Danes. The shallower Danish ships, afloat before ours, were able to row off and escape.

g. With these severe losses they could not row past the Sussex coast and two of the three ran aground. The captured crews were brought to Winchester before the king, who had them all hanged. A single ship reached port in East Anglia, with heavy loss.

h. This year they lost twenty ships and crews on the south coast.

i. Marshal Wulfric the Welsh-reeve died.

The action of this war shifted abruptly from the London region to the Severn valley or Cheshire and then suddenly back again. Whenever the Vikings made a dash for new, unravaged territory, as they did so often in the 860s and 870s, the English followed in close pursuit. We can follow the action from the *Chronicle* without much comment.

At one stage in 893, when Alfred himself was in Devon, relieving Exeter from a Viking assault, large reinforcements of Danes from Northumbria and East Anglia arrived at the main Viking camp near Southend in Essex. This combined force set off overland to raid along the Thames and Severn valleys. They were trapped, blockaded and fought to a standstill at Buttington in Montgomeryshire by three of Alfred's provincial governors, Ethelred of Mercia, Ethelnoth of Somerset, both of whom we have encountered above, and Ethelhelm of Wiltshire. Showing a mobility to equal that of the Vikings, the last two and their fighting men had ridden 300km from home.

After two more seasons' campaigning up and down the Midlands, with raids to Chester and Bridgnorth, the Vikings finally dispersed. Those who had accumulated enough loot to be able to afford it went to buy land and settle among their recent allies in East Anglia, the East Midlands or the north. 'Those that were moneyless' had to return to their old life raiding along the Seine. The crisis revealed the need for some additional defence points and Oxford must have been established at this time as one of them, most probably in 895. This was the year that saw the end of the long-range raids up and down across the Midlands.

897–899: PEACE AT LAST

The peaceful final years of Alfred's reign are poorly documented. There was no external threat to the kingdom and no writer emerged with the dramatic flair of the author of the *Chronicle* up to 891 or the craving for tedious military detail of the scribe whose account of the years 892–896 forms the next major section. The *Chronicle*'s long-running narrative which has formed the backbone of this book tells only of two minor details before leaving the last full two years of the reign blank:

897
a. Nine days before midsummer governor Ethelhelm of Wiltshire died.
b. Bishop Heahstan of London [*c.*890–897] also died.

In fact we are driven to conclude that the *Chronicle* was set aside and not kept up at all for some years, perhaps as much as two decades, until an ambitious protégé of King Edward the Elder took it up in the second decade of the tenth century, when Edward embarked on his conquest of the Midlands and all the Viking settlers there. The writer of this new set of annals may have intended them to be a new history of Edward's reign, a free-standing work of its own, that happened casually to be copied by another scribe to fill the last few folios of a copy of the *Chronicle*.

Without any real narrative, we make the best use we can of the other evidence we can rely on. A charter dated 898 by which Alfred granted to governor Sigilm an estate at Farleigh on the Medway in Kent fills some of our needs. The document, a single sheet of parchment, survives in the cathedral archives at Canterbury. Experts have, as so often, found fault with it: in 1904 as composed in a 'language ... considerably later than Alfred's time' and in 1931 as written in a hand that was 'probably un-English' and 'somewhat later in date' than Alfred's reign, which are good reasons to believe it original.[1]

+In the name of our Lord I Ælfræd, by the grace of God king of the Saxons, grant in perpetual ownership to my faithful governor Sigelm one hide of land of my own property at the place which is known as Fearnleag [*with a large marsh of six acres of meadow fields north of the property bounding on Eadwald Sibirhtigne's land*] for a satisfactory payment, for him to have and hold as long as he lives; and after he has left this life, he is to have the power of granting it to whoever he wishes. This grant was made in the year *DCCCXCVIII* since Christ

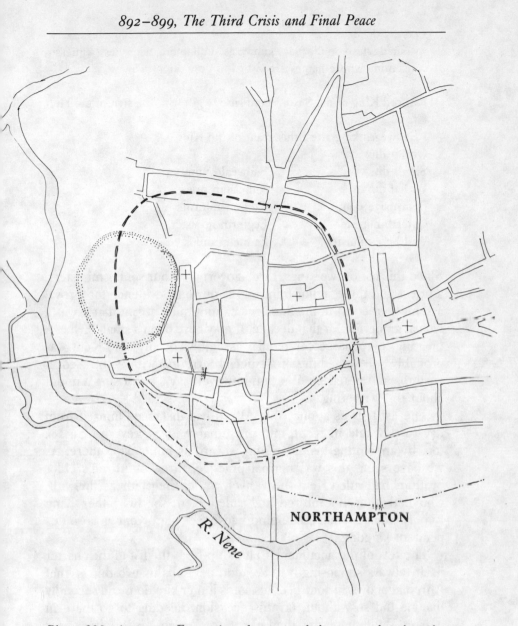

NORTHAMPTON

R. Nene

Plan of Northampton. Excavations have revealed a stone church and a nearby stockade and ditch (marked) of about the eighth century and many house remains. A Viking army based here raided the Cotswolds in 913 and submitted to Alfred's son Edward in 914. A probable Viking defence is marked with dashes, the medieval line by double-dotted dashes, the castle with dots and crosses indicate churches.

was made flesh, in the place known as Wulfamere, with these witnesses consenting whose names are sworn to be written below

I Alfred King of the Saxons confirm my gift with the sign of the Holy Cross
I Eadweard king attest this grant of the King
Ordlaf dux

Sigulf dux	Eadweald minister
Wullaf dux	Æthelstan priest
Beorhtsige minister	Cuthulf minister
Osferth minister	Ecgferth minister
Wulfhere minister	Eadhelm minister

Since this list of two kings, three governors, four senior ministers, a priest and three junior ministers is our only evidence for a royal assembly or court in the 890s, we cannot quite affirm that it was a typical gathering for that decade. It may have been a small business meeting, not a large ceremonial assembly. In any case Kent was probably still something of a 'special territory' with its own court customs and practices. We can, however, say a surprising amount about this gathering.

The list tells us at once that Alfred had distanced himself from day-to-day rule in Kent, and presumably in Surrey and Sussex too, by appointing his elder son Edward as junior king there. As we have seen, this was normal practice; three of Alfred's elder brothers had ruled Kent successively under their father Ethelwulf, who had himself captured and ruled Kent for his father King Egbert, whose father Ealhmund had once ruled Kent as an independent kingdom.

The text of the document, to look up from the list to the charter itself (always supposing it to be genuine), tells us two things, that Alfred kept overall control of his son's junior kingdom and secondly that he did so without, on this occasion, needing to go there in person. Wulfamere, the 'the Lake of the Wolves', is Woolmer near Selborne in Hampshire, not a place but a forest a mile or two from the Surrey border. Alfred was presumably there for a few days' hunting and chose to combine it with holding court for Kentish matters. Or perhaps he knew that he had to sit as an appeal court checking judgements in a series of Kentish cases and chose

Woolmer as a spot convenient for himself and for witnesses and officials from Kent, where he could get some sport with his son and the Kentish nobles.

Of the fourteen men involved in this charter, more than one-third were dead within five years, Alfred himself by natural causes at the age of fifty and the other four in battle, in the worst succession crisis ever to affect Alfred's family. Sigelm, Sigulf and Eadwald died because of their own lack of discipline, ignoring the orders of King Edward, also mentioned in this charter. The last, Beorhtsige, died fighting against Edward, having joined the rebels supporting Edward's cousin Ethelwold. The resumed *Chronicle*, probably written up retrospectively, tells us about the action, which took place in 903, in some detail.

Sigelm's daughter Eadgifu became the third wife of King Edward the Elder, probably long after his death in battle in 903. His own insubordination as a commander of the Kentish contingent brought about the disaster, in which his son Sigeberht was also killed. Governor Sigewulf, perhaps a brother or cousin of Sigelm, was also involved in the delay and defeat in 903, in which he too lost his life.

We have already discussed Ordlaf and Wullaf, and the Wulf family; Beorhtsige was from a family of chiefs or princes who had ruled in Essex or the Home Counties. He fell in battle in 903 as Brihtsige, as a commander in the Viking army of Alfred's nephew Ethelwold. His father Beornnoth has appeared as a Mercian governor under every regime from the 840s to the 880s.

Osferth

Minister Osferth was one of Alfred's closest relatives and most intimate associates throughout his reign, most likely a cousin on his mother's side and probably not, as has recently been suggested, a bastard son.[2] In the early 880s in his 'will' Alfred earmarked seven estates, all in Sussex, for 'my kinsman Osferth', who was also to receive a hundred mancuses, as were Alfred's nephews, Ethelhelm and Ethelwold, and each of his governors. Osferth does not appear in any record between the early 880s and the late 890s. He figures in the witness-lists of many charters between 898 and 934, in a variety of roles in five charters, all at least partly authentic, before 909 and then invariably as a governor under Edward the Elder.

In 898 Osferth was seventh of thirteen signatories and second of seven ministers; in 901 next after King Edward he was second of twenty-nine witnesses; in 903 he was twelfth of twenty-five witnesses at the court of the province of Mercia, after the king, the joint governors, the archbishop and bishops and Edward's younger brother Ethelward; in 904 he was third of thirty-six witnesses directly after King Edward and his brother Ethelward; and in 909 he was described as *propinquus regis*, the 'king's kinsman', and listed tenth of fifty-one witnesses.[3]

Osferth was born, we can infer, in about the early 860s, the son of a brother or close cousin of Alfred's mother; perhaps his father was governor Osric of Hampshire. During the 880s and early 890s he served as one of Alfred's close personal attendants and was thus not eligible to be named as a witness. As a minister between 898 and 909, in Alfred's last years and the first years of his son's reign, he was a particularly intimate royal adviser. In his mid-forties Osferth was promoted governor. He was to hold this high office throughout the reign of King Edward the Elder and well into that of Alfred's grandson Athelstan, when he must have been in his seventies, a grizzled veteran of unimaginable experience, a companion and survivor of Alfred's darkest days at Athelney. In his teens he may have commanded a company of the royal guards at Edington. But until very recently historians have mentioned him only in footnotes. His fellow minister Eadwald has been noted in our short 'Life' of his father Acca.

THE LESSER RANKS OF SOCIETY

Below the tiny ruling class, about which we can discover and deduce a certain amount, we can dimly perceive small and varied groups, who may be lumped together to form almost a kind of middle class, of full-time artisans, warriors, merchants and priests. Our knowledge of these people is poor; we have no real idea which craft-skills had become specialised and which were broadly spread among the serfs and peasants. We can distinguish from the peasantry those specialist craftsmen who worked full-time for a wage, perhaps most often in the retinue of kings, bishops and noblemen.

One particular group about which we have a large mass of data from independent sources is the moneyers. Almost all silver pennies of the ninth century carry the name of the king, usually around a schematic representation of his head on the front, or as numismatists say the obverse, and the name of the man responsible for making it, the moneyer, quite often with the place of issue, on the back or reverse. The coin supply was evidently privatised and contracted out by the crown. We should perhaps look on most moneyers of Alfred's time as goldsmith-bankers from established dynasties of goldsmiths who had long specialised in or had a side-line in minting coins. But some may be royal ministers who later moved on up the career ladder of public service.

Several of these dynasties are evident from their often-repeated name-root, for example the Torht–s of Canterbury and the Dud–s and Lud–s of London in the ninth century, and the Leof–s of tenth- and eleventh-century Northampton.[4] Another can be perceived in the Bern–s or Beorn–s of Canterbury active from the 770s, perhaps descended from a younger brother of Offa's governor Beornheard who had estates in what is now Gloucestershire from the 760s.[5] We find a moneyer Biornfred working for King Coenwulf of Mercia (796–822) who must be the Beornfred who issued pennies for Coenwulf's brother and dependent King Cuthwulf of Kent (798–807) and was perhaps a brother of Bishop Beornmod of Rochester (*c.*804–843) and a kinsman of the Mercian governor Beornoth, the grandfather of Alfred's supporter. Money, land and the Church were, of course, inextricably connected then and for centuries after and nothing is more likely than that the head of a great family sponsored and promoted his relatives' attempts to find lucrative posts.

After Mercia lost Kent to Wessex in the late 820s, the Bern–family seems to have split and one branch retired with their equipment to Mercia proper, where we find Burnwald on coins of King Berhtwulf (839–853) and Bearnea, perhaps his son, on coins of Burgred, while Beornnoth and Bernmod remained in Canterbury issuing coins for Archbishop Ceolnoth (833–870). We can perhaps identify Bearnea as the Beornheah who turned out pennies for King Edmund of East Anglia, the future martyr and saint, perhaps commuting there or on a contract basis. We have of course no idea at all about whether any of these moneyers were goldsmiths at court, specialist minters dealing only in silver coins or large-scale merchants buying and selling Welshmen, iron, wool and any other profitable commodities, who employed illiterate or semi-literate operatives to fulfil their government contracts.

In the 860s we can find four Bern–s working at Canterbury, Beornnoth and Biarnmod being joined by Biarnvine and Byrnvald. In the 870s and 880s the last-named continued to issue pennies, being joined in the business by Beorneah, who can only be Bearnea from Mercia and Beornhaeh from East Anglia fleeing to the old family home with his pack-mules loaded with moulds, dies and ingots as the Vikings slaughtered King Edmund in 870 and then drove King Burgred into exile in 874. With these two we also read on the coins the names of Beornmær, Beornred and Beornwulf, the last two of whom remained in business well into the next century. We can legitimately arrange these names into putative generations and construct possible genealogical trees, with lines showing some cousins working in Mercia and others for Wessex, as long as we remember that we are building hypothesis on hypothesis and look out constantly for minor points of similarity between coins that might tend to confirm and for little discrepancies that could destroy the whole theoretical structure of the family. At the same time we must wonder whether all the Bern–s together formed a kind of family bank with branches here and there across England, or whether they each set up on their own.

Byrnvald, of Canterbury in the 860s, 870s and 880s, struck coins for Alfred's middle brother Ethelbert, junior king of Kent in the late 850s and then king of Wessex (860–865/6), and continued minting coins at Canterbury through the next two reigns, of Alfred's next brother Ethelred and of Alfred himself. Early in the 890s all the familiar minor details of coins struck at Canterbury cease; one great numismatist concluded from this sign that the city was sacked by the Vikings in 892 and that in Alfred's last years 'the bulk of the English coinage was issued from London'.[6] The first part of this conclusion goes too far; the *Chronicle* makes no reference to any Viking attack on Canterbury in its verbose and detailed account of the war of 892–896. But the second part may well be correct, as there are many signs that Alfred moved the financial centre of his kingdom away from Canterbury.

Bernwald, either the moneyer of the 860s–880s or a son and namesake, struck an issue in about 895 with the place-name, almost uniquely, on the obverse with the king's name: *Orsna/ Ælfred/ Forda*, 'of the oxen/ Alfred/ at the ford', and only his own name on the reverse: *Bernv/ ald.mo*, 'by Bernw/ ald [the] mo[neyer]'. He continued to strike coins for Edward the Elder and for Athelstan, the former's being (like all his coins) unlocated, the latter's being issued from Wallingford. We can suggest that Alfred intended Wallingford to be a major new base and transferred Bernwald there from Canterbury in about 890 and that Bernwald struck the Oxford coins there. We can suggest too that Bernwald engaged poor craftsmen who took very little care and 'scrambled' the inscriptions on most of the coin-dies, setting many of the letters on their side or upside-down, using an 'r' for an 'x' or 'chs' and so on, to explain the defects of most of the coins of this type, which have long been hailed as crude Viking copies or forgeries. So many of the scrawled, misspelt and misdated charters that used to be dismissed as forgeries are now considered genuine, but perhaps written by a long-sighted old priest with no spectacles using the back of his mule as a writing-desk, that it is fair to look on coins in the same generous light.

We should perhaps admit that all the inferior issues, like Alfred's Oxford pennies, were a desperate rush-job completed in a week or two to be available for a solemn inauguration of a new fort, itself constructed in a great rush during a Viking invasion to block a familiar raiding route. All the surviving examples of these coins are strikingly similar and well up to standard weight.

Great men employed other expert craftsmen full-time for a wage. Swordsmiths forged weapons and stone-masons and carvers worked on churches and chapels, while goldsmiths, whether the same as the moneyers or not, made jewellery. In the ninth century military skills may have been sternly restricted to a particular social group, almost a 'caste', of warriors, who got their keep and pay as household bodyguards.

By far the largest proportion of the population were peasants, many of them descended from the long-settled native Celtic population who had begun to assimilate to their Anglo-Saxon overlords as they had, centuries before, to the Romans. These small farmers are very poorly documented. All or almost all of them were tied to the land, but less miserably so than the serfs with certain rights to some land of their own but with even less personal freedom. There were also landless slaves who could be bought and sold. They are even worse documented and we cannot begin to guess what proportion of a whole population they formed, how many were born slaves, how many were captives with no hope of ransom and how many were peasants and artisans driven by debt into slavery.

Our knowledge of how these working people occupied themselves is equally sketchy. We have no real idea which craft skills had become specialised and which were broadly spread among the serfs and peasants. Most women were able to weave coarse woollen cloth and cut and sew garments, which they could sell, as well as dig plots with the spade and grow particular small-scale crops, which they could also sell. No doubt also most men had rough and ready skills in tanning and leatherwork, in making tools and the like from bone and antler and in basic carpentry, as well as managing beasts and cultivating large-scale crops to produce a surplus in good years, selling their crops and products and buying others. Meticulous studies of small finds from excavations are slowly providing material for debate, if not for conclusive answers. To judge from the number of moneyers and coin-issues, small-scale local commerce was both widespread and often transacted in cash;[7] no doubt barter was also used.

The peasants were accustomed to disruption, looting and the destruction of their homes and crops. As well as these hazards, kings and great lords engaged in schemes of conquest or colonisation regularly transferred their serfs and peasant-farmers to new regions to ensure food supplies.[8]

As we have said, the notion that all peasants took up arms and went to war is a myth or wishful fantasy that grew up in the late eighteenth and nineteenth centuries to justify the military practice, imposed on most European nations from the late eighteenth century, of two or three years' conscription in the ranks followed by long availability of these trained soldiers in the reserve. Even the English, whose army was unusual in being made up of long-service volunteers, enthusiastically embraced this myth. With it they gave credence to two more, both equally fantastic and quite unsupported by sound evidence and common sense. One was that a primitive form of 'democracy' was exercised by 'lordless' peasant communities; this has its origin in some idiosyncrasy of political idealism. The other myth, widely adopted in most parts of Europe but not in Scandinavia, was that in about the fifth to the ninth centuries AD, invading tribes, the ancestors of the present population, exterminated the previous inhabitants. This belief has never been comprehensively rebutted and still affects scholarly thinking. But over the last thirty years it has been undermined by detailed studies of all kinds and now seems fundamentally implausible.

Alfred's life came to an end and he passed his realm and his responsibilities on to the next generation.

900

a. Alfred son of Ethelwulf died six days before All Saints [26 October 899]. He was king of all the English, apart from those under Danish control, and ruled for twenty-eight and a half years.

14

Postscript:
The Kingdom of England

ALFRED'S SON EDWARD THE ELDER and daughter Ethelfleda together continued the expansion of his kingdom to the north and may be said, more than any others, to have created the English kingdom which the next generation finally consolidated. Between 910 and 920 they conquered all Viking territories south of Yorkshire. Alfred had begun the process when he annexed south-west Mercia in the early 880s. His youngest grandson King Eadred completed it when he finally reduced the Viking kingdom of York, once the English kingdom of Northumbria, to submission in 954.

Alfred's eldest child, his daughter Ethelfleda, had a remarkable political and military career in her father's lifetime as joint governor with her husband Ethelred of the kingdom's largest province and in her brother's lifetime as joint and then sole governor of a rather reduced version of the province. She commanded her armies in the field for seven seasons as the western or left-hand arm of a great pincer movement, while her brother, King Edward, led the forces of the other provinces as the eastern or right-hand arm.

In poetry she appears memorably, transposed into biblical imagery as Judith in the fragmentary epic of that name, slaying the would-be conqueror of her land, the Danish commanders who figure collectively as Holofernes.[1] Her own special chronicle survives, very much abbreviated, in a distinct Mercian addition to or version of the *Chronicle*. This text, briefly recounting Ethelfleda's military achievements, comes down to us in two copies, both in

216

the British Library, one (the B-text) copied out in the 970s and the other (the C-text) in the 1050s.

902
a. Ealhswith [Alfred's wife, of Mercian royal blood] died.
b. The men of Kent fought the Danes at the Holme.

904
a. There was an eclipse of the moon.

905
a. A comet was observed.

907
a. Chester was repaired.

909
a. St Oswald's body was taken into Mercia from Bardney.

910
a. The English fought the Danes at Tettenhall and beat them.
b. Ethelfleda built the fort at Bremesbyrig [not identified].

911
a. Ethelred, lord of the Mercians, died.

912
a. On the eve of the Discovery of the Holy Cross Ethelfleda, lady of the Mercians, went to Scergeat [not identified] and made the fort there.
b. She built a fort at Bridgnorth.

913
a. At the beginning of summer, by God's grace, Ethelfleda, lady of Mercia, marched the Mercian forces to Tamworth and made the fort there.
b. After that, before Lammas, she built the fort at Stafford.

217

914
a. She made the fort at Eddisbury early in summer.
b. At the start of autumn she fortified Warwick.

915
a. After Christmas, she made forts at Chirbury and Weardbyrig [not identified].
b. Before Christmas the same year she built a fort at Runcorn.

916
a. The abbot Egbert and his retainers were murdered without cause on June 16, the feast of St Cyriac the Martyr before Midsummer.
b. Three days later Ethelfleda sent an armed force into Wales, destroyed Brecenanmere and seized the king's wife and thirty-three others as hostages.

917
a. With God's help Ethelfleda, lady of Mercia, captured the fortress known as Derby with all its assets. Four of her favoured ministers were slain inside the gates.

918
a. With the help of God she won control of the fortress of Leicester early in the year and most of the Viking host based there submitted to her.
b. And the men of York had given her their word, some by promises and some by sworn guarantees, to submit to her governance.
c. Just after they had given this undertaking, she died at Tamworth twelve days before Midsummer, in the eighth year that she had rightfully governed Mercia on her own.
d. She was buried at Gloucester in the eastern chapel of St Peter's church.

919 This year, three weeks before Christmas the governorship of Mercia was taken from Elfwyn, daughter of Ethelred lord of Mercia, and she was removed into Wessex.

These remarkable achievements of a royal princess, who is recorded as having built one fortress during her husband's lifetime and then, as a widow during six years of campaigning, constructed nine fortresses and captured two enemy bases, were entirely ignored in the *Chronicle*'s main version, the A-text. This gives a very full account of the campaigns of Ethelfleda's brother, King Edward, and makes it clear that brother and sister were following carefully laid plans and commanding closely co-ordinated armies.

Ethelfleda, Asser tells us, was Alfred's first-born child.[2] She must have been born before 871, as we must assume that she was about fifteen or sixteen by 887, when she appears in a charter about Brightwell Baldwin and Watlington, Oxon as joint governor of the province of south-west Mercia, with her husband, Ethelred.[3] She can have been no more than forty when he died in 911 and perhaps only about forty-seven when she herself died in 918. To the Welsh and Irish annalists who recorded her death, and ignored her father's and her brother's, Ethelfleda was *famosissima regina Saxonum*, 'the most famous queen of the Saxons'.[4]

Ethelfleda herself led the western army in the field, acting in every way as the most senior and responsible of her brother's provincial governors. We have read the record of her construction of ten new fortresses and of how she sent her warriors in to storm Derby with heavy loss and personally accepted the surrender of Leicester. In talks with her, the Viking leaders in York had agreed to surrender. But when she died suddenly in 918 they broke off negotiations and fought Edward for another two years.

We have seen that Ethelfleda sent a punitive expedition into the Welsh kingdom of Brycheiniog in 916 to avenge the murder of an abbot and his men, taking thirty-four hostages, including the queen, whom she must have felt was fair game.[5] Beating up the Welsh had long been a family pastime. In 853 her grandfather, King Ethelwulf of Wessex, had invaded Wales on a joint expedition at the request of King Burgred of Mercia. One almost immediate result of this co-operation was Burgred's marriage to Ethelfleda's aunt. We may suspect that if the Vikings were not the constant enemy in the *Chronicle*, the Welsh would have figured in that role as the villains and victims of raids and counter-raids and other such warlike excitements.

Ethelfleda's daughter and only recorded child, Elfwyn, may have been about fifteen years old in 903 when she was listed as witnessing King Edward's confirmation of a charter, lost by fire, about land at Risborough, Bucks.[6] She appears in one charter as her mother's deputy governor;[7] here a thirteenth-century Abingdon scribe miscopied his text and put her down as a bishop, making some amends for his all too characteristic slip by giving us an attractive little portrait of Ethelfleda (Pl. 3). She was perhaps aged thirty in 918 when, as we have just seen, she succeeded to her mother's governorship only to be deprived of it after a short time. The *Chronicle*'s terse record implies that she actually took over and began to rule her mother's province before her uncle, King Edward, rounded her up and took her into custody in Wessex, thus putting a firm stop to any prospect of a dynasty of powerful female governors in the Midlands. There does not seem to be any indication of husband or children, but we have no reason to suppose that she had none.

Alfred had two younger daughters who survived to adulthood: Ethelgifu, whom he made abbess of his new nunnery at Shaftesbury, and Elfthryth who married Count Baldwin of Flanders, son, by her third marriage, of Alfred's stepmother Judith.

Alfred's son, Edward the Elder, succeeded to his kingdom and ruled from 899 until his death in 924. The main A-text of the *Chronicle* gives us a rather long-winded account of his reign which we can set beside the short summary of his sister's war record:

900

a. . . . and then his son Edward followed on the throne.

b. His first cousin Prince Ethelwold hastened to seize the royal halls at Wimborne [in Dorset] and Twinham [Christchurch in Hampshire] without the authority of the king and his council. The king rode with his guards and bivouaced at Badbury by Wimborne. Ethelwold and the men loyal to him stayed inside the stockade with the gateways barricaded, swearing to live or die there.

c. The prince then stole away under cover of dark and fled to Northumbria where the Danish army leaders chose him as their king and swore loyalty to him.

d. His girlfriend, a professed nun with whom he had lived without the king's leave and against the bishop's orders, was put under arrest.

e. Governor Ethelred of Devon had died that year four weeks before King Alfred.

901

a. Governor Ethelwulf, the king's uncle on his mother's side, died, as did Abbot Virgil in Ireland and the priest Grimbald.

902

a. Ethelwold invaded Essex with the largest sea-borne force he could recruit and forced the people to submit to him.

903

a. Ethelwold persuaded the Vikings of East Anglia to break the peace-treaty and raid all Mercia as far as Cricklade. They crossed the Thames and pillaged the Braydon area [in north Wiltshire west of Cricklade] before withdrawing.

b. King Edward mustered his forces and hastened after them, ravaging their territory between the old dykes and the Ouse northward as far as the Fens.

c. When he planned to withdraw, he instructed his commanders to march closed up, but the Kent division put off their move despite the king sending seven despatch-riders.

d. The Danes caught them there and a battle ensued, in which we lost governors Sigcwulf and Sigehelm, minister Ealdwold, abbot Cenwald, Sigewulf's son Sigeberht, Acca's son Eadwold and many less distinguished men. Danish casualties included King Eric [of East Anglia], Prince Ethelwold whom they had made king, Brihtsige son of prince Beornoth, two brigade commanders, Isopa and Oscetel and many whom we have no space to list. Although they won the battle, the Danes suffered higher losses.

e. Ealhswith [Alfred's queen] died during the year.

[No entries for 904 or 905]

906

a. Alfred the reeve of Bath died.

b. An armistice was reached at Tiddingford [in Buckinghamshire] as outlined by King Edward, with the East Anglians and the Northumbrians.

[no entry for 907]

908
a. Bishop Denewulf of Winchester died.

909
a. Frithustan became bishop of Winchester and Bishop Asser of Sherborne died.
b. King Edward ordered an attack on the north. His forces from Wessex and Mercia killed many Danes on this five-week invasion, plundering the lands of the northern army and raiding men and cattle.

910
a. The army of Northumbria broke the cease-fire and looted all across Mercia, spurning the peace-terms that King Edward and his advisers put on the table.
b. The king, at that time in Kent, had recruited a hundred ships which were sailing along the south coast to join him. Assuming that his main force was on board, the Danish forces set off on an inland plundering raid, unopposed as they thought.
c. When he heard this, the king mobilised the main forces of Wessex and Mercia to intercept the retreating Danes [at Wednesfield near Wolverhampton in Staffordshire, as Ethelward tells us[8]] and rout them with very heavy casualties including King Eowils [and two other kings, Healfdene and Inwær, according to Ethelward].

911
a. Governor Ethelred of Mercia died and King Edward took over London and Oxford and their districts.

912
a. In November [911] King Edward had the north fort made at Hertford between the Mimran, the Bean and the Lea.
b. The following summer, in late May and early June, he marched to Maldon in Essex to cover the construction of the fort at Witham; many former subjects of the Danes came over to him.
c. A detached brigade built the fort at Hertford south of the Lea.

913
a. The Viking armies of Northampton and Leicester broke the cease-

fire and went raiding after Easter, killing many people around Hook Norton [Oxfordshire] and that area.

b. As they withdrew they chanced to meet another warband making a thrust against Luton [Bedfordshire]; attacking them when they realised what was happening, our local forces drove them in flight, recovering all the booty and most of their horses and weapons.

914

a. A great fleet led by Earl Othere and Earl Harald crossed the Channel from Brittany and coasted round to the Severn mouth, plundering in Wales and wherever they felt like as they sailed. They kidnapped Bishop Cyfeiliog of Archenfield [Herefordshire, west of the River Wye] and charged the king forty pounds to ransom him.

b. They landed to raid Archenfield, but the men of Hereford and Gloucester and the nearby forts intercepted them, brought them to battle and defeated them, killing Earl Harald and Othere's brother with much of the force. They penned them in and surrounded them until they offered hostages and promised to leave the kingdom.

c. The king ordered a line of outposts to be on watch along the south coast of the [Bristol] Channel, from the Avon mouth to Cornwall to ensure that they made no major invasion. In fact they crept ashore twice, east of Watchet and at Porlock [both in west Somerset], being counter-attacked both times with the result that only the swimmers escaped.

d. They camped on Steepholme [a small island out in the Severn estuary] until their supplies ran out and many of them died of famine. They moved on to west Wales and then to Ireland in the autumn.

e. In October King Edward marched to Buckingham and spent four weeks constructing the forts on both sides of the river before leaving.

f. Earl Thurcetyl came and submitted to him with all the earls and leading men of Bedford and many from Northampton.

915

a. King Edward marched against and took Bedford in October, accepting the submission of the leading men and staying there four weeks; before marching home he left orders for the fort south of the river to be built.

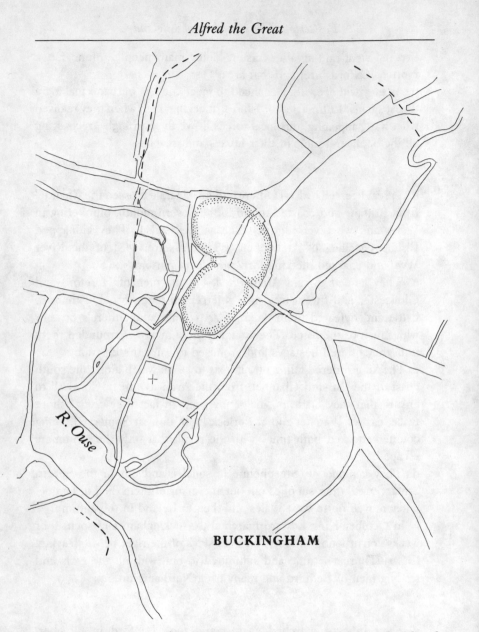

BUCKINGHAM

Plan of Buckingham. Alfred's son Edward built a fort on each side of the river; no trace of these has yet been found. Possible defence-lines are marked by dashes, the former church by a cross, the supposed castle by dots. The long market-place stretching north-east is like the wide streets at St Giles', north of Oxford, and Dance Common south of Cricklade.

916

a. King Edward marched to Maldon in June and constructed the fort there before he left.

b. Earl Thurcetyl and a number of his followers left for France with King Edward's blessing and assistance.

917

a. In March King Edward had the fort at Towcester [the small Roman walled town of Lactodorum] manned and built.

b. In May he gave orders for the fort at Wigingamere [not identified].

c. In July the Vikings from Leicester and Northampton and further north broke the cease-fire and attacked Towcester in an attempt to storm it, but the garrison held out until reinforcements came up and the enemy abandoned their attempt and withdrew.

d. Immediately afterwards a warband crossed the frontier and captured many cattle and their herdsmen between Bernwood and Aylesbury [both in mid-Buckinghamshire].

e. A larger force from Huntingdon and East Anglia concentrated at Tempsford [in Bedfordshire, on the Ivel just above its confluence with the Ouse] and moved into a fort which they built there, abandoning their base at Huntingdon as Tempsford appeared better placed for offensive action and raiding.

f. They marched against Bedford; the garrison came out, formed a battle-line and drove them back with heavy loss.

g. A large force of Vikings from eastern Mercia and East Anglia mustered and tried to take the Wigingamere fort by escalade, keeping up their assaults far into the day while they drove off the cattle from the meadows. The garrison held out and the Vikings left them and retreated.

h. In the summer King Edward assembled a striking force from the nearby forts to attack Tempsford, which they took by storm, killing Earl Toglos, his son Earl Manna and his brother and all those who fought on. The rest surrendered with all their supplies and equipment.

i. Almost immediately afterwards, in autumn he mobilised a large army from Kent, Surrey and Essex and the nearby forts, marched to Colchester and besieged that stronghold [the great Roman walled city of Camulodunum], keeping up the attack until they broke in and slaughtered everyone they found there and seizing all the supplies; a few men escaped over the wall.

j. Later that autumn the Vikings assembled a great army from East Anglia with everyone else they could persuade to join in and take reprisals. Advancing to Maldon they cut off the fort and attacked it until a relieving force arrived to reinforce the garrison, when they began to retreat. Our combined forces promptly attacked and defeated them, massacring several hundred, both men from the ships and locals.

k. A little later that autumn King Edward marched his main army to Passenham, where he remained while the fort at Towcester was equipped with a stone wall. Earl Thurferth and his brigadiers offered the king their allegiance, as did all the army of Northampton as far as the River Welland [which skirts the northern edge of Northamptonshire], seeking his lordship and protection.

l. As that division went off service, the king recalled their reliefs and sent them to capture the Viking base at Huntingdon, which he had repaired and refurbished. All surviving local leaders accepted King Edward and came under his peace and authority.

m. In October King Edward marched the army of Wessex to Colchester to repair and refurbish the fortress. Many men who had been subject to Danish rule in East Anglia and Essex came to submit to him. The army of East Anglia made a formal sworn treaty on the king's terms, aligning themselves with his allies by land and sea; and the army of Cambridge invited him specially to be their overlord and guardian, settling the matter with solemn oaths as the king ordered.

918

a. In May King Edward marched his main army to Stamford and had the fort south of the river put up; all the Viking forces of the north fort surrendered and accepted him as their ruler.

b. While he was there his sister Ethelfleda died at Tamworth two weeks before midsummer. The king took possession of Tamworth and the whole province of Mercia which she had governed.

c. The Welsh kings Hywel, Clydog and Idwal came to give him their allegiance and all the tribes of Wales welcomed him as their lord.

d. He advanced to Nottingham and captured the Viking fort, which he had repaired for manning by a joint Anglo-Danish garrison; and all the leaders of Mercia, English and Danes gave him their homage.

When his brother-in-law, governor Ethelred of Mercia, died in 911, or more likely at the end of 910, Edward took over London and Oxford as bases for his long series of small-scale campaigns across the eastern side of the country while his sister Ethelfleda led the fighting men of her reduced Mercian province through the West Midlands, each of them founding fort after fort and taking Viking base after base, keeping up their relentless pressure until they broke the will of the small Viking earldoms and petty kingdoms. In the end all of them submitted to English rule.

A glance at King Edward's four daughters shows us how his standing had grown in Europe. One of them, named as Eadgyth by a much later chronicler, married the Viking king Sihtric of Dublin and, for a few years, of York. Four of her sisters married rulers across the Channel. Eadgifu married the king of France, Charles the Simple; Eadhild married the Frankish duke Hugh the Great; Eadgyth married the German emperor, Otto the Great (936–973); and Elfgifu married an unknown count, perhaps Alberic of Narbonne or Conrad the Peaceable of Burgundy.

Alfred's younger son, Ethelward, born perhaps in the late 870s, died in his mid-forties in about 920–922, if we can trust later chroniclers quoting unknown sources. His great-nephew and namesake in the 980s, one of the greatest of English nobles and governor of the south-west, laboriously produced a history of the world and particularly of his forebears for his cousin Abbess Matilda of Essen on the Rhine, written in his own flamboyant and idiosyncratic Latin.[9]

Alfred's grandson Athelstan succeeded to the throne in 924 and reduced the northern Vikings and their Scottish allies much more firmly to subjection before his death in 939. He ruled with imperial splendour and could summon a court that comprised, in 934, two archbishops, four lesser kings, seventeen bishops, four abbots, twelve earls and governors and fifty-two ministers, a total of ninety-one great men.[10]

He was succeeded by his brother Edmund (939–946) who lost and recovered the Danish areas of the East Midlands, and he by his brother Eadred (946–955) who finally eliminated the kingdom of York. All of them built on the foundations that Alfred had laid in the distant days of the 870s and 880s, when the survival of any English kingdom was a very doubtful matter. Eadred and his descendants and successors can fairly be called kings of England.

15

Alfred in Later Centuries

KING ALFRED THE GREAT WAS A PHILOSOPHER-KING who wrote and issued his own versions of spiritual and pastoral classics for his administrators and churchmen and a heroic and successful battle-leader with rare strategic insights who three times saved his kingdom of Wessex from devastating invasions. He became the supreme figure of an heroic age through personal courage in eight ferocious hand-to-hand battles; this period saw the destruction of the three other English kingdoms. Although beaten in four of his battles, Alfred showed himself to be thoroughly realistic and adaptable when in trouble. He bought off an implacable enemy when he could raise the money, renewed the fight within a few days when he could raise the men and, when he could do neither, endured a winter in hiding in the Somerset marshes. In victory he was generous and humane to his enemies, repaying brutal and destructive attacks with compulsory baptism, feasting and freedom. During his reign he established at least thirty forts or *burhs*, some of which have since developed into major towns and cities. A small and enigmatic jewel with his name as maker, but evidently 'wrought' for him by one of his most skilful goldsmiths, is the greatest treasure of the University of Oxford, which for centuries claimed him, without evidence, as its founder.

In his lifetime King Alfred must have been the object of much comment and countless tales; we can hardly doubt that he was the main subject of epic poems on the general lines of *Beowulf* or *The Battle of Maldon*, composed to be chanted in the feasting halls of great lords. Several tales about him are still recounted in children's

228

books, how he reconnoitred the enemy camp disguised as a minstrel, and how, posing as a working man, he begged for shelter
from a storm in a remote cottage; the swineherd's wife left him to
watch her cakes baking in the embers and scolded him for letting
them burn. At that point her husband the swineherd came home
and recognised his king, fell on his knees and begged for forgive-
ness. This must be the last echo of an incident from a great epic
poem once familiar to all Englishmen. Succeeding centuries have
seen Alfred in a great variety of roles. Within about a century of
his death, this strange and interesting tale was written down, but
its true meaning may have been forgotten eight centuries ago.[1]

In the mid-twelfth century a monk of Abingdon abbey, not far
from Oxford, compiled, as an enlarged form of a property book,
a *Chronicle* of the history of his house, based partly on his own
imagination and partly on documents he found among the abbey
records. He accused King Alfred of seizing the abbey's site and
lands for himself and making Abingdon a royal manor; and he
compared him to Judas. It is hard to know whether we should take
this charge at all seriously, as the first church of Abingdon was
not on the site of the present town but on the crest of a hill not
far off, while the foundation-documents and charters that the monk
was using were those of a quite different early minster church
some way off. He may have been consciously creating a legend of
an early church within medieval and modern Abingdon.[2] Apart
from this isolated accusation, Alfred had has a remarkably good
press.

In the fourteenth century Andrew Horn, Chamberlain of
London in the 1320s, presented Alfred as summoning a parliament
regularly every two years, listening to the advice of his great lords
and scrutinising his lawgivers so sternly that he ended up hanging
many of his judges;[3] he saw Alfred as an even bigger bully than
King Edward I. In the 1340s Alfred may have been represented
as a large figure-statue on the west front of Exeter cathedral. Later
in the century an academic legend grew up that Alfred had founded
or at least refounded Oxford University, in reality a casual development mostly of the 1180s. The scholars responsible mischievously
ignored the impeccable evidence of documents then and now in
the University Archives, which show the art-loving but politically
inept King Henry III (1216–1272) as the university's most signifi-

cant patron, and hailed Alfred as their founder, when he moved their forebears from Cricklade in Wiltshire and Lechlade in Gloucestershire, two small market towns further up the Thames valley.[4]

It was really a matter of prestige coupled with fund-raising: their first priority was to be able to claim royal patronage; their second to establish Oxford's seniority over Cambridge as England's premier university. Cricklade was brought in because the name's first element sounds a bit like 'Greek', even though the Lech– of Lechlade would have to be a very debased form of 'Latin'. But this ridiculous and fraudulent claim was put forward and soon nobly developed in the 1380s with a claim that he had also founded University College, then just a hundred and thirty years old and even better documented than the university itself; it had begun soon after 1249 as something between a charitable foundation and a theology training school. This secondary claim was upheld in the highest London courts, sublimely ignorant then as now of historical truth, in a complex and bitterly fought property dispute.[5]

In 1441 King Henry VI, who was something of a religious enthusiast, sent an embassy to Pope Eugenius IV with a formal petition for Alfred's canonisation, without the slightest success as Eugenius was completely involved in religious schisms and Italian politics.

In the sixteenth century serious scholars began to work on Alfred. Archbishop Matthew Parker, whose great collection of Anglo-Saxon manuscripts is at Corpus Christi College, Cambridge, published Asser's *Life of Alfred* in Latin in 1574. In 1602 the great antiquary William Camden included Asser's biography in a new large collection of English, Irish, Welsh and Norman chronicles and sources; but he was the victim of a notorious and elaborate spoof. His research assistants, including a kinsman of his associate Henry Savile, the Warden of Merton College, Oxford, concocted and added some paragraphs describing how Alfred refounded a university at Oxford with the help of the Flemish priest Grimbald. A strange long-term consequence of this prank was that by attributing the early twelfth-century crypt of the Oxford church of St Peter in the East to Grimbald, who died in 901, the hoaxers incidentally falsified the dating of Romanesque architecture for two centuries.

Sir Robert Cotton MP (1571–1631) assembled a wonderful library with great numbers of original Anglo-Saxon charters, many of which are referred to here, at his house among the buildings of Westminster Palace close by the House of Commons. His grandson Sir John Cotton MP handed the whole library over to become national property in 1702, fulfilling his father's wishes. In 1731 the collection narrowly escaped destruction and some volumes were damaged, others quite destroyed by a fire in its temporary accommodation in Westminster. Luckily the generosity of the Cotton family in opening their library to scholars meant that many of the manuscripts that suffered had been copied.

Some men of the seventeenth century saw Alfred as a symbol of absolutism. In 1634 an obscure Gloucestershire attorney Robert Powell published a bizarre eulogy of King Charles I under the guise of a *Life of Alfred or Alured, the first Institutor of sub-ordinate government*. He recommends Charles's policy of 'divide and rule', grossly flattering him with nearly seventy pages of comparison with Alfred. In 1642–1643 Sir John Spelman wrote a much more critical evaluation of Alfred's life based, like Powell's, on the *Chronicle* and Asser's *Life*. His objective, both educational and political, was to instruct the future King Charles II in the duties of monarchy, as a boy living at Oxford, the Royalist capital during the Civil War. The original much-corrected manuscript survives in the Bodleian Library.[6]

In the late seventeenth and early eighteenth centuries Oxford scholars continued to work on Alfred, particularly his quite mythical links with the university and ignoring his well-attested foundation of the town. They hailed Alfred as a beacon of learning and in 1678 Obadiah Walker, master of University College, Oxford, published a Latin translation of Spelman's biography with notes and appendices by his friends and colleagues; he himself wrote a section on Anglo-Saxon coins and illustrated it with engraved plates. I discovered the actual copperplates from which these were printed mouldering on the floor of the college archive-store, which I had care of for some years; in the college library too I found Walker's roughly stitched page-proofs, abandoned when he fled Oxford ten years later.

For a hitherto empty niche over the main gate of the college Robert Plot, soon to be first Keeper of the Ashmolean Museum, presented a new life-sized statue of King Alfred in 1682/3. In 1686 the college moved it inside to a niche over the entrance to the dining-hall, to balance a new statue of St Cuthbert which Obadiah Walker gave for the niche over the chapel door. Both were taken down in 1802 and a dilapidated Alfred survived in the Master's garden until recent years.

Walker was a secret Roman Catholic, 'coming out' in the mid-1680s, no doubt in the hope of becoming a bishop and even a cardinal in King James II's Catholic regime. The most dramatic event of his eventful life was his arrest with James as they fled in disguise from London in 1688. He was expelled from his college post and imprisoned for a few years, and then spent the 1690s living in quiet obscurity near London, continuing his work on Saxon numismatics with support from the great court doctor John Radcliffe, his old pupil.

In 1693 the Alfred Jewel was discovered in farming-works or digging drainage ditches at North Petherton in Somerset. The full tale of how it was recognised and how it was given to Oxford in 1718 has never been adequately investigated and placed in a wider social context of family and academic links among the ramifications of the Palmer family's political and antiquarian interests. No doubt it will prove to be as relentlessly high-minded as all the rest of the seventeenth century's interest in Alfred[6b].

In about 1700 the first Lord Weymouth, one of the four lords who went to Holland in 1688 to invite William of Orange to take the throne, excavated at Athelney in Somerset and discovered timbers of what he took to be King Alfred's 'domicile' there. A 'staff' cut from one of these timbers was exhibited at the Bodleian Library in Oxford until the 1780s; it does not survive among the remains of the Bodleian and Anatomy School collections at the Ashmolean Museum.

In 1703 Dr Thomas Hickes, the redoubtable ex-dean of Worcester cathedral and outspoken opponent of both James II and William III, first published the Alfred Jewel. He had evaded exile and prosecution while on the run for nine years during the preparation of his great three-volume *Thesaurus* of northern languages. In the first volume of this vast work, Hickes recognised the Jewel as an example of an *aestel* or pointer, mentioned in Asser's *Life*, for teaching sacred and other important texts. We still accept this identification but forget that we owe this vital insight to Hickes.

In 1709 Thomas Hearne, under-librarian at the Bodleian Library and thus curator of the Athelney 'staff', published his own edition of the English text that Spelman wrote on Alfred in the 1640s. The friend and patron for whom he did this and to whom he gave a touchingly signed copy, Walter Charlett, the current master of University College, instantly disowned it and promoted a rival version, Francis Wise's 1722 edition of Asser's *Life*. Wise was under-keeper of the Bodleian Library and later keeper of the University Archives and Radcliffe Librarian. The edition was quite scholarly, going back, if not to the only extant early manuscript in the Cotton collection, at least to a new transcript of it.[7] In keeping with the dramatic and sometimes violent lives of the seventeenth- and early eighteenth-century scholars, the manuscript was destroyed when the Cotton Library, by now a national possession, went up in flames in 1731. The damage was not so serious as to destroy more than a fraction of the library, which became one of the founding collections of the British Museum, and since of the British Library.

In the 1720s there was a bitter dispute, all too characteristic of Oxford at that time, about the succession to the Mastership of University College. The opposing parties went to law and took the case to London. The first result was a firm legal decision, by the London courts, that Alfred had indeed founded it in the ninth century. Immediately afterwards Dr William Smith, a former fellow of the college (who had flouted the college statutes, which required celibacy, by keeping a secret wife at Windsor until he was forced to retire), published a book in Newcastle upon Tyne which proved, with abundant quotations from the college archives, that the college had no valid claim to royal patronage and was founded four centuries after Alfred's birth.

In this decade Alfred began to be commemorated in architecture as well as sculpture. Encouraged by a literary and political circle which included Alexander Pope, Lord Bathurst built 'Alfred's Hall' in 1721 as a wooden picnic-shelter in the grounds of Cirencester Park; hailed as 'the first of all castellated follies . . . a true sham', this park pavilion was several times rebuilt and extended in stone and further embellished in 1732 with details from a demolished Tudor manor house.[8] Bathurst himself treated it as a bit of a joke and ventured 'to assert that all Europe cannot show such a pretty little plain work in the Brobdingnag style'.

In 1733 Viscount Cobham included a bust of King Alfred in the 'Temple of British Worthies' which the painter-turned-architect William Kent designed for him at his palatial country house at Stowe, Buckinghamshire. Two years later the Princess of Wales commissioned Rysbrack to carve statues of Alfred and the Black Prince for Kent's octagon pavilion at Carlton House on the edge of St James's Park in the first of all informal gardens.[9] A vicious pamphleteering war about the date of the White Horse at Uffington in Berkshire (now Oxfordshire) kept Alfred in the public eye in the late 1730s.[10]

On 1 August 1740 George II's disaffected son, Frederick Prince of Wales, staged an open-air spectacular in the grounds of his country retreat at Cliveden in Buckinghamshire. He commissioned *Alfred: a Masque* from the poet James Thomson, who brought David Mallet in to help him, with music by Thomas Arne. The rousing final chorus, familiar to every Englishman, brings tears to our eyes and pride to our heart as it is still performed, almost ritualistically, every year. In 1751 the *Masque*, extensively rewritten by Mallet, was produced at the Theatre Royal, Drury Lane with an all-star cast led by the greatest actor of the age, David Garrick in the role of Alfred. Also playing 'a Friend', he spoke the prologue:

> In arms renown'd, for arts of peace ador'd
> ALFRED, the nations father, more than lord,
> A British author has presum'd to draw . . .

Having defeated the Danes, he speaks in triumph from an outstandingly confident mid-eighteenth-century pre-imperial standpoint:

> BRITONS, proceed, the subject Deep command,
> Awe with your Navies every hostile Land;
> In vain their Threats, their Armies all are vain,
> They rule the balanc'd World, who rule the Main.

Two years later, in 1753, the next Alfred script demands some ambitious scene changes, from the Danish camp, near Wilton, on Salisbury Plain to a garden at Dulverton, the outside of a cottage at Athelney and Kinwith Castle in Devon. In the moment of triumph the Anglo-Saxon warriors chant:

> Victoria, Victoria, the bold Britons cry;
> Now the Victory's won
> To the Plunder we run;
> We'll return to our Lasses like fortunate Traders,
> And triumph in Spite of the vanquished Invaders.

Elfleda, Alfred's warrior daughter, speaks the epilogue 'in Mans Apparel':

> Perhaps some here, may think my part too bold
> And hardly can believe, our Dames of old
> Would quit their Petticoats, and put on Breeches,
> Or risk their lives; – but they were cunning Witches.
> Breeches they wore, and very oft wou'd rent 'em
> And who, besides their Husbands, would prevent 'em?
> But Raillery apart, the History,
> Which furnishes the Matter of this Play,
> Makes Alfred's Daughter brave, as may be seen,
> If you'll please to consult Monsieur Rapin;
> She fought by her Husband's side, but made a vow
> Such as few married Women can keep now:
> Supported thus, by History I stand,
> And over Mercia's kingdom had command.
> Britons, we don't presume to give you Laws.
> But gladly shall accept your kind Applause.

Reading this we cannot feel that either Hollywood's view of the Vikings or more recent dramatised history on TV have debased things significantly.

As Alfred somehow became a symbol of aristocratic consensus against the crown, he remained a familiar theme on the London stage and was never quite forgotten at Oxford. Inspired by reading Voltaire on Alfred, the banker Henry Hoare built the strikingly tall Alfred's Tower on his Wiltshire estate at Stourhead as a landmark and memorial, partly for patriotic reasons, partly for political ones as a monument to national aspirations under Whig government, and partly to outdo other landowners with ambitious plans to embellish their grounds. It is a vast project which took some time to reach fruition. The idea occurred to Hoare in 1762; in 1764 he commissioned a marble bust of Alfred from Rysbrack for £100; in 1765 he obtained a design from the Office of Works architect Henry Flitcroft; building began in 1769 and the tower was at length completed in 1772.[11]

By this time more Alfred memorials had sprouted at Oxford. In 1766 Sir Roger Newdigate MP and a group of friends paid for a grand architectural fireplace for the dining-hall at University College, his *alma mater*. Designed by Henry Keene and carved by Hayward, the jambs and canopy are modelled on Aymer de Valence's early fourteenth-century tomb in Westminster abbey, with an elegant, if anachronistic, profile bust of Alfred in a central roundel.[12] The roundel is still visible, the Gothic fripperies of the fire-surround unfortunately hidden behind clumsy Edwardian woodwork. In 1771 another former undergraduate of the college, Viscount Folkestone, gave a marble bust of King Alfred copied by Wilton (for £51.18.0) from the Rysbrack bust at Stourhead.[13]

Plays, recitations and other dramatic performances on the theme of Alfred and his descendants, such as his grandson Athelstan, remained a staple of London and provincial playwrights and stages, as reliefs and busts did of sculptors, decorative artists and artificial stone casters. No antiquarian-minded magnate or virtuoso seems to have contrived or commissioned any coherent Alfredian or even Anglo-Saxon interiors, in London or in their country houses.

With the country under threat of invasion in the 1790s, spectacular shows on the anti-invader theme were constantly put on in London, from Charles Dibdin's Boadicea in ballet to mockery of a windmill-powered French invasion fort on a giant raft nearly half a mile long. Alfred of course came up trumps at Sadlers Wells in a 'Grand Historical Ballet of Action (entirely new)' in 1798, which played to 'crowded houses with great applause'. In Scene I, set on the 'Skirts of a Danish Encampment', Guthrum 'invites his army to fresh acts of Plunder and offers a high reward for the capture of Alfred'. In Scene II, in 'An open Country, A party of Danes concert means for plundering an English Monastery, and proceed in disguise to execute their purpose'. In Scene III, set inevitably in 'The Neatherd's Cottage, Alfred, in disguise of a peasant is reproved by the Neatherd's wife for negligence in letting the cakes burn' and, by a lucky coincidence, 'Oddune Earl of Devon casually taking shelter during a storm, discovers the King in this state of concealment, and proposes to conduct him to a place [of] security on the Isle of Athelney'. Much of the action takes place in the Danish camp, where Alfred rescues his wife, but loses his sister Judith (Mr Lonsdale, the author, had read his sources in too much of a hurry, or decided to spice them up). She is to be sacrificed as an offering to victory while the Danish scalds chant:

> God of War to thee we pour
> Sanguine streams of victim gore.
> Odin! every soul unite
> To consecrate revenge's rite,

assigning to the surrogate French atrocities as terrible as any scene at the guillotine. The recitative after the battle and before the final scene, a 'Grand Historical Pageant' or 'Temple of History' which takes us breathlessly from Cnut ordering the sea to retreat by way of Magna Carta to George III with Earls Howe, St Vincent and Duncan, greets the victorious Alfred:

> Behold the guardian genius of this Isle
> The watchful Witness of thy gallant deeds!
> Alfred go on – the noble task pursue . . .
> Give to the Land that owns thee for its king
> A Guardian and a Father. – Albion thou,
> First taught by thee – shall teach invading foes,
> That Britain's king reigns in his Subjects hearts
> And firmly great, Britannia rules the waves.

The show ended with the inevitable familiar climax borrowed from the *Masque* of 1740, with two extra verses added to gloss over the problems of the doubtful sanity of George III and the risk of having his unsatisfactory son as regent.

Even the French took to this kind of thing in a short-lived anglophile phase after the signing of the Treaty of Amiens in 1802 and found themselves sitting through a three-act melodrama about

Alfred's grandfather King Egbert as first king of a united England.

The Italians too were affected a little later, five years after Waterloo, when a splendid Alfred opera was put on at La Scala in Milan, although at this time there was only a trickle of new and rather abstruse books on Alfred coming out, always some in German or translated from the German. As part of the tortuous process of finding suitable decorations for the rebuilt Houses of Parliament many groups and statues were exhibited in Westminster Hall in 1844, including several representations of Alfred. F. S. Archer's *Alfred the Great with the Book of Common Law* was castigated as a 'tame spiritless specimen of vulgarity'. The enlightened and energetic millionaire coal-owner and statesman Francis Egerton MP, ennobled as the Earl of Ellesmere, found time to write a short Alfred play when not engaged in translating Schiller, sponsoring free trade and London University, and presiding over the Camden Historical Society and the British Association. He was ably backed by the precipitate scholar J. A. Giles, whose Alfred biography of 1848 was timed to set off a new wave of interest.

In 1849 a festival to celebrate the millenary of Alfred's birth drew ten thousand people to his birthplace, the little Berkshire market town of Wantage. Giles edited and brought out as a part-work during 1849–51, planned on this occasion, a great co-operative multi-volume series which put translations of Alfred's works and assessments of every aspect of his life and works before the mid-Victorian reader; it was reprinted in 1858. For Christmas 1850 this continuing public interest made an unusual and dramatic appearance in an unforgettable Alfred pantomime, which also served as a trailer for the Great Exhibition of 1851. In the now mandatory 'Danish camp' scene, Guthrum the Danish king is 'drinking and laughing' while 'seated on a sort of rude Throne'. Around him, among the large Oak Trees with which the stage is scattered, Girls and Soldiers are dancing a very spirited dance to the air of 'Jolly Nose'. Guthrum interrupts:

> Enough of that! A strain more brave and gallant,
> Something *recherché* – I hate all native talent.

And, to answer his whim, Alfred and his associates, Hogseye the Swineherd and Sweeney, 'a rural gent of a thousand years ago', prance on to the stage dressed as black-and-white minstrels, Alfred with a banjo and Hogseye with a concertina, singing, to the tune of 'Zip Coon':

> Alfred de Great, he was a learned skolar,
> Alfred de Great, he was a learned skolar,
> But Guthrum was a great chap
> Who made him hoop and holler . . .

At the end, as the oaks become ships to the familiar chorus of 1740, and Hope turns Alfred and his rescued queen Ethelswitha (again the author had scanned his sources too hastily or cared little for them) into Harlequin and Columbine, and Despair transforms Guthrum into the Clown and Hogseye into Pantaloon, Hope concludes:

> Now, then, pursue your Pantomimic fun
> But Hope will come again in '51
> When former foes will seem as fond relations
> Despair: And where will that be at?
> Hope: The Industrial Exhibition of All Nations,

with a last magical change of scene to 'Hyde Park as it will be', with the as yet unnamed Crystal Palace.

From then until the First World War, books on every aspect of Alfred poured from the presses in England, Germany, Denmark and America. From the 1870s to the first decade of this century, this special vogue for Alfred was also manifested in stained-glass windows, monumental public statues and vast narrative paintings, some of them stressing Alfred's role as the first founder of the Royal Navy, then dominant throughout the world. All witnessed Alfred's extraordinarily persistent and widespread reputation and influence. In 1870 Dvorak wrote his first opera, *Alfred*, to symbolise the Czech struggle against the imperial might of Austria, with the sinister Viking chiefs standing in for the Hapsburgs. Fortunately for his reputation, this singularly tuneless work was never performed in his lifetime.

In Wantage a life-sized statue set up in the market-place in 1877 to commemorate Alfred has, carved on its high stone base, a record of the main achievements of his reign, which lasted from 871 until his death in 899:

ALFRED FOUND LEARNING DEAD
AND HE RESTORED IT
EDUCATION NEGLECTED
AND HE REVIVED IT
THE LAWS POWERLESS
AND HE GAVE THEM FORCE
THE CHURCH DEBASED
AND HE RAISED IT
THE LAND RAVAGED BY A FEARFUL ENEMY
FROM WHICH HE DELIVERED IT

ALFRED'S NAME WILL LIVE AS LONG
AS MANKIND SHALL RESPECT THE PAST

This admirably summarises Alfred's main deeds without either romanticising and over-dramatising them or distorting them in order to exploit them. A retired British naval officer, Prince Victor of Hohenlohe-Langenburg, or Count Gleichen as this cousin of Queen Victoria preferred to be known, designed and carved the Wantage statue in 1877. In Winchester Hamo Thornycroft's great 1901 statue of Alfred is brandishing his sword in the air not so much in defiance against the Danes as 'probably annoyed by the way in which the County Hall closes his view in the distance', as Sir Nicholas Pevsner wryly comments.[14]

After the First World War Alfred, so long favoured in Germany as a symbol of Anglo-German cohesion, fell abruptly from favour here and the flood of books dropped to a trickle. But despite a less enthusiastically patriotic and sometimes anti-war public, the 1930s saw four biographies and three specialist books; the 1940s only two, both specialist and both published in neutral countries during the Second World War. Every decade since then has seen at least five Alfred books come out, without mentioning any learned articles and general books referring to him.

How can we sum up Alfred's influence and repute in the twentieth century? Perhaps the only thing we can do is to run our eye through the Appendix, which attempts to list the main books about him, and remember that every year on the last night of London's Promenade Concerts in the Royal Albert Hall a ribald audience of five thousand roars out to an international TV audience of millions that all-time smash-hit, first performed more than two and a half centuries ago on the banks of the Thames to a select audience, the troubled Prince of Wales's guests: 'Rule Britannia!', the climax of *Alfred: a Masque* in 1740.

Notes

A NOTE ON SOURCES

The written sources that survive from King Alfred's own day and enable us to assemble a reasonably full account of his life and times are of four kinds: a history, the *Anglo-Saxon Chronicle*; a biography, Asser's *Life of Alfred* which is partly based on the *Chronicle*; some improving literature, remarkable for having been written or sponsored by Alfred himself, books that he had adapted or had translated into English; and legal papers, the code of law and, more particularly, the surviving charters or property records of the time. The study and publication of the texts has a remarkable history going back to the sixteenth and seventeenth centuries; we can only refer to this in passing. Coins, a specialised kind of document, have also been studied and published intensively since the seventeenth century.

The reader who looks through the notes and sees the letter B followed by a number can appreciate the extent of the extra data that I have included from the charters. B stands here for Birch and for the three great volumes of charters and related documents that Walter de Gray Birch of the Department of Manuscripts at the British Museum published as *Cartularium Saxonicum*, the 'Saxon charter book *or* property book' in 1885–93. The value of Birch's meticulous editing of 1354 obscure and difficult documents and his contribution to any study of the seventh to tenth centuries cannot be over-estimated.

Various attempts of the last forty years to make the information they contain more widely accessible include P. H. Sawyer's full and reliable list, *Anglo-Saxon Charters, an annotated list and bibliography* (1968), published by the Royal Historical Society in 1968, which gives 1875 charters up to 1066, arranged in a different order by kingdoms, lay landowners, bishops, other churchmen and so on.

The list gives new numbers to all the charters which, unforgivably, makes for a great deal of unnecessary work and worry. But the thousands of references provide endless food for thought and even entertainment on various experts' differing opinions about how authentic the documents are.

Two other attempts on the charters are Leicester University's series arranged by county, and numbered consecutively through each volume by county and date; these volumes summarise the contents, but omit many details:

H. P. R. Finberg, *Early Charters of Devon and Cornwall* (1953, 2nd ed. 1963)
C. R. Hart, *Early Charters of Essex* (1957, 2nd ed. 1971)
H. P. R. Finberg, *Early Charters of the West Midlands* (1961)
H. P. R. Finberg, *Early Charters of Wessex* (1964)
C. R. Hart, *Early Charters of Eastern England* (1966)
C. R. Hart, *Early Charters of Northern England and the North Midlands* (1975)
M. Gelling, *Early Charters of the Thames Valley* (1979)

and the British Academy's series arranged and numbered by land-owning institution, which prints the texts in full with not always reliable comments on authenticity and language and a sketchy discussion of the topography and later history of the estates:

A. Campbell, *Charters of Rochester* (Anglo-Saxon Charters I, 1973)

Besides this excellent work in collecting the sources and making them available, if with a good deal of overlapping effort and far too many numbers, historians can also lay some very strange false trails. Their judgements and opinions can be quite remarkably unsound. In his later years the late Professor V. H. Galbraith of Oxford got a 'bee in his bonnet' about Alfred's adviser, the Welsh Bishop Asser, and became convinced that his *Life of Alfred* was a forgery made by the eleventh-century Bishop Leofric of Crediton/ Exeter. When young research students were first introduced to him at receptions, he used to buttonhole them, saying: 'Hm, I suppose *you* think Asser is real.' He finally wrote up his fantasy in

1964, only to be comprehensively demolished by Professor Dorothy Whitelock in 1967.

In 1973 Professor A. Campbell, also of Oxford, brought out the pioneer *Charters of Rochester* in the British Academy series, just noted, which has been charitably described to me as 'embarrassing', condemning as it does several perfectly sound charters as 'highly suspicious' or 'a crude forgery'. Other aberrations of this sort, historians ignoring reliable evidence for a whim, and boldly asserting the opposite is true, have been pointed out in the appropriate places.

Two other approaches, topography and archaeology, appear to be independent of historical documents and are too often practised without much reference to the written evidence which, in this period, is all-important. All of us can walk round a place, a village or a town and draw our own conclusions about how it developed and what it was like at a particular time in the past; these are all guesses or, at best, informed hypotheses. Only a few archaeologists seem to be able to excavate and provide clear and impeccable evidence to confirm or destroy hypotheses of this kind. This should be the archaeologists' proper job but it must be said that their capacity to ask the right questions in the first place and their standards of observation, of interpretation and of coming to tenable conclusions are uneven. Too often they draw sweeping conclusions that will not stand up to close examination; many of them are not conclusions at all, but mere notions that should be expressed as suggestions.

The reader who wishes to discover more can easily turn to Dorothy Whitelock, ed., *English Historical Documents* 1 (2nd ed., 1979) and Simon Keynes and Michael Lapidge, *Alfred the Great, Asser's Life of King Alfred and other contemporary sources* (1983). The former, a rather monumental 900-page hardback volume, can be found in all large reference libraries; the latter is a much smaller paperback volume widely available. Each quotes in whole or in part from the *Chronicle*, from Asser's *Life*, from the law code that Alfred collected and edited from his forebears and himself promulgated and from the translations and adaptations of the classics which he himself made or sponsored; but each of them gives only a single charter of Alfred's.

CHAPTER 1

1. Asser (trans. S. Keynes and M. Lapidge) *Life of King Alfred* (1983, Penguin Classics) para 1
2. F. M. Stenton, *Anglo-Saxon England* (3rd ed. 1971), 245
3. *Anglo-Saxon Chronicle*, year 757
4. B591, trans. in D. Whitelock, *English Historical Documents* (2nd ed. 1979), 545
5. Bede (trans. L. Sherley Price) *History of the English Church and People* (1955 etc., Penguin Classics)
6. Æthelward (trans. A. Campbell) *Chronicle of Æthelweard* (1962)
7. *Anglo-Saxon Chronicle*, year 784
8. *Anglo-Saxon Chronicle*, year 839
9. B370, 373
10. B395, 396
11. B395, a charter exploded as 'highly suspicious' in 1973; but now discussed as authentic
12. B418
13. B396
14. B419
15. B444
16. B389
17. B377
18. B390, 398
19. B395
20. B411, 418

CHAPTER 2

1. Asser, *Life of Alfred*, para 2
2. B496, MS Cotton Augustus II, 66
3. Bede, *History of the English Church and People*, I.15
4. *Anglo-Saxon Chronicle*, year 757
5. B395, 411
6. N. Brooks, *Early History of the Church of Canterbury* (1984), 197
7. B227, Cotton Charters viii 34
8. B228

9. B257
10. B282
11. B258, from MS Cotton Claudius B vi
12. B377, Add MS 15,350
13. B395, wrongly considered 'highly suspicious' by A. Campbell, *Charters of Rochester* (1973), xxxiii, no. 18; but as genuine by S. Keynes, *Early Medieval Europe (Journal)* 2 (1993), 122–3. He believes Dudda and Osmod to be Kentish nobles; I suggest they were part of the Wessex regime
14. B416, MS Cotton Augustus ii, 9
15. MS Cotton Tiberius A xiii
16. B421C (with 421A, B), MS Cotton Augustus II, 37 (with II, 20 and II, 21); N. Brooks, *Early History of the Church of Canterbury* (1984), 323–5
17. Add MS 46487, H. P. R. Finberg, *Early Charters of Wessex* (1964), no. 567
18. B487, MS Cotton Tiberius A xiii
19. H. P. R. Finberg, *Early Charters of Wessex* (1964) no. 566
20. B439
21. B442, Stowe Charters 16
22. B457

CHAPTER 3

1. *Annals of St Bertin*, year 839
2. J. L. Nelson in *Journal of Ecclesiastical History* 18 (1967), 145–163
3. B467, MS Cotton Augustus II,71
4. B468–481
5. B469, Cotton Charters viii, 35
6. *Early Charters of Wessex* (1964), 187–213. S. Keynes and M. Lapidge suspect the charters noted in Notes 7–9 to be based on an 11th-century forgery; see their Asser's *Life* (1983), 233
7. B473 (perhaps a forgery copying a forgery), 475, 476, 493
8. B478
9. B468, 470, 471, 472, 474
10. B486, translated in D. Whitelock, *English Historical Documents* I (2nd ed. 1979), 525–6

11. Asser, *Life of Alfred*, para 23
12. Asser, *Life*, para 16
13. Asser, *Life*, para 11
14. J. L. Nelson, as in Note 2 above, developing an idea of R. H. C. Davis in *History* 56 (1971)
15. Einhard's *Life of Charlemagne* is readily available in translations such as that by S. Painter (1960)
16. V. H. Galbraith, *An Introduction to the Study of History* (1964), 88–128 and D. Whitelock, *The Genuine Asser* (1968)
17. S. Gibson and B. Ward-Perkins in *Papers of the British School at Rome* 47 and 51 (1979, 1983); L. Pani Ermini, 'Renovatio Murorum', *Centro Italiano di Studi sull' alto medioevo* 39 ii (1992), 485–530
18. A. Silvagni, *Monumenta Epigraphica Christiana* 1 (1943), pl xv
19. L. Duchesne (ed.), *Liber Pontificalis* 2 (1892), 124–5
20. J. B. de Rossi, *Inscriptiones Christianae Urbis Romae* 2i (1888), 325
21. L. Duchesne (ed.), *Liber Pontificalis* 2 (1892), 82; U. Broccoli, 'Ricerche su Gregoriopoli' *Archaeologia Laziale* 7 (1983), 170
22. R. Lanciani, *The Destruction of Ancient Rome* (1899), 126–7
23. L. Duchesne (ed.), *Liber Pontificalis* 2 (1892)
24. L. Duchesne (ed.), *Liber Pontificalis* 2 (1892), 131, 421; O. Marucchi, 'La inscrizione monumentale di Leopoli', *Nuovo bulletino di archeologia cristiana* 6 (1900), 195–203 and tav. vi
25. B438
26. B384
27. B395; B411; B426
28. B437
29. B439, 442, 449, 460 and perhaps 538
30. B1428; B426 and 449; B1195; B1198, 1200; B403, 501. Miss F. Harmer discussed and translated most of these documents in her *Select English Historical Documents* (1914). N. P. Brooks has refined her conclusions and worked out these three generations of Ealhhere's family from the records of the church of Canterbury in *Early History of the Church of Canterbury* (1984), 147–9
31. B442, Stowe Charters 16
32. B404

CHAPTER 4

1. Bede, *History of the English Church and People*, iv.16
2. A. D. Morton, *Excavations at Hamwic* 1 (1992)
3. H. P. R. Finberg, *Early Charters of Wessex* (1964) no. 27, discussed on pp. 230–241; M. Biddle in *Vor- und Frühformen der europäischen Stadt* 2 (1973), 246
4. J. Cook and T. Rowley (eds), *Dorchester through the Ages* (1985), 30–39 with Bibliography
5. B1210, by which Ethelred gave Navestock, Essex to St Paul's cathedral; M. Gibbs, *Early Charters of St Paul's* (Royal Hist. Soc. 1939) no. 2 is a better text of this badly copied charter
6. G. Milne, *From Roman Basilica to Medieval Market* (1992), 29–33
7. A. G. Vince, *Saxon London: an archaeological investigation* (1990)
8. R. Hodges, *Dark Age Economics: the origins of towns and trade* (2nd ed. 1989)
9. B37
10. P. Manning in *Berks, Bucks and Oxon Archaeol Jnl* 4 (1898), 24–5; P. Manning and E. T. Leeds in *Archaeologia* 71 (1921), 253, both listings being early versions of a 'sites and monuments record'
11. R. H. C. Davis, 'The Ford, the River and the City', *Oxoniensia* 38 (1973), 258–267
12. B. Durham in *Oxoniensia* 42 (1977), 174–5
13. *Oxoniensia* 53 (1988), 61
14. F. M. Stenton, 'St Frideswide and her Times', *Oxoniensia* 1 (1936), 103–112; J. Blair, 'St Frideswide reconsidered', *Oxoniensia* 52 (1987), 71–127; J. Blair trans., *St Frideswide patron of Oxford, the early texts* (1988)
15. Summary in G. Jackson, *Making of Medieval Spain* (1972), 14, 32
16. A. C. Floriano, *Diplomatica española del Periodo astur* 1 (1949)
17. N. Wand, 'Oppidum Buraburg' in H. Jankuhn etc., eds, *Vor- und Frühformen der europäischen Stadt* 1 (1973), 163–201
18. R. Schindler, *Ausgrabungen im Alt-Hamburg* (1957)
19. The series of excavation reports include those edited by H.

Jankuhn etc., 1–8 (1937–1983) and K. Schietzel etc., pts 1–30 (1969–1991)

20. M. Solle, *Stará Kourim* (1966)
21. V. Hrubý, *Stará Mesto, velkomoravsky Velehrad* (1965)
22. J. Poulík, *Mikulcice* (1975)
23. S. Michailov, *Preslav Sbornik* 1 (1968) &c
24. I. Welkow, 'Pliska', *Antiquity* **13** (1939), 293–303
25. P. A. Rappaport in *Materialy i Issledovaniya po Arkheologii SSSR* **62** (1958), 1–84; M. I. Artamonov, *Materialy* **75** (1959), **109** (1963)

CHAPTER 5

1. *Annals of the kingdom of the Franks*, year 782, available in the translation by B. W. Scholz, *Carolingian Chronicles* (1970, paperback 1972), cited here as *AF*
2. *Chronicle*, year 789; the ships' origin is noted in the D/E-text, revised in the north, the reeve's name in Ethelward's *Chronicon*
3. *Chronicle*, year 793; D/E text
4. *Chronicle*, year 794; D/E text
5. *AF*, year 798
6. *AF*, year 800
7. *AF*, year 804
8. *AF*, year 808
9. *AF*, year 810
10. *AF*, year 813
11. *AF*, year 820
12. *AF*, year 827
13. *AF*, year 828
14. J. L. Nelson (trans.), *Annals of St Bertin* (Ninth-century Histories 1, 1991) cited here as *AB*, followed by the year, in this case 836
15. *AB*, 839
16. *AB*, 847
17. *AB*, 850
18. *AB*, 854
19. *AB*, 855
20. *AB*, 834

21. *AB*, 835
22. *AB*, 840
23. Asser, *Life of Alfred*, para 83

CHAPTER 6

1. J. L. Nelson's translation of the *Annals of St Bertin* (Ninth-century Histories 1, 1991) has a good introduction and notes; it will be cited here as *AB*, with the year
2. *AB*, 834
3. *AB*, 841
4. *AB*, 842
5. *AB*, 844
6. *Chronicle*, year 843(?)
7. *AB*, 861
8. *AB*, 859

CHAPTER 7

1. D. Whitelock, *English Historical Documents* 1 (2nd ed. 1979), 282. This is an early 13th-century monk of St Albans quoting a lost northern chronicle
2. Asser, *Life*, para 38
3. Asser, *Life*, para 39
4. Asser, *Life*, para 35
5. Asser, *Life*, para 36
6. Asser, *Life*, para 43
7. B502, Cotton Charters viii 29
8. A. Campbell, *Charters of Rochester* (1974) xxiv no. 24
9. *Asser's Life of King Alfred* (1904), 230 n2
10. B510, not in Latin, but entirely in Old English; Add MS 46478; the witness-list and a translation were first printed in 1939 with detailed notes by Miss A. J. Robertson, *Anglo-Saxon Charters*, (1939) no. xi
11. B520, MS Add 15350
12. B522, MS Cotton Claudius B.vi and C.ix
13. B537, MS Cotton Tiberius A xiii

14. B541, MS Cotton Tiberius A xiii
15. B550
16. *Chronicle*, year 883.c
17. B552
18. B576, Chart Ant F 150

CHAPTER 8

1. B450
2. D. Whitelock, *English Historical Documents* 1 (2nd ed. 1979), 282 year 872
3. D. Whitclock, *English Historical Documents* 1 (2nd ed. 1979), 307
4. B506
5. B438
6. B567, trans by S. Keynes and M. Lapidge, *Alfred the Great, Asser's Life* (1983), 179–181; discussed in some detail, 326–330
7. B507
8. B504/5
9. A. Campbell trans., *Chronicon Æthelweardi* (1962), 13
10. B508
11. B496
12. in B531/2 of about 876
13. B549, 550; B565; B576
14. B520, 522, 539
15. B508, 1210
16. B529
17. B558, Stowe charters 20
18. B550
19. B610
20. B467, MS Cotton Augustus ii.71
21. B486
22. B505, MS Cotton Claudius B.vi and C.ix
23. B502, 518
24. B567, 568
25. A. Campbell trans., *Chronicon Æthelweardi* (1962), 42
26. A. Campbell trans., *Chronicon Æthelweardi* (1962), 51; revised

translation in S. Keynes and M. Lapidge, *Alfred the Great, Asser's Life* (1983), 190, 337

27. B496; 502; 506; 507
28. B529; 740; 550
29. B443; F. M. Stenton, *Anglo-Saxon England* (3rd ed. 1971), 234, 249
30. B522
31. A. Campbell trans., *Chronicon Æthelweardi* (1962), 37
32. B531/2 of about 876
33. B590
34. B757
35. B474, 532
36. B595
37. Asser, *Life* para 55
38. B549
39. B1210
40. B550, 567
41. B449, 467
42. B496
43. B502
44. B550, p. 121f; B576, p. 123, 206, 208f

CHAPTER 9

1. B595, trans. by D. Whitelock, *English Historical Documents* I (2nd ed. 1979), 541–2
2. *Anglo-Saxon Chronicle*, year 878.a
3. Asser, *Life* para 52
4. Asser, *Life* para 53
5. Asser, *Life* para 54
6. A. Campbell trans, *Chronicon Æthelweardi* (1962), 43
7. A. Campbell trans, *Chronicon Æthelweardi* (1962), 42
8. Asser, *Life* para 56
9. S. Lewis, *Topographical Dictionary of England* (1842) 1, 349
10. Asser, *Life* para 38
11. *Anglo-Saxon Chronicle*, year 757
12. F. L. Attenborough, *Laws of the Earliest English Kings* (1922) 40–1, Clause 13, section 1

13. Asser, *Life* para 38; R. P. Abels, *Lordship and Military Obligation in Anglo-Saxon England* (1988), is a sensible and scholarly appreciation
14. B1210, 550
15. B567
16. B1210, 740, 549
17. B581
18. B617
19. B623, 1150
20. B740, 568, 549, 550
21. B581, 567
22. B581
23. B595
24. B620
25. B469, 475&c, 568, 550
26. B531, 550
27. H. P. R. Finberg, *Early Charters of Wessex*, (1964) no. 567; B576
28. B550, 594, 596
29. B588
30. B620

CHAPTER 10

1. B540
2. B541, see p. 120f
3. *Chronicle*, year 877
4. B551
5. C. R. Hart, *Early Charters of northern England and the north Midlands* (1975), 291, 292, 299 etc.
6. Asser, *Life*, para 29; B537
7. B603
8. Asser, *Life*, para 75
9. B575
10. B539
11. Asser, *Life*, para 83
12. B553–5, MS Stowe 944
13. B531–2

14. B536
15. B536
16. B531, a summary in Middle English translated in A. J. Robertson, *Anglo-Saxon Charters* (1913), no. 13; B532, a paraphrase in medieval Latin.
17. B568
18. B545, H. P. R. Finberg, *Early Charters of Wessex*, no. 415
19. B549, H. P. R. Finberg, *Early Charters of Wessex*, no. 416
20. B550, see also page 121
21. B551
22. B547
23. B561

CHAPTER II

1. Mrs E. S. Armitage, *Early Norman Castles of the British Isles* (1912); J. Counihan, 'Mrs Ella Armitage, J. H. Round . . . and Early Norman Castles', *Anglo-Norman Studies* 7 (1986), 73–87
2. *Annals of St Bertin*, year 868 and compare 862, 864, 865, 866 and 869
3. *Anglo-Saxon Chronicle*, year 914 for a fort built at Buckingham in 4 weeks
4. L. Pani Ermini, *Centro Italiano di Studi sull' alto Medioevo* **39** ii (1992), 485–530
5. G. Gondi, 'Excursus sulla paleografia medievale', *Dissertaz. del Pont. Acad.* ser. II, **13** (1918), 160 n.36
6. F. L. Ganshof, *Étude sur le Développement des Villes entre Loire et Rhin au Moyen Age* (1943)
7. J. A. Trimpe Burger, 'The geometrical fortress of Oost-Souburg', *Château Gaillard* 7 (1975), 215–9; English summary of O. Olsen and H. Schmidt, *Fyrkat* 1 (1977), 214–7
8. J. D. Richards, *Viking Age England* (1991) 19, fig. 9a; M. Biddle etc., 'Coins . . . from Repton, Derbyshire' *in* M. A. S. Blackburn, *Anglo-Saxon Monetary History* (1986), 111–132
9. B1335; A. J. Robertson, *Anglo-Saxon Charters* (1939), 246–9, 494–6; D. Hill, 'The Burghal Hidage, the establishment of a

text', *Medieval Archaeology* **14** (1970), 83–103; S. Keynes and M. Lapidge, *Alfred the Great, Asser's Life* (1983), 193–4, 339–341

10. *Annals of St Bertin*, year 869
11. B613; in 904 King Edward, son of Alfred, gave the estate later known as Bishops Waltham to the bishop of Winchester in exchange for Portchester; perhaps as much as twenty years before Alfred had taken this for a fort.
12. E. M. Jope in *Oxoniensia* **23** (1958) Figs 1–3; D. Sturdy in *Oxoniensia* **50** (1985) Fig. 2
13. restated by M. Biddle and D. Hill, 'Late Saxon planned towns', *Antiquaries Journal* **51** (1971), 70–85, but already fully developed in T. H. Hughes and E. A. G. Lamborn, *Towns and Town Planning Ancient and Modern* (1923), 50–3, 73–4 from a suggestion in H. E. Salter, *Records of Mediæval Oxford* (1912) which was not entirely original.
14. M. Biddle, *Winchester in the early Middle Ages* (Winchester Studies 1, 1976), 449–453; forecast and quoted in many other less substantial works.

CHAPTER 12

1. Asser, *Life* paras 73–106
2. H. P. R. Finberg, *Early Charters of Wessex* (1964) nos. 567, B507; A. J. Robertson, *Anglo-Saxon Charters*, (1939) no. XI; S. Keynes discusses Heahmund and his colleague Heremod as likely members of a royal secretariat, *English Hist. Review* **109** (1994), 1132–4
3. B452, 488
4. B487, 503
5. B851
6. B402
7. B464
8. B448, Stowe Charters 18
9. B468, 469, 471, 472, 470, 474; B473, 475–6, 477–8; B481, 491, 502
10. B553
11. B447, 457

12. H. P. R. Finberg, *Early Charters of Wessex* (1964) nos. 417, 418 and 419
13. B579
14. B547
15. B561, 577
16. B534
17. B567
18. Asser, *Life*, para. 77
19. B533–4, 559–60, 570, 580, 609, 560

CHAPTER 13

1. B576; Canterbury, Dean and Chapter records, Red Book no. 11 (Chart. Ant. F150)
2. J. L. Nelson, 'Reconstructing a Royal Family', I. Wood and N. Lund, *People and Places in Northern Europe* (1991), 59–61
3. B576, B588, B603, B611, B624
4. R. S. Kinsey in *Spinks Numismatic Circular*, vol. 63 '1955', 269–272 and *British Numismatic Journal* vol. 29i (1958), 12–50; I. Stewart in *Numismatic Chronicle* (1935), 219–229
5. B218
6. M. Dolley, *Anglo-Saxon Pennies* (1964), 20
7. D. N. Metcalf, 'Prosperity of north-western Europe', *Economic History Review*, 2nd. s, vol. 20 (1967), 344–357
8. B547

CHAPTER 14

1. R. Hamer, *A Choice of Anglo-Saxon Verse* (1970), 137–157 is a good verse translation available in paperback
2. Asser, *Life*, para. 75
3. B547
4. F. T. Wainwright, 'Æthelflæd Lady of the Mercians', in P. Clemoes ed., *The Anglo-Saxons* (1959), 65, quoting the *Annals of Ulster*
5. M. Aston and Channel 4's *Time Team* made a detailed and scholarly field-investigation of this incident, screened on 18

December 1994; their identification of likely royal and monastic sites around Llangorse Lake is of permanent value
6. B603
7. B632; she must be the second witness 'Ælfwyn bishop', the third being 'Ælfwine bishop' (of Lichfield)
8. A. Campbell trans, *Chronicon Æthelweardi* (1962), 53
9. A. Campbell trans, *Chronicon Æthelweardi* (1962)
10. B702

CHAPTER 15

1. S. Keynes and M. Lapidge, *Alfred the Great, Asser's Life* (1983), 197–202
2. J. Stevenson, *Chronicon Monasterii de Abingdon* 1 (1858); R. Fleming developed the charge in *English Hist. Rev.* **395** (1985), 247–265, probably going too far; J. Blair, *Anglo-Saxon Oxfordshire* (1994), 64–5
3. A. Horn, *Mirror of Justices* (1624)
4. J. Parker, *Early History of Oxford* (Oxf. Hist. Soc. 3 1885), 1–52
5. D. Cox, 'University College, King Alfred and Edmund Francis', *University College Record* (1952/3), 14–24
6. MS e Mus 75, in a later eighteenth-century binding; the Library also has a seventeenth-century transcript, MS Ballard 55
6b. But see S. Keynes in *Somerset Archaeol Nat His* 136 (1992), 1–8.
7. S. Gibson, 'Francis Wise B.D.', *Oxoniensia* 1 (1936), 174
8. D. Verey, *Gloucestershire* 1 (Buildings of England; 2nd ed., 1979), 186; M. McCarthy, *Origins of the Gothic Revival* (1987), 27 and pl. 21
9. R. Gunnis, *Dictionary of British Sculptors* (2nd ed. n.d.), 334
10. S. Gibson, 'Francis Wise B.D.', *Oxoniensia* 1 (1936), 176–182
11. K. Woodbridge, *Landscape and Antiquity, aspects of English culture at Stourhead* (1970), 52–68; R. Gunnis, *Dictionary of British Sculptors*, 337
12. M. McCarthy, *Origins of the Gothic Revival* (1987), 133, pl.174; pl.77 in R. Brown ed., *The Architectural Outsiders* (1985)

13. R. Gunnis, *Dictionary of British Sculptors*, 437; *Victoria County History, Oxon* 3 (1954), 81
14. N. Pevsner and D. Lloyd, *Hampshire and the Isle of Wight* (Buildings of England, 1967), 713

Appendix

ALFRED THE GREAT in books, plays and poetical dramas of the sixteenth to the twentieth centuries

1574 Matthew Parker (archbishop of Canterbury, 1559–1575) ed., Asser, *Ælfredi Regis Res Gesta*. London

1596 H. Savile, ed., Æthelweard, *Chronicon* in *Rerum Anglicarum scriptores*, pp. 472–483. London (repr. Frankfurt, 1601)

1602 W. Camden ed., Asser, *Life* in *Anglica . . . a veteribus Scripta*, Frankfurt, (2nd ed. Frankfurt 1603)

1618 B. Vulcanius ed., Alfred's Gregory, *Cura Past* in *Goth&Lang script* vol. 4

1634 R. Powell, *Life of Alfred . . . the first institutor . . .* London

1642/3 Sir J. Spelman, 'Life of Alfred' (for Prince Charles) in Bodleian Library

1644 A. Whelock, ed., *Venerabilis Bedae Historia Ecclesiae.* (with first publication of *Anglo-Saxon Chronicle.*, the G-text). Cambridge

1678 O. Walker, ed., Sir J. Spelman, *Vita Alfredi* (Latin tr. by C. Wase). Oxford

1698 C. Rawlinson, ed., Alfred's Boethius, *Consolation*. Oxford

1709 T. Hearne, ed., Sir J. Spelman, *Life of Ælfred . . .* Oxford

1722 F. Wise, ed., Asser, *Annales . . . Ælfridi Magni*. Oxford

1733 A. Bussaeus, ed., Ari Thorgilson, *Schedae seu Libellus de Is-landia* or *Periplus*, with extract from Spelman, 1678. Copenhagen

1738 F. Wise, *Letter to Dr Mead . . . White Horse . . . A.D.871*. Oxford

1739 'Philalethes Rusticus', *Impertinence and Imposture of Modern Antiquaries*

1740 J. Thomson and D. Mallet, *Alfred, a Masque* at Cliveden, Bucks

1741 G. North, *Answer to a scandalous libel . . .*

1743 F. Wise, *Further Observations upon the White Horse*

1751 D. Mallet's rewritten *Masque* at Drury Lane, London

1753 (Author of *Friendly Rivals*), *Alfred . . . Deliverer of his country. A Tragedy*, London

1773 Baron A. von Halle, *Alfred, König der Angeln-sachsen.* (reprinted 1779, French ed. 1775)

1777 Alex Bicknell, *Life . . .*

1777 John Home, *Alfred, a Tragedy*. Dublin (reprinted 1778)

1784 J. C. Ryland, *The life and character of Alfred . . .* London

1788 T. Astle, ed., *The will of king Alfred*. Oxford

1789 Ebenezer Rhodes, *Alfred, a Historical Tragedy*. Sheffield

1798 Mr Lonsdale, 'Alfred the Great: or the Danish Invasions (Grand Historical Ballet of Action)', at Sadlers Wells Theatre, London

1809 J. Whitaker, *The Life of St Neot, oldest of brothers to King Alfred*

1816 R. Rask, ed., Alfred's Othere's & Wulfstan's *Voyages*. Copenhagen

1820 B. Merelli, *Alfredo il Grande*, opera at La Scala, Milan

1828 T. Astle, ed., *The will of king Alfred*. London (2nd ed., see 1788) Sharon Turner, *Gesischte* . . .

1829 J. S. Cardale, trans., Alfred's Boethius, *Consolation*. London

1835 S. Fox, trans., Alfred's Boethius, verses, *Consolation*. London

1835 P. de Rapin-Thoyras, *The beginner's French bk. Life* . . . +vocab. London

1836 Count F. L. zu Stolberg, *Leben Alfreds der Grosse*

1840 Earl of Ellesmere, *Alfred, a Drama in one Act*

1840 Agnes M. Stewart, *Stories about Alfred the Great for children*. Dublin

1848 H. Petrie, ed., Asser, *Vita* . . . in *Mon hist Brit*, 467–498 (see 1722)

1848 H. Petrie, ed Æthelweard, *Chron.* in *Mon hint Brit*, 499–521

1848 J. A. Giles, *The life and times of Alfred the Great*. London

1849 Anon, *The life of Alfred* . . . London

1849 F. Steinitz, ed., A. v. Haller, *The moderate monarchy . . . the life and maxims . . .* London (see 1773)

1849 'Spectator' (F. Reyroux), *The . . . jubilee . . . at Wantage*. Littlemore.

1849–51 J. A. Giles, ed., *King Alfred the Great's Works* (Jubilee edition; repr. 1858)

1850 Jacob Abbott, *Hist of king AlfredT*. London (repr 1853 etc.)

1850 Author of *Bluff King Hal, Harlequin Alfred the Great, or the Magic Banjo & the Mystic Raven*. London

1850 M. F. Tupper, trans., *King A's poems . . . turned into Engl metres*. London

c.1850 Anon, *The life of Alfred* . . . London

1851 G. R. Pauli, *König Alfred und seine Stelle* . . . Berlin

1852 G. R. Pauli, tr. T. Wright, *The life of king* . . . London

1852 J. B. v. Weiss, *Geschichte Alfreds des Grossen mit Sendschreiben . . . Boethius.* Schaffhausen

1852 J. Bosworth, ed., Alfred's Othere & Wulfstan, *A . . . voyage*. London

1853 B. Thorpe, ed., G. R. Pauli, *The life . . . with Alfred's Orosius*. London

1854 J. A. Giles, *The life and times* . . . London

1855 Alfred's Othere & Wulfstan, ed. Bosworth, *A descr* . . . (no facs). London

1859 L. G. Nilsson, ed., Alfred, *Proverbs*. Copenhagen

1859 Anon, *King Alfred contemplating Oxford at the present day* (Newdigate poem). Oxford

1863 M. G. Guizot, *Alfred le Grand*

1864 D. Alcock, *Great & good; or, Alfred the father of his people*. London

1864 S. Fox, *Alfred's Boethius's Consolations* . . . London (see 1835)

1864 G. S. Smith, *Great and good* . . .

1866 I.P.E.T., *König Alfred der Grosse*, in six acts. Bamberg

1869 Thomas Hughes, *Life* . . . (Sunday library for household reading). London

1870 Antonin Dvorak, *Alfred* (opera, not performed until much later). Prague

1871 'A classical scholar', *Alfred, king of England*. Westbury

1871 Anon, *Alfred the Great, and other stories from history*. London

1871–2 H. Sweet, Alfred's Gregory's *Pastoral Care* (Early Engl Texts). London

1872 R. Morris, *King Alfred's Proverbs*

1878 M. G. Guizot, *Alfred le Grand* . . . London (Hachette series)

1880 A. G. Knight, *The life of king Alfred*. London (Quarterly series; vol. 32)

1881 F. Y. Powell, *Alfred the great and William the conqueror*. London

1883 J. Abbott, *Hist of king Alfred*. London (3rd ed; see 1850. 4th ed. 1889, reprinted 1890)

1890–98 T. Miller, ed., Alfred's Bede, *Eccl Hist.* (Early Engl Text 95–6, 110–11)

1893 P. Askin, *Life* . . .
1893 M. H. Turk, *The legal code of Ælfred the Great*. Halle
1894 J. D. Bruce, *The Anglo-Saxon version of the Book of Psalms*. Baltimore
1894–1901 J. E. Wulfing, *Die Syntax in den Werken Alfreds*, 3 pts. Bonn
1896 E. S. Holt, *Light in the Darkness*
1897 F. Harrison, '*The millenary* . . .', *an address*. Birmingham
1898 Sir W. Besant, *Alfred, a lecture*. London (3rd ed. 1899)
1898 M. Burrows, *King Alfred the great*. London
1898 W. H. Stevenson, 'The Date of King Alfred's Death', *Eng Hist. R* 13, 71–77
1899 A. Bowker, *Alfred, Chapters on his Life and Times*. London
1899 J. H. Cooke, *Life of king Alfred* . . . London
1899 Sir F. Pollock, *King Alfred, a paper*. London (Roy. Inst. of G.B. lect.)
1899 W. J. Sedgefield, Alfred's Boethius, *Consolatio*. London and 1900

1900 F. Conybeare, ed., *Alfred in the chroniclers*. London
1900 Mary Douglas, *The story of Alfred and his times*. London
1900 Sir P. A. H. Gibbs, *Alfred, model of* . . . *kings*. London (Founders of Empire)
1900 W. Hawkins and E. T. Smith, *The story of Alfred* . . . London
1900 Jesse Page, *Alfred the great: the father of the English*. London
1900 J. C. Wall, *Alfred the Great, his abbey of Hyde, Athelney and Shaftesbury*
1900–07 H. Hecht, Werferths Gregory, *Dialoge*. Leipzig
c.1900 J. Abbott, *History of* . . . New York (5th ed., see 1850, 1883)
1901 Sir W. Besant, *The story of* . . . *Alfred*. London (Library of useful stories)
1901 G. F. Bosworth, *Alfred the great, his life and times*. London
1901 British Museum, *Millenary Exhibition*
1901 S. A. Brooke and K. M. Warren, *Alfred as educator of his people* . . . London
1901 W. H. Draper, *Alfred the great* . . . *seven studies*. London (2nd ed. 1901)
1901 C. R. L. Engstrom, *The Millenary* . . ., *a sermon*
1901 F. Harrison, *The writings of king Alfred, an address*. New York
1901 F. B. Jeffery, *A perfect prince*. London
1901 D. Macfadyen, *Alfred the West Saxon, king* . . . London (Saintly lives)
1901 H. Molenaar, *Alfred der Grosse*
1901 G. Philip and Son, pub, *The Alfred Millenary*
1901 Portland Historical Society, *Commemoration*. Maine
1901 Earl of Rosebery, *Alfred the truthteller, a speech*. London
1901 J. H. Swann, *Millenary, annotated study list*. Manchester, Public Lib.
1901 'A Saxon', *Was Alfred king of England? A political review*. London
1901 Anon, *Programme* . . . *commemoration of the millenary* . . . Winchester
1902 H. L. Hargrove, trans., Alfred's Augustine, *Soliloquies*. New York (1904)
1902 A. Bowker, *Millenary proceedings of national commemoration*. London
1902 L. W. Miles, *King Alfred in Literature*. Baltimore
1902 C. Plummer, *The life and times of Alfred* . . . Oxford (Ford lectures, 1901)
1902 Mary M. C. M. Scott, *Life* . . .
1903 S. Harris, *Alfred the great, a paper*. Hull
1904 W. H. Stevenson, ed., Asser, *Life* . . . *with Annals of Saint Neots*. Oxford
1904 H. Geidel, *Alfred der Grosse als Geograph*. Munich (Munch Geog Stud)
1906 A. S. Cook, trans., Asser, *Life* . . . transl. Boston
1907 W. W. Skeat, ed., *Proverbs of Alfred*. Oxford
1908 L. C. Jane, trans., Asser, *Life* (Kings Classics). London
1908 E. Borgström, *Proverbs of king Alfred*. Lund

1908 R. K. H. Münch, *Die sprachliche Bedeutung . . . Alfreds des Grossen*. Halle
1908 Katrina Spencer Trask, *King Alfred's Jewel, a Drama in Verse*. London
1912 Sir W. Besant, *The story of . . .* (Useful knowledge ser; see 1901). London
1914 J. W. E. Conybeare, *Alfred in the chroniclers*. Cambridge (2nd ed., 1900)
1914 Annie E. McKilliam, *The story of . . . Alfred*. (Heroes of all time). London
1915 Beatrice A. Lees, *A the g, the truth teller*. New York
1919 Beatrice A. Lees, *A the g, the truth teller*. (Heroes of the nations) New York
1920 G. F. Browne, *King Alfred's Books*
1922 W. Endter, *König Alfreds Soliloquien*. Hamburg, repr. Darmstad '64
1931 G. P. Baker, *The fighting kings of Wessex*. London
1931 H. P. South, ed., *Proverbs of King Alfred . . . Maidstone MS*. New York
1934 Ludwig Borinski, *Der Stil Konigs Alfreds*. Leipzig
1934 H. Sweet, ed., tr., Alfred's Gregory, *Pastoral Care* (Early Eng Texts)
1935 F. H. Hayward, *Life . . .* (Great Lives) London
1938 G. L. May, *Life . . .*
1939 J. C. Rimington, *A man of his people . . .*
1942 O. S. A. Arngart, ed., *The proverbs of Alfred*. Lund
1944 A. W. Green, ed., Alfred, *The will . . .* Dublin
1955 C. E. Wright, ed., Bald, *Leechbook*. Copenhagen Facs 5
1955 G. P. Baker, *Golden Dragon, the story of Alfred the great*. London
1956 N. R. Ker, Alfred's Gregory's *Regula Pastoralis*. Facsimile Copenhagen
1956 L. du G. Peach, *King Alfred the g*. (Ladybird Books) Loughborough
1957 Eleanor Duckett, *Alfred the Great, The King and his England*. Chicago
1958 K. Freeman (as Mary Fitt), *Alfred . . .* (Nelsons' picture biogs) Edinburgh
1959 D. Whitelock, re-ed., Stevenson's Asser, *Life* (see 1904). London
1963 P. J. Helm, *Life of Alfred the great*, London
1964 K. Otten, ed., *König Alfreds Boethius*. Tubingen (Stud z engl Phil nf 3)
1967 H. R. Loyn, *Alfred the Great*. (Clarendon biographies) London
1968 Anne F. Payne, *King Alfred and Boethius: An Analysis . . .* Madison
1969 T. A. Carnicelli, Alfred's Augustine, *Soliloquies*. Cambridge, Mass
1970 W. H. Brown, *A syntax of king Alfred's Pastoral Care*. The Hague
1974 J. D. Woodruff, *The Life and Times of Alfred the Great*. London
1975 I. Carlson, trans., Alfred's Gregory, *Pastoral Care . . .* Stockholm
1977 D. A. Hinton, *A's Kingdom: Wessex and the South 800–1500*. London
1977 J. Pelling, *Alfred the great*. (Teachers' Notes). Cambridge
1978 J. B. Westwood, *Alfred the great*
1979 S. S. Jessup, *Remembrance in good works . . . the prose translations . . . of king A*
1980 J. Bately, Alfred's Orosius, *Histories against pagans* (Early Engl Texts s s 6)
1980 J. Bately, *The Literary Prose of King Alfred's Reign*. London
1981 J. Peddie, *Alfred's defeat of the Vikings*. Devizes
1983 S. Keynes and M. Lapidge, Asser's *Life . . . and other . . . sources*. London
1984 R. S. May, *Alfred the great and the Saxons*
1989 J. Peddie, *Alfred the good soldier*
1993 R. M. Scott, *Alfred the Great*

Index